4 Plays by
William Inge

4 Plays BY
William Inge

Come Back, Little Sheba

Picnic

Bus Stop

The Dark at the Top of the Stairs

RANDOM HOUSE, NEW YORK

ISBN: 1-56865-109-0

Manufactured in the United States of America

FOREWORD

The experience of my first production on Broadway was frantic and bewildering. The play was *Come Back, Little Sheba*, and it was a modest success. I had always hoped for an overwhelming success, but I felt myself very satisfied at the time that *Sheba* had come off as well as it did. Anticipating success (of any degree), I had always expected to feel hilarious, but I didn't. Other people kept coming to me saying, "Aren't you thrilled?" Even my oldest friends, who had known me during the years when I gave myself no peace for lack of success, were baffled by me. There was absolutely no one to understand how I felt, for I didn't feel anything at all. I was in a funk. Where was the joy I had always imagined? Where were the gloating satisfactions I had always anticipated? I looked everywhere to find them. None were there.

A few weeks after *Sheba* opened, a newspaper woman from the Midwest came dancing into my apartment to interview me, bringing with her a party spirit that could not counter with my persisting solemnity. "Where's the celebration?" she wanted to know, looking about the room as though for confetti. "Where's the champagne?" I knew I was not meeting success in the expected way but I was too tired to fake it. I endured her disappointment in me. I could tell by her twitching features that she was wondering what in the world she would tell her readers. Obviously, she couldn't tell them the truth, that the man who had written a (modestly) successful play was one of the saddest-looking creatures she had ever seen. But she didn't let the facts bother her. She returned home and wrote of the play's success and my reaction to it in a fitting way that wouldn't let her readers down. At the time I was too depressed to care.

Other people, friends and aquaintances, couldn't imagine why I had started being psychoanalyzed at this time. "But you're a success now," they would assure me. "What do you want to get analyzed for?" As though successful people automatically became happy, and psychoanalysis were only a remedy for professional failure. But if the personal rewards of my success were a disillusionment to others, they also were to me. My plays since *Sheba* have been more successful, but none of them has brought me the kind of joy, the hilarity, I had craved as a boy, as a young man, living in Kansas and Missouri back in the thirties and forties. Strange and ironic.

Once we find the fruits of success, the taste is nothing like what we had anticipated.

Maybe the sleight of hand is performed during the brief interval of rehearsals, out-of-town tryouts, and opening night. A period of six or more weeks that pack a lifetime of growing up. During that period, the playwright comes to realize, maybe with considerable shock, that the play contains something very vital to him, something of the very essence of his own life. If it is rejected, he can only feel that he is rejected, too. Some part of him has been turned down, cast aside, even laughed at or scorned. If it is accepted, all that becomes him to feel is a deep gratefulness, like a man barely escaping a fatal accident, that he has survived.

All my plays have survived on Broadway. All have met with success in varying degrees. And I feel a fitting gratefulness, because they all represent something of me, some view of life that is peculiarly mine that no one else could offer in quite the same style and form. Success, it seems to me, would be somewhat meaningless if the play were not a personal contribution. The author who creates only for audience consumption is only engaged in a financial enterprise. There must always be room for both kinds of theatre, but it is regrettable that they must always compete together in our commercial theatre. For commercial theatre only builds on what has already been created, contributing only theatre back into the theatre. Creative theatre brings something of life itself, which gives the theatre something new to grow on. But when new life comes to us, we don't always recognize it. New life doesn't always survive on Broadway. It's considered risky.

People still come to me sometimes to tell me how much they admired *Come Back, Little Sheba*, referring to the play as though it had been "a smash hit" (a term which we are too eager to apply to shows). Actually, *Sheba* made out well with about half of the reviewers, its total run being something less than six months. Some of the reviews showed an almost violent repugnance to the play. We did good business for only a few weeks and then houses began to dwindle to the size of tea parties. At one time, the actors all took salary cuts, and I took a cut in my royalties. The show was cheap to run, and so, with a struggle, we survived. We always held a small audience of people who were most devoted to the play and came to see it many times. It is remembered now as "a smash hit" or "a hit," probably because the far greater success of the movie shed more glorious reflections on the play.

Now, I don't see how it could have been otherwise with *Sheba*. It is probably a bad omen if any author's first play is "a smash hit." It takes the slow-moving theatre audience one or two plays by a new author, who brings them something new from life outside the theatre, before they can feel sufficiently comfortable with him to consider fairly what he has to say. A good author insists on being accepted on his own terms, and audiences must bicker awhile before they're willing to give in. One learns not to be resentful about this condition but to credit it to human nature.

I have a tendency, after a play of mine is produced, to look back on it disparagingly, seeing only its faults (before production, I see only its virtues). But after the hiatus of opening night, after enough time passes for me to regard each play seriously, as something finally distinct from myself, I have felt that each one gave me some feeling of personal success, that each one contributed something to the theatre out of my life's experience.

I have never sought to write plays that primarily tell a story; nor have I sought deliberately to create new forms. I have been most concerned with dramatizing something of the dynamism I myself find in human motivations and behavior. I regard a play as a composition rather than a story, as a distillation of life rather than a narration of it. It is only in this way that I feel myself a real contemporary. *Sheba* is the closest thing to a story play that I have written, and it is the only play of mine that could be said to have two central characters. But even this play was a fabric of life, in which the two characters (Doc and Lola) were species of the environment. After *Sheba*, I sought deliberately to fill a larger canvas, to write plays of an overall texture that made fuller use of the stage as a medium. I strive to keep the stage bubbling with a restless kind of action that seeks first one outlet and then another before finally resolving itself. I like to keep several stories going at once, and to keep as much of the playing area on stage as alive as possible. I use one piece of action to comment on another, not to distract from it. I don't suppose that in any of my later plays I found the single dramatic intensity of action that I found in the drunk scene in *Sheba*, in which Doc threatens Lola's life. I have deliberately sought breadth instead of depth in my plays since *Sheba*, and have sought a more forthright humor than *Sheba* could afford.

In an article I once wrote on *Picnic*, I compared a play to a journey, in which every moment should be as interesting as the destination. I despair of a play that requires its audience to sit through two hours of plot construction, having no reference outside the immediate setting, just to be rewarded by a big emotional pay-off in the last act. This, I regard as a kind of false stimulation. I think every line and every situation in a play should "pay off," too, and have its extensions of meaning beyond the immediate setting, into life. I strive to bring meaning to every moment, every action.

I doubt if my plays "pay off" for an audience unless they are watched rather closely. Writing for a big audience, I deal with surfaces in my plays, and let whatever depths there are in my material emerge unexpectedly so that they bring something of the suddenness and shock which accompany the discovery of truths in actuality. I suppose none of my plays means anything much unless seen as a composite, for I seek dramatic values in a relative way. That is, one character in a play of mine might seem quite pointless unless seen in comparison with another character. For instance, in *Bus Stop*, the cowboy's eagerness, awkwardness, and naïveté in seeking love were interesting only when seen by comparison, in the same setting, with the amorality of Cherie, the depravity of the professor, the casual earthiness of Grace and Carl, the innocence of the schoolgirl Elma, and the defeat of his buddy Virgil. In themselves, the characters may have been entertaining, but not very meaningful.

    Bus Stop, I suppose, has less real story than any play that ever survived on Broadway. I meant it only as a composite picture of varying kinds of love, ranging from the innocent to the depraved. With the play's success, I felt quite proud of the fact that I had held the audience's interest long after what would normally be considered the final "pay-off" (when the cowboy and his girl are reunited and go off together). I guess maybe I was trying to prove that a play's merits can exist, not in the dramatization of one soul-satisfying event, but in the over-all pattern and texture of the play. I insisted that the audience be just as interested in what happened to all the characters as they were in Bo and Cherie.

    I was sure enough of my craft by the time I started writing *The Dark at the Top of the Stairs* to be able to take my craftsmanship more easily for granted. This play was developed out of the first play I ever wrote, called *Farther Off From Heaven*. Margo Jones produced it in her Dallas Theatre in June, 1947, and I didn't know what to do with it at the time but felt it contained too much good material to keep on the shelf. I had been working on the play off and on for over six years, then in the winter of 1957, settled down on it for serious. It is formed from pretty nostalgic memories of childhood, without being very autobiographical. I suppose it represents my belated attempt to come to terms with the past, to rearrange its parts and make them balance, to bring a mature understanding to everyday phenomena that mystified me as a boy. Again, the story is very slight. I deliberately divert the audience from the main story in order to bring them back to it at the end of the play with a fresher viewpoint. In the play, I try to explore some of man's hidden fear in facing life and to show something of the hidden fears that motivate us all. There is a suicide in the play, of a young, homeless, part Jewish boy who has no sure connection with anyone in the world. Some people felt upon reading the play, and others upon first seeing it, that the announcement of the suicide came as too much of a shock; but every suicide I ever heard of came to me in the same way, with no preparation. I have never heard of a suicide that I expected. We always find the reasons for such events after they happen, in re-exploring the character to find motivations we had previously overlooked. It was this kind of dynamism I wanted most to achieve. And I felt also that maybe I was drawing a little on Christian theology to show something of the uniting effect human suffering can bring into our lives.

The success of these four plays, I must share in each case with my director. This is not just a pleasant compliment. I have come to learn how important good direction is to a play, and to realize that good directors are as scarce as good playwrights. I was most fortunate in finding Daniel Mann, unknown at the time, to do *Sheba*. He sensed all the play's implied values and projected them superbly. Joshua Logan, with *Picnic*, was my second director. We had our ups and downs with that play, which I attribute mainly to my second-play nervousness and indecision. An unstable author, who isn't sure what he wants, is a great liability to a director; so if *Picnic* did not come off entirely to please me (as rumor had it), it was my own fault. Josh only sensed my indecision and tried to compensate for it. Still, I feel *Picnic* was a good show. Josh gave it lovely picturesqueness (he is perhaps the most visual of all directors) and feeling of size. I worked on the play with him for a year and a half, during which time he gave of himself very spontaneously. I can never cease being grateful for all that I learned from him.

Harold Clurman is the only real intellectual I know in the theatre. He seems to me a man who has channeled very powerful emotions into a vitally rational life. I was a little dubious about taking *Bus Stop* to him. I didn't see how he, the most metropolitan man I know, could bring understanding to the play's rural types. But he understood them perfectly, I felt, as though by contrast with himself. And he gave me a beautifully felt production.

Working with Elia Kazan sometimes borders on the supernatural, he intuitively senses so quickly all the dim feelings about a play that lie in an author's subconscious. During production, he is the gentlest, humblest man I've ever known. He talks with actors like a ministering angel, infusing them with courage and insight. His range of understanding is from the most delicately sensitive to the most cataclysmically violent. He is a great creative talent.

I also feel very indebted to the superb actors who have taken part in my plays. I would like to list them here, but I truly would not know where to stop in compiling the list. Anyway, I am deeply grateful for the many talented people who have given of their own freshness and vitality to the parts I have written. If there have been poor performances in my plays, I don't recall them now.

"Success is counted sweetest by those who ne'er succeed," according to Emily Dickinson, and I realize what she meant when I compare the success

I once anticipated with the success I found. They are not the same things, at all. But the four plays in this volume represent almost a decade in my life, a decade that was very intensely lived. Publishing the plays now is like tying those years together to file away, years in which I managed to find some expression for my life and experience, and to find response. Maybe this is all that success means.

WILLIAM INGE

CONTENTS

CONTENTS

Come Back, Little Sheba

COME BACK, LITTLE SHEBA *was first presented by The Theatre Guild at the Booth Theatre, New York City, on February 15, 1950, with the following cast:*

(IN ORDER OF APPEARANCE)

DOC	*Sidney Blackmer*
MARIE	*Joan Lorring*
LOLA	*Shirley Booth*
TURK	*Lonny Chapman*
POSTMAN	*Daniel Reed*
MRS. COFFMAN	*Olga Fabian*
MILKMAN	*John Randolph*
MESSENGER	*Arnold Schulman*
BRUCE	*Robert Cunningham*
ED ANDERSON	*Wilson Brooks*
ELMO HUSTON	*Paul Krauss*

DIRECTED BY Daniel Mann
SETTING AND LIGHTING DESIGNED BY Howard Bay
COSTUMES BY Lucille Little
PRODUCTION UNDER THE SUPERVISION OF Lawrence Langner and Theresa Helburn
ASSOCIATE PRODUCER, Phyllis Anderson

Scenes

An old house in a run-down neighborhood of a Midwestern city.

ACT ONE	SCENE I. SCENE II.	Morning in late spring. The same evening, after supper.

ACT TWO	SCENE I. SCENE II. SCENE III. SCENE IV.	The following morning. Late afternoon the same day. 5:30 the next morning. Morning, a week later.

ACT ONE | Scene One

SCENE: *The stage is empty.*

It is the downstairs of an old house in one of those semi-respectable neighborhoods in a Midwestern city. The stage is divided into two rooms, the living room at right and the kitchen at left, with a stairway and a door between. At the foot of the stairway is a small table with a telephone on it. The time is about 8:00 A.M., a morning in the late spring.

At rise of curtain the sun hasn't come out in full force and outside the atmosphere is a little gray. The house is extremely cluttered and even dirty. The living room somehow manages to convey the atmosphere of the twenties, decorated with cheap pretense at niceness and respectability. The general effect is one of fussy awkwardness. The furniture is all heavy and rounded-looking, the chairs and davenport being covered with a shiny mohair. The davenport is littered and there are lace antimacassars on all the chairs. In such areas, houses are so close together, they hide each other from the sunlight. What sun could come through the window, at right, is dimmed by the smoky glass curtains. In the kitchen there is a table, center. On it are piled dirty dishes from supper the night before. Woodwork in the kitchen is dark and grimy. No industry whatsoever has been spent in making it one of those white, cheerful rooms that we commonly think kitchens should be. There is no action on stage for several seconds.

DOC comes downstairs to kitchen. His coat is on back of chair, center. He straightens chair, takes roll from bag on drainboard, folds bag and tucks it behind sink. He lights stove and goes to table, fills dishpan there and takes it to sink. Turns on water, tucks towel in vest for apron. He goes to chair and says prayer. Then he crosses to stove, takes frying pan to sink and turns on water.

MARIE, a young girl of eighteen or nineteen who rooms in the house, comes out of her bedroom (next to the living room), skipping airily into the kitchen. Her hair is piled in curls on top of her head and she wears a sheer dainty negligee and smart, feathery mules on her feet. She has the cheerfulness only youth can feel in the morning.

MARIE *(Goes to chair, opens pocketbook there)*   Hi!

DOC   Well, well, how is our star boarder this morning?

MARIE   Fine.

DOC   Want your breakfast now?

MARIE   Just my fruit juice. I'll drink it while I dress and have my breakfast later.

DOC *(Places two glasses on table)*   Up a little early, aren't you?

MARIE   I have to get to the library and check out some books before anyone else gets them.

DOC   Yes, you want to study hard, Marie, learn to be a fine artist some day. Paint lots of beautiful pictures. I remember a picture my mother had over the mantelpiece at home, a picture of a cathedral in a sunset, one of those big cathedrals in Europe somewhere. Made you feel religious just to look at it.

MARIE   These books aren't for art, they're for biology. I have an exam.

DOC   Biology? Why do they make you take biology?

MARIE *(Laughs)*   It's required. Didn't you have to take biology when you were in college?

DOC   Well . . . yes, but I was preparing to study medicine, so of course I *had* to take biology and things like that. You see—I was going to be a real doctor then—only I left college my third year.

MARIE   What's the matter? Didn't you like the pre-med course?

DOC   Yes, of course . . . I had to give it up.

MARIE   Why?

DOC *(Goes to stove with roll on plate—evasive)*   I'll put your sweet roll in now, Marie, so it will be nice and warm for you when you want it.

MARIE   Dr. Delaney, you're so nice to your wife, and you're so nice to me, as a matter of fact, you're so nice to everyone. I hope my husband is as nice as you are. Most husbands would never think of getting their own breakfast.

DOC *(Very pleased with this)*   . . . Uh . . . you might as well sit down now and . . . yes, sit here and I'll serve you your breakfast now, Marie, and we can eat it together, the two of us.

MARIE *(A light little laugh as she starts dancing away from him)*   No, I like to bathe first and feel that I'm all fresh and clean to start the day. I'm going to hop into the tub now. See you later.
(She goes upstairs)

DOC *(The words appeal to him)*   Yes, fresh and clean—
(DOC shows disappointment but goes on in businesslike way setting his breakfast on the table)

MARIE *(Offstage)*   Mrs. Delaney.

LOLA *(Offstage)*   'Mornin', honey.
(Then LOLA comes downstairs. She is a contrast to DOC's neat cleanliness, and MARIE's. Over a nightdress she wears a lumpy kimono. Her eyes are dim with a morning expression of disillusionment, as though she had had a beautiful dream during the night and found on waking none of it was true. On her feet are worn dirty comfies)

LOLA *(With some self-pity)*   I can't sleep late like I used to. It used to be I could sleep till noon if I wanted to, but I can't any more. I don't know why.

DOC   Habits change. Here's your fruit juice.

LOLA *(Taking it)*   I oughta be gettin' your breakfast, Doc, instead of you gettin' mine.

DOC   I have to get up anyway, Baby.

LOLA *(Sadly)*   I had another dream last night.

DOC *(Pours coffee)*   About Little Sheba?

LOLA *(With sudden animation)*   It was just as real. I dreamt I put her on a leash and we walked downtown—to do some shopping. All the people on the street turned around to admire her, and I felt so proud. Then we started to walk, and the blocks started going by so fast that Little Sheba couldn't keep up with me. Suddenly, I looked around and Little Sheba was gone. Isn't that funny? I looked everywhere for her but I couldn't find her. And I stood there feeling sort of afraid. *(Pause)* Do you suppose that means anything?

DOC   Dreams are funny.

LOLA   Do you suppose it means Little Sheba is going to come back?

DOC   I don't know, Baby.

LOLA *(Petulant)* I miss her so, Doc. She was such a cute little puppy. Wasn't she cute?

DOC *(Smiles with the reminiscence)* Yes, she was cute.

LOLA Remember how white and fluffy she used to be after I gave her a bath? And how her little hind-end wagged from side to side when she walked?

DOC *(An appealing memory)* I remember.

LOLA She was such a cute little puppy. I hated to see her grow old, didn't you, Doc?

DOC Yah. Little Sheba should have stayed young forever. Some things should never grow old. That's what it amounts to, I guess.

LOLA She's been gone for such a long time. What do you suppose ever happened to her?

DOC You can't ever tell.

LOLA *(With anxiety)* Do you suppose she got run over by a car? Or do you think that old Mrs. Coffman next door poisoned her? I wouldn't be a bit surprised.

DOC No, Baby. She just disappeared. That's all we know.

LOLA *(Redundantly)* Just vanished one day . . . vanished into thin air. *(As though in a dream)*

DOC I told you I'd find you another one, Baby.

LOLA *(Pessimistically)* You couldn't ever find another puppy as cute as Little Sheba.

DOC *(Back to reality)* Want an egg?

LOLA No. Just this coffee. *(He pours coffee and sits down to breakfast.* LOLA, *suddenly)* Have you said your prayer, Doc?

DOC Yes, Baby.

LOLA And did you ask God to be with you—all through the day, and keep you strong?

DOC Yes, Baby.

LOLA Then God will be with you, Docky. He's been with you almost a year now and I'm so proud of you.

DOC *(Preening a little)*   Sometimes I feel sorta proud of myself.

LOLA   Say your prayer, Doc. I like to hear it.

DOC *(Matter-of-factly)*   God grant me the serenity to accept the things I cannot change, courage to change the things I can, and wisdom always to tell the difference.

LOLA   That's nice. That's so pretty. When I think of the way you used to drink, always getting into fights, we had so much trouble. I was so scared! I never knew what was going to happen.

DOC   That was a long time ago, Baby.

LOLA   I know it, Daddy. I know how you're going to be when you come home now.
(She kisses him lightly)

DOC   *I* don't know what I would have done without you.

LOLA   And now you've been sober almost a year.

DOC   Yep. A year next month.
(He rises and goes to the sink with coffee cup and two glasses, rinsing them)

LOLA   Do you have to go to the meeting tonight?

DOC   No. I can skip the meetings now for a while.

LOLA   Oh, good! Then you can take me to a movie.

DOC   Sorry, Baby. I'm going out on some Twelfth Step work with Ed Anderson.

LOLA   What's that?

DOC *(Drying the glasses)*   I showed you that list of twelve steps the Alcoholics Anonymous have to follow. This is the final one. After you learn to stay dry yourself, then you go out and help other guys that need it.

LOLA   Oh!

DOC *(Goes to sink)*   When we help others, we help ourselves.

LOLA   I know what you mean. Whenever I help Marie in some way, it makes me feel good.

Doc   Yah. (LOLA *takes her cup to* DOC *and he washes it*) Yes, but this is a lot different, Baby. When I go out to help some poor drunk, I have to give him courage—to stay sober like I've stayed sober. Most alcoholics are disappointed men. . . . They need courage . . .

LOLA   You weren't ever disappointed, were you, Daddy?

DOC   *(After another evasive pause)*   The important thing is to forget the past and live for the present. And stay sober doing it.

LOLA   Who do you have to help tonight?

DOC   Some guy they picked up on Skid Row last night. *(Gets his coat from back of chair)* They got him at the City Hospital. I kinda dread it.

LOLA   I thought you said it helped you.

DOC *(Puts on coat)*   It does, if you can stand it. I did some Twelfth Step work down there once before. They put alcoholics right in with the crazy people. It's horrible—these men all twisted and shaking—eyes all foggy and full of pain. Some guy there with his fists clamped together, so he couldn't kill anyone. There was a young man, just a *young* man, had scratched his eyes out.

LOLA *(Cringing)*   Don't, Daddy. Seems a shame to take a man there just 'cause he got drunk.

DOC   Well, they'll sober a man up. That's the important thing. Let's not talk about it any more.

LOLA *(With relief)*   Rita Hayworth's on tonight, out at the Plaza. Don't you want to see it?

DOC   Maybe Marie will go with you.

LOLA   Oh, no. She's probably going out with Turk tonight.

DOC   She's too nice a girl to be going out with a guy like Turk.

LOLA   I don't know why, Daddy. Turk's nice.
(Cuts coffee cake)

DOC   A guy like that doesn't have any respect for *nice* young girls. You can tell that by looking at him.

LOLA   I never saw Marie object to any of the love-making.

DOC   A big brawny bozo like Turk, he probably forces her to kiss him.

LOLA   Daddy, that's not so at all. I came in the back way once when they were in the living room, and she was kissing him like he was Rudolph Valentino.

DOC (*An angry denial*) Marie is a nice girl.

LOLA I know she's nice. I just said she and Turk were doing some tall spooning. It wouldn't surprise me any if . . .

DOC Honey, I don't want to hear any more about it.

LOLA You try to make out like every young girl is Jennifer Jones in the *Song of Bernadette*.

DOC I do not. I just like to believe that young people like her are clean and decent. . . .
(MARIE *comes downstairs*)

MARIE Hi!
(*Gets cup and saucer from drainboard*)

LOLA (*At stove*) There's an extra sweet roll for you this morning, honey. I didn't want mine.

MARIE One's plenty, thank you.

DOC How soon do you leave this morning?
(LOLA *brings coffee*)

MARIE (*Eating*) As soon as I finish my breakfast.

DOC Well, I'll wait and we can walk to the corner together.

MARIE Oh, I'm sorry, Doc. Turk's coming by. He has to go to the library, too.

DOC Oh, well, I'm not going to be competition with a football player. (*To* LOLA) It's a nice spring morning. Wanta walk to the office with me?

LOLA I look too terrible, Daddy. I ain't even dressed.

DOC Kiss Daddy good-bye.

LOLA (*Gets up and kisses him softly*) 'Bye, 'bye, Daddy. If you get hungry, come home and I'll have something for you.

MARIE (*Joking*) Aren't you going to kiss *me*, Dr. Delaney? (LOLA *eggs* DOC *to go ahead*)

DOC (*Startled, hesitates, forces himself to realize she is only joking and manages to answer*) Can't spend my time kissing all the girls.
(MARIE *laughs.* DOC *goes into living room while* LOLA *and* MARIE *continue talking.* MARIE'S *scarf is tossed over his hat on chair, so he picks it up, then*

looks at it fondly, holding it in the air inspecting its delicate gracefulness. He drops it back on chair and goes out)

MARIE   I think Dr. Delaney is so nice.

LOLA   *(She is by the closet now, where she keeps a few personal articles. She is getting into a more becoming smock)*   When did you say Turk was coming by?

MARIE   Said he'd be here about nine-thirty. (DOC *exits, hearing the line about* TURK) That's a pretty smock.

LOLA   *(Goes to table, sits in chair and changes shoes)*   It'll be better to work around the house in.

MARIE   *(Not sounding exactly cheerful)*   Mrs. Delaney, I'm expecting a telegram this morning. Would you leave it on my dresser for me when it comes?

LOLA   Sure, honey. No bad news, I hope.

MARIE   Oh, no! It's from Bruce.

LOLA   (MARIE'S *boy friends are one of her liveliest interests)*   Oh, your boy friend in Cincinnati. Is he coming to see you?

MARIE   I guess so.

LOLA   I'm just dying to meet him.

MARIE   *(Changing the subject)*   Really, Mrs. Delaney, you and Doc have been so nice to me. I just want you to know I appreciate it.

LOLA   Thanks, honey.

MARIE   You've been like a father and mother to me. I appreciate it.

LOLA   Thanks, honey.

MARIE   Turk was saying just the other night what good sports you both are.

LOLA   *(Brushing hair)*   That so?

MARIE   Honest. He said it was just as much fun being with you as with kids our own age.

LOLA   *(Couldn't be more flattered)*   Oh, I like that Turk. He reminds me of a boy I used to know in high school, Dutch McCoy. Where did you ever meet him?

MARIE   In art class.

LOLA Turk take art?

MARIE *(Laughs)* No. It was in a life class. He was modeling. Lots of the athletes do that. It pays them a dollar an hour.

LOLA That's nice.

MARIE Mrs. Delaney? I've got some corrections to make in some of my drawings. Is it all right if I bring Turk home this morning to pose for me? It'll just take a few minutes.

LOLA Sure, honey.

MARIE There's a contest on now. They're giving a prize for the best drawing to use for advertising the Spring Relays.

LOLA And you're going to do a picture of Turk? That's nice. *(A sudden thought)* Doc's gonna be gone tonight. You and Turk can have the living room if you want to. *(A little secretively)*

MARIE *(This is a temptation)* O.K. Thanks.
(Exits to bedroom)

LOLA Tell me more about Bruce.
(Follows her to bedroom door)

MARIE *(Offstage in bedroom. Remembering her affinity)* Well, he comes from one of the best families in Cincinnati. And they have a great big house. And they have a maid, too. And he's got a wonderful personality. He makes three hundred dollars a month.

LOLA That so?

MARIE And he stays at the best hotels. His company insists on it.
(Enters)

LOLA Do you like him as well as Turk?
(Buttoning up back of MARIE'S blouse)

MARIE *(Evasive)* Bruce is so dependable, and . . . he's a gentleman, too.

LOLA Are you goin' to marry him, honey?

MARIE Maybe, after I graduate from college and he feels he can support a wife and children. I'm going to have lots and lots of children.

LOLA I wanted children, too. When I lost my baby and found out I couldn't have any more, I didn't know what to do with myself. I wanted to get a job, but Doc wouldn't hear of it.

MARIE   Bruce is going to come into a lot of money some day. His uncle made a fortune in men's garters.
(Exits into her room)

LOLA *(Leaning on door frame)*   Doc was a rich boy when I married him. His mother left him twenty-five thousand when she died. *(Disillusioned)* It took him a lot to get his office started and everything . . . then, he got sick. *(She makes a futile gesture; then on the bright side)* But Doc's always good to me . . . *now.*

MARIE *(Re-enters)*   Oh, Doc's a peach.

LOLA   I used to be pretty, something like you. *(She gets her picture from table)* I was Beauty Queen of the senior class in high school. My dad was awful strict, though. Once he caught me holding hands with that good-looking Dutch McCoy. Dad sent Dutch home, and wouldn't let me go out after supper for a whole month. Daddy would never let me go out with boys much. Just because I was pretty. He was afraid all the boys would get the wrong idea—*you* know. I never had any fun at all until I met Doc.

MARIE   Sometimes I'm glad I didn't know my father. Mom always let me do pretty much as I please.

LOLA   Doc was the first boy my dad ever let me go out with. We got married that spring.
(Replaces picture. MARIE *sits on couch, puts on shoes and socks)*

MARIE   What did your father think of that?

LOLA   We came right to the city then. And, well, Doc gave up his pre-med course and went to chiropractor school instead.

MARIE   You must have been married awful young.

LOLA   Oh, yes. Eighteen.

MARIE   That must have made your father really mad.

LOLA   Yes, it did. I never went home after that, but my mother comes down here from Green Valley to visit me sometimes.

TURK *(Bursts into the front room from outside. He is a young, big, husky, good-looking boy, nineteen or twenty. He has the openness, the generosity, vigor and health of youth. He's had a little time in the service, but he is not what one would call disciplined. He wears faded dungarees and a T-shirt. He always enters unannounced. He hollers for* MARIE)   Hey, Marie! Ready?

MARIE *(Calling. Runs and exits into bedroom, closing door)*   Just a minute, Turk.

LOLA *(Confidentially)*   I'll entertain him until you're ready. *(She is by nature coy and kittenish with any attractive man. Picks up papers—stuffs them under table)*   The house is such a mess, Turk! I bet you think I'm an awful housekeeper. Some day I'll surprise you. But you're like one of the family now. *(Pause)* My, you're an early caller.

TURK   Gotta get to the library. Haven't cracked a book for a biology exam and Marie's gotta help me.

LOLA *(Unconsciously admiring his stature and physique and looking him over)*   My, I'd think you'd be chilly running around in just that thin little shirt.

TURK   Me? I go like this in the middle of winter.

LOLA   Well, you're a big husky man.

TURK *(Laughs)*   Oh, I'm a brute, *I* am.

LOLA   You should be out in Hollywood making those Tarzan movies.

TURK   I had enough of that place when I was in the Navy.

LOLA   That so?

TURK *(Calling)*   Hey, Marie, hurry up.

MARIE   Oh, be patient, Turk.

TURK *(To LOLA)*   She doesn't realize how busy I am. I'll only have a half hour to study at most. I gotta report to the coach at ten-thirty.

LOLA   What are you in training for now?

TURK   Spring track. They got me throwing the javelin.

LOLA   The javelin? What's that?

TURK *(Laughs at her ignorance)*   It's a big, long lance. *(Assumes the magnificent position)* You hold it like this, erect—then you let go and it goes singing through the air, and lands yards away, if you're any good at it, and sticks in the ground, quivering like an arrow. I won the state championship last year.

LOLA *(She has watched as though fascinated)*   My!

TURK *(Very generous)*   Get Marie to take you to the track field some afternoon, and you can watch me.

LOLA   That would be thrilling.

MARIE *(Comes dancing in)*   Hi, Turk.

TURK   Hi, juicy.

LOLA *(As the young couple move to the doorway)*   Remember, Marie, you and Turk can have the front room tonight. All to yourselves. You can play the radio and dance and make a plate of fudge, or anything you want.

MARIE *(To TURK)*   O.K.?

TURK *(With eagerness)*   Sure.

MARIE   Let's go.
       (Exits)

LOLA   'Bye, kids.

TURK   'Bye, Mrs. Delaney. *(Gives her a chuck under the chin)* You're a swell skirt.
       (LOLA couldn't be more flattered. For a moment she is breathless. They speed out the door and LOLA stands, sadly watching them depart. Then a sad, vacant look comes over her face. Her arms drop in a gesture of futility. Slowly she walks out on the front porch and calls)

LOLA   Little Sheba! Come, Little She-ba. Come back . . . come back, Little Sheba! *(She waits for a few moments, then comes wearily back into the house, closing the door behind her. Now the morning has caught up with her. She goes to the kitchen, kicks off her pumps and gets back into comfies. The sight of the dishes on the drainboard depresses her. Clearly she is bored to death. Then the telephone rings with the promise of relieving her. She answers it)* Hello—Oh, no, you've got the wrong number— Oh, that's all right. *(Again it looks hopeless. She hears the POSTMAN. Now her spirits are lifted. She runs to the door, opens it and awaits him. When he's within distance, she lets loose a barrage of welcome)* 'Morning, Mr. Postman.

POSTMAN   'Morning, ma'am.

LOLA   You better have something for me today. Sometimes I think you don't even know I live here. You haven't left me anything for two whole weeks. If you can't do better than that, I'll just have to get a new postman.

POSTMAN *(On the porch)*   You'll have to get someone to write you some letters, lady. Nope, nothing for you.

LOLA   Well, I was only joking. You knew I was joking, didn't you? I bet you're thirsty. You come right in here and I'll bring you a glass of cold water. Come in and sit down for a few minutes and rest your feet awhile.

POSTMAN   I'll take you up on that, lady. I've worked up quite a thirst. *(Coming in)*

LOLA   You sit down. I'll be back in just a minute. *(Goes to kitchen, gets pitcher out of refrigerator and brings it back)*

POSTMAN   Spring is turnin' into summer awful soon.

LOLA   You feel free to stop here and ask me for a drink of water any time you want to. *(Pouring drink)* That's what we're all here for, isn't it? To make each other comfortable?

POSTMAN   Thank you, ma'am.

LOLA   *(Clinging, not wanting to be left alone so soon; she hurries her conversation to hold him)*   You haven't been our postman very long, have you?

POSTMAN   *(She gives him the glass of water, stands holding pitcher as he drinks)*   No.

LOLA   You postmen have things pretty nice, don't you? I hear you get nice pensions after you been working for the government twenty years. I think that's dandy. It's a *good* job, too. *(Pours him a second glass)* You may get tired but I think it's good for a man to be outside and get a lot of exercise. Keeps him strong and healthy. My husband, he's a doctor, a *chiro*practor; he has to stay inside his office all day long. The only exercise he gets is rubbin' people's backbones. *(They laugh. LOLA goes to table, leaves pitcher)* It makes his hands strong. He's got the strongest hands you ever did see. But he's got a poor digestion. I keep tellin' him he oughta get some fresh air once in a while and some exercise. (POSTMAN *rises as if to go, and this hurries her into a more absorbing monologue)* You know what? My husband is an Alcoholics Anonymous. He doesn't care if I tell you that 'cause he's proud of it. He hasn't touched a drop in almost a year. All that time we've had a quart of whiskey in the pantry for company and he hasn't even gone near it. Doesn't even want to. You know, alcoholics can't drink like ordinary people; they're *allergic* to it. It affects them different. They get started drinking and can't stop. Liquor transforms them. Sometimes they get mean and violent and wanta fight, but if they let liquor alone, they're perfectly all right, just like you and me. (POSTMAN *tries to leave)* You should have seen Doc before he gave it up. He lost all his patients, wouldn't even go to the office; just wanted to stay drunk all day long and he'd come home at night and . . . You just wouldn't believe it if you saw him now. He's got his patients all back, and he's just doing fine.

POSTMAN   Sure, I know Dr. Delaney. I deliver his office mail. He's a fine man.

LOLA   Oh, thanks. You don't ever drink, do you?

POSTMAN   Oh, a few beers once in a while.
(He is ready to go)

LOLA   Well, I guess that stuff doesn't do any of us any good.

POSTMAN   No. *(Crosses down for mail on floor center)* Well, good day, ma'am.

LOLA   Say, you got any kids?

POSTMAN   Three grandchildren.

LOLA *(Getting it from console table)*   We don't have any kids, and we got this toy in a box of breakfast food. Why don't you take it home to them?

POSTMAN   Why, that's very kind of you, ma'am.
(He takes it, and goes)

LOLA   Good-bye, Mr. Postman.

POSTMAN *(On porch)*   I'll see that you get a letter, if I have to write it myself.

LOLA   Thanks. Good-bye. *(Left alone, she turns on radio. Then she goes to kitchen to start dishes, showing her boredom in the half-hearted way she washes them. Takes water back to icebox. Then she spies MRS. COFFMAN hanging baby clothes on lines just outside kitchen door. Goes to door)* My, you're a busy woman this morning, Mrs. Coffman.

MRS. COFFMAN *(German accent. She is outside, but sticks her head in for some of the following)*   Being busy is being happy.

LOLA   I guess so.

MRS. COFFMAN   I don't have it as easy as you. When you got seven kids to look after, you got no time to sit around the house, Mrs. Delaney.

LOLA   I s'pose not.

MRS. COFFMAN   But you don't hear me complain.

LOLA   Oh, no. You never complain. *(Pause)* I guess my little doggie's gone for good, Mrs. Coffman. I sure miss her.

MRS. COFFMAN   The only way to keep from missing one dog is to get another.

LOLA *(Goes to sink, turns off water)*   Oh, I never could find another doggie as cute as Little Sheba.

MRS. COFFMAN   Did you put an ad in the paper?

LOLA   For two whole weeks. No one answered it. It's just like she vanished —into thin air. *(She likes this metaphor)* Every day, though, I go out on the porch and call her. You can't tell; she might be around. Don't you think?

MRS. COFFMAN   You should get busy and forget her. You should get busy, Mrs. Delaney.

LOLA   Yes, I'm going to. I'm going to start my spring house-cleaning one of these days real soon. Why don't you come in and have a cup of coffee with me, Mrs. Coffman, and we can chat awhile?

MRS. COFFMAN   I got work to do, Mrs. Delaney. I got work. (LOLA *turns from the window, annoyed at her rejection. Is about to start in on the dishes when the* MILKMAN *arrives. She opens the back door and detains him)*

MILKMAN   'Morning, Mrs. Coffman.

MRS. COFFMAN   'Morning.

LOLA   Hello there, Mr. Milkman. How are you today?

MILKMAN   'Morning, lady.

LOLA   I think I'm going to want a few specials today. Can you come in a minute?
(Goes to icebox)

MILKMAN *(Coming in)*   What'll it be?
(He probably is used to her. He is not a handsome man, but is husky and attractive in his uniform)

LOLA *(At icebox)*   Well, now, let's see. You got any cottage cheese?

MILKMAN   We always got cottage cheese, lady. *(Showing her card)* All you gotta do is check the items on the card and we leave 'em. Now I gotta go back to the truck.

LOLA   Now, don't scold me. I always mean to do that but you're always here before I think of it. Now, I guess I'll need some coffee cream, too—half a pint.

MILKMAN Coffee cream. O.K.

LOLA Now let me see . . . Oh, yes, I want a quart of buttermilk. My husband has liked buttermilk ever since he stopped drinking. My husband's an alcoholic. Had to give it up. Did I ever tell you? *(Starts out. Stops at sink)*

MILKMAN Yes, lady.
(Starts to go. She follows)

LOLA Now he can't get enough to eat. Eats six times a day. He comes home in the middle of the morning, and I fix him a snack. In the middle of the afternoon he has a malted milk with an egg in it. And then another snack before he goes to bed.

MILKMAN What'd ya know?

LOLA Keeps his energy up.

MILKMAN I'll bet. Anything else, lady?

LOLA No, I guess not.

MILKMAN *(Going out)* Be back in a jiffy.
(Gives her a slip of paper)

LOLA I'm just so sorry I put you to so much extra work. *(He goes. Returns shortly with dairy products)* After this I'm going to do my best to remember to check the card. I don't think it's right to put people to extra work. *(Goes to icebox, puts things away)*

MILKMAN *(Smiles, is willing to forget)* That's all right, lady.

LOLA Maybe you'd like a piece of cake or a sandwich. Got some awfully good cold cuts in the icebox.

MILKMAN No, thanks, lady.

LOLA Or maybe you'd like a cup of coffee.

MILKMAN No, thanks.
(He's checking the items, putting them on the bill)

LOLA You're just a young man. You oughta be going to college. I think everyone should have an education. Do you like your job?

MILKMAN It's O.K.
(Looks at LOLA)

LOLA You're a husky young man. You oughta be out in Hollywood making those Tarzan movies.

MILKMAN *(Steps back. Feels a little flattered)* When I first began on this job I didn't get enough exercise, so I started working out on the bar-bell.

LOLA Bar-bells?

MILKMAN Keeps you in trim.

LOLA *(Fascinated)* Yes, I imagine.

MILKMAN I sent my picture in to *Strength and Health* last month. *(Proudly)* It's a physique study! If they print it, I'll bring you a copy.

LOLA Oh, will you? I think we should all take better care of ourselves, don't you?

MILKMAN If you ask me, lady, that's what's wrong with the world today. We're not taking care of ourselves.

LOLA I wouldn't be surprised.

MILKMAN Every morning, I do forty push-ups before I eat my breakfast.

LOLA Push-ups?

MILKMAN Like this. *(He spreads himself on the floor and demonstrates, doing three rapid push-ups. LOLA couldn't be more fascinated. Then he springs to his feet)* That's good for shoulder development. Wanta feel my shoulders?

LOLA Why . . . why, yes. *(He makes one arm tense and puts her hand on his shoulder)* Why, it's just like a rock.

MILKMAN I can do seventy-nine without stopping.

LOLA Seventy-nine!

MILKMAN Now feel my arm.

LOLA *(Does so)* Goodness!

MILKMAN You wouldn't believe what a puny kid I was. Sickly, no appetite.

LOLA Is that a fact? And, my! Look at you now.

MILKMAN *(Very proud)* Shucks, any man could do the same . . . if he just takes care of himself.

LOLA Oh, sure, sure.
(A horn is heard offstage)

MILKMAN There's my buddy. I gotta beat it. *(Picks up his things, shakes hands, leaves hurriedly)* See you tomorrow, lady.

LOLA 'Bye.
(She watches him from kitchen window until he gets out of sight. There is a look of some wonder on her face, an emptiness, as though she were unable to understand anything that ever happened to her. She looks at clock, runs into living room, turns on radio. A pulsating tom-tom is heard as a theme introduction. Then the ANNOUNCER*)*

ANNOUNCER *(In dramatic voice)* TA-BOOoooo! *(Now in a very soft, highly personalized voice.* LOLA *sits on couch, eats candy)* It's Ta-boo, radio listeners, your fifteen minutes of temptation. *(An alluring voice)* Won't you join me? *(*LOLA *swings feet up)* Won't you leave behind your routine, the dull cares that make up your day-to-day existence, the little worries, the uncertainties, the confusions of the work-a-day world and follow me where pagan spirits hold sway, where lithe natives dance on a moon-enchanted isle, where palm trees sway with the restless ocean tide, restless surging on the white shore? Won't you come along? *(More tom-tom. Now, in an oily voice)* But remember, it's TA-BOOOOOOOOOOOOOO! *(Now the tom-tom again, going into a sensual, primitive rhythm melody.* LOLA *has been transfixed from the beginning of the program. She lies down on the davenport, listening, then slowly, growing more and more comfortable)*

WESTERN UNION BOY *(At door)* Telegram for Miss Marie Buckholder.

LOLA *(Going to door)* She's not here.

WESTERN UNION BOY Sign here.
*(*LOLA *does, then she closes the door and brings the envelope into the house, looking at it wonderingly. This is a major temptation to her. She puts the envelope on the table but can't resist looking at it. Finally she gives in and takes it to the kitchen to steam it open. Then* MARIE *and* TURK *burst into the room.* LOLA, *confused, wonders what to do with the telegram, then decides, just in the nick of time, to jam it in her apron pocket)*

MARIE Mrs. Delaney! *(Turns off radio. At the sound of* MARIE'S *voice,* LOLA *embarrassedly slips the message into her pocket and runs in to greet them)* Mind if we turn your parlor into an art studio?

LOLA Sure, go right ahead. Hi, Turk.
*(*TURK *gives a wave of his arm)*

MARIE *(To* TURK, *indicating her bedroom)* You can change in there, Turk.
(Exit to bedroom)

LOLA *(Puzzled)* Change?

MARIE He's gotta take off his clothes.

LOLA Huh?
(Closes door)

MARIE These drawings are for my life class.

LOLA *(Consoled but still mystified)* Oh.

MARIE *(Sits on couch)* Turk's the best male model we've had all year. Lotsa athletes pose for us 'cause they've all got muscles. They're easier to draw.

LOLA You mean . . . he's gonna pose *naked?*

MARIE *(Laughs)* No. The women do, but the men are always more proper. Turk's going to pose in his track suit.

LOLA Oh. *(Almost to herself)* The women pose naked but the men don't. *(This strikes her as a startling inconsistency)* If it's all right for a woman, it oughta be for a man.

MARIE *(Businesslike)* The man always keeps covered. *(Calling to* TURK) Hurry up, Turk.

TURK *(With all his muscles in place, he comes out. He is not at all self-conscious about his semi-nudity. His body is something he takes very much for granted.* LOLA *is a little dazed by the spectacle of flesh)* How do you want this lovely body? Same pose I took in art class?

MARIE Yah. Over there where I can get more light on you.

TURK *(Opens door. Starts pose)* Anything in the house I can use for a javelin?

MARIE Is there, Mrs. Delaney?

LOLA How about the broom?

TURK O.K.
*(*LOLA *runs out to get it.* TURK *goes to her in kitchen, takes it, returns to living room and resumes pose)*

MARIE *(From her sofa, studying* TURK *in relation to her sketch pad, moves his leg)* Your left foot a little more this way. *(Studying it)* O.K., hold it. *(Starts sketching rapidly and industriously.* LOLA *looks on, lingeringly)*

LOLA *(Starts unwillingly into kitchen, changes her mind and returns to the scene of action.* MARIE *and* TURK *are too busy to comment.* LOLA *looks at sketch, inspecting it)* Well . . . that's real pretty, Marie. (MARIE *is intent.* LOLA *moves closer to look at the drawing)* It . . . it's real artistic. *(Pause)* I wish I was artistic.

TURK   Baby, I can't hold this pose very long at a time.

MARIE   Rest whenever you feel like it.

TURK   O.K.

MARIE *(To* LOLA) If I make a good drawing, they'll use it for the posters for the Spring Relays.

LOLA   Ya. You told me.

MARIE *(To* TURK) After I'm finished with these sketches I won't have to bother you any more.

TURK   No bother. *(Rubs his shoulder—he poses)* Hard pose, though. Gets me in the shoulder.
(MARIE *pays no attention.* LOLA *peers at him so closely, he becomes a little self-conscious and breaks pose. This also breaks* LOLA's *concentration)*

LOLA   I'll heat you up some coffee.
(Goes to kitchen)

TURK *(Softly to* MARIE) Hey, can't you keep her out of here? She makes me feel naked.

MARIE *(Laughs)* I can't keep her out of her own house, can I?

TURK   Didn't she ever see a man before?

MARIE   Not a big beautiful man like you, Turky.
(TURK *smiles, is flattered by any recognition of his physical worth, takes it as an immediate invitation to lovemaking. Pulling her up, he kisses her as* DOC *comes up on porch.* MARIE *pushes* TURK *away)* Turk, get back in your corner. (DOC *comes in from outside)*

DOC *(Cheerily)* Hi, everyone.

MARIE   Hi.

TURK   Hi, Doc. (DOC *then sees* TURK, *feels immediate resentment. Goes into kitchen to* LOLA) What's goin' on here?

LOLA *(Getting cups)* Oh, hello, Daddy. Marie's doin' a drawin'.

DOC *(Trying to size up the situation.* MARIE *and* TURK *are too busy to speak)* Oh.

LOLA   I've just heated up the coffee, want some?

DOC   Yeah. What happened to Turk's clothes?

LOLA   Marie's doing some drawings for her *life* class, Doc.

DOC   Can't she draw him with his clothes on?

LOLA   *(With coffee. Very professional now)*   No, Doc, it's not the same. See, it's a *life* class. They draw bodies. They all do it, right in the classroom.

DOC   Why, Marie's just a young girl; she shouldn't be drawing things like that. I don't care if they do teach it at college. It's not right.

LOLA   *(Disclaiming responsibility)*   I don't know, Doc.

TURK   *(Turns)*   I'm tired.

MARIE   *(Squats at his feet)*   Just let me finish the foot.

DOC   Why doesn't she draw something else, a bowl of flowers or a cathedral . . . or a sunset?

LOLA   All she told me, Doc, was if she made a good drawing of Turk, they'd use it for the posters for the Spring Relays. *(Pause)* So I guess they don't want sunsets.

DOC   What if someone walked into the house now? What would they think?

LOLA   Daddy, Marie just asked me if it was all right if Turk came and posed for her. Now that's all she said, and I said O.K. But if you think it's wrong I won't let them do it again.

DOC   I just don't like it.

MARIE   Hold it a minute more.

TURK   O.K.

LOLA   Well, then you speak to Marie about it if . . .

DOC   *(He'd never mention anything disapprovingly to* MARIE*)*   No, Baby. I couldn't do that.

LOLA   Well, then . . .

DOC   Besides, it's not her fault. If those college people make her do drawings like that, I suppose she has to do them. I just don't think it's right she should have to, that's all.

LOLA   Well, if you think it's wrong . . .

DOC *(Ready to dismiss it)*   Never mind.

LOLA   I don't see any harm in it, Daddy.

DOC   Forget it.

LOLA *(Goes to icebox)*   Would you like some buttermilk?

DOC   Thanks.
    (MARIE *finishes sketch*)

MARIE   O.K. That's all I can do for today.

TURK   Is there anything I can do for *you?*

MARIE   Yes—get your clothes on.

TURK   O.K., coach.
    (TURK *exits*)

LOLA   You know what Marie said, Doc? She said that the women pose naked, but the men don't.

DOC   Why, of course, honey.

LOLA   Why is that?

DOC *(Stumped)*   Well . . .

LOLA   If it's all right for a woman it oughta be for a man. But the man always keeps covered. That's what she said.

DOC   Well, that's the way it should be, honey. A man, after all, is a man, and he . . . well, he has to protect himself.

LOLA   And a woman doesn't?

DOC   It's different, honey.

LOLA   Is it? I've got a secret, Doc. Bruce is comin'.

DOC   Is that so?

LOLA *(After a glum silence)*   You know Marie's boy friend from Cincinnati. I promised Marie a long time ago, when her fiancé came to town, dinner was on me. So I'm getting out the best china and cooking the best meal you ever sat down to.

DOC   When did she get the news?

LOLA   The telegram came this morning.

DOC That's fine. That Bruce sounds to me like just the fellow for her. I think I'll go in and congratulate her.

LOLA *(Nervous)* Not now, Doc.

DOC Why not?

LOLA Well, Turk's there. It might make him feel embarrassed.

DOC Well, why doesn't Turk clear out now that Bruce is coming? What's he hanging around for? She's engaged to marry Bruce, isn't she?
(TURK *enters from bedroom and goes to* MARIE, *starting to make advances*)

LOLA Marie's just doing a picture of him, Doc.

DOC You always stick up for him. You encourage him.

LOLA Shhh, Daddy. Don't get upset.

DOC *(Very angrily)* All right, but if anything happens to the girl I'll never forgive you.
(DOC *goes upstairs.* TURK *then grabs* MARIE, *kisses her passionately*)

CURTAIN

SCENE: *The same evening, after supper. Outside it is dark. There has been an almost miraculous transformation of the entire house.* LOLA, *apparently, has been working hard and fast all day. The rooms are spotlessly clean and there are such additions as new lampshades, fresh curtains, etc. In the kitchen all the enamel surfaces glisten, and piles of junk that have lain around for months have been disposed of.* LOLA *and* DOC *are in the kitchen, he washing up the dishes and she puttering around putting the finishing touches on her house-cleaning.*

LOLA *(At stove)*   There's still some beans left. Do you want them, Doc?

DOC   I had enough.

LOLA   I hope you got enough to eat tonight, Daddy. I been so busy cleaning I didn't have time to fix you much.

DOC   I wasn't very hungry.

LOLA *(At table, cleaning up)*   You know what? Mrs. Coffman said I could come over and pick all the lilacs I wanted for my centerpiece tomorrow. Isn't that nice? I don't think she poisoned Little Sheba, do you?

DOC   I never did think so, Baby. Where'd you get the new curtains?

LOLA   I went out and bought them this afternoon. Aren't they pretty? Be careful of the woodwork, it's been varnished.

DOC   How come, honey?

LOLA *(Gets broom and dustpan from closet)*   Bruce is comin'. I figured I had to do my spring house-cleaning some time.

DOC   You got all this done in one day? The house hasn't looked like this in years.

LOLA   I can be a good housekeeper when I want to be, can't I, Doc?

DOC *(Holding dustpan for* LOLA) I never had any complaints. Where's Marie now?

LOLA I don't know, Doc. I haven't seen her since she left here this morning with Turk.

DOC *(With a look of disapproval)* Marie's too nice to be wasting her time with him.

LOLA Daddy, Marie can take care of herself. Don't worry. *(Returns broom to closet)*

DOC *(Goes into living room)* 'Bout time for Fibber McGee and Molly.

LOLA *(Untying apron. Goes to closet and then back door)* Daddy, I'm gonna run over to Mrs. Coffman's and see if she's got any silver polish. I'll be right back. (DOC *goes to radio.* LOLA *exits. At the radio* DOC *starts twisting the dial. He rejects one noisy program after another, then very unexpectedly he comes across a rendition of Schubert's famous "Ave Maria," sung in a high soprano voice. Probably he has encountered the piece before somewhere, but it is now making its first impression on him. Gradually he is transported into a world of ethereal beauty which he never knew existed. He listens intently. The music has expressed some ideal of beauty he never fully realized and he is even a little mystified. Then* LOLA *comes in the back door, letting it slam, breaking the spell, and announcing in a loud, energetic voice)* Isn't it funny? I'm not a bit tired tonight. You'd think after working so hard all day I'd be pooped.

DOC *(In the living room; he cringes)* Baby, don't use that word.

LOLA *(To* DOC *on couch. Sets silver polish down and joins* DOC) I'm sorry, Doc. I hear Marie and Turk say it all the time, and I thought it was kinda cute.

DOC It . . . it sounds vulgar.

LOLA *(Kisses* DOC) I won't say it again, Daddy. Where's Fibber McGee?

DOC Not quite time yet.

LOLA Let's get some peppy music.

DOC *(Tuning in a sentimental dance band)* That what you want?

LOLA That's O.K. (DOC *takes a pack of cards off radio and starts shuffling them, very deftly)* I love to watch you shuffle cards, Daddy. You use your hands so gracefully. *(She watches closely)* Do me one of your card tricks.

DOC   Baby, you've seen them all.

LOLA   But I never get tired of them.

DOC   O.K. Take a card. (LOLA *does*) Keep it now. Don't tell me what it is.

LOLA   I won't.

DOC   *(Shuffling cards again)*   Now put it back in the deck. I won't look. *(He closes his eyes)*

LOLA   *(With childish delight)*   All right.

DOC   Put it back.

LOLA   Uh-huh.

DOC   O.K. *(Shuffles cards again, cutting them, taking top half off, exposing* LOLA'*s card, to her astonishment)* That your card?

LOLA   *(Unbelievingly)*   Daddy, how did you do it?

DOC   Baby, I've pulled that trick on you dozens of times.

LOLA   But I never understand how you do it.

DOC   Very simple.

LOLA   Docky, show me how you do that.

DOC   *(You can forgive him a harmless feeling of superiority)*   Try it for yourself.

LOLA   Doc, you're clever. I never could do it.

DOC   Nothing to it.

LOLA   There is *too*. Show me how you do it, Doc.

DOC   And give away all my secrets? It's a gift, honey. A magic gift.

LOLA   Can't you give it to me?

DOC   *(Picks up newspaper)*   A man has to keep some things to himself.

LOLA   It's not a gift at all, it's just some trick you *learned*.

DOC   O.K., Baby, any way you want to look at it.

LOLA   Let's have some music. How soon do you have to meet Ed Anderson?
    (DOC *turns on radio*)

DOC I still got a little time.
(Pleased)

LOLA Marie's going to be awfully happy when she sees the house all fixed up. She can entertain Bruce here when he comes, and maybe we could have a little party here and you can do your card tricks.

DOC O.K.

LOLA I think a young girl should be able to bring her friends home.

DOC Sure.

LOLA We never liked to sit around the house 'cause the folks always stayed there with us. *(Rises—starts dancing alone)* Remember the dances we used to go to, Daddy?

DOC Sure.

LOLA We had awful good times—for a while, didn't we?

DOC Yes, Baby.

LOLA Remember the homecoming dance, when Charlie Kettlekamp and I won the Charleston contest?

DOC Please, honey, I'm trying to read.

LOLA And you got mad at him 'cause he thought he should take me home afterwards.

DOC I did not.

LOLA Yes, you did—Charlie was all right, Doc, really he was. You were just jealous.

DOC I *wasn't* jealous.

LOLA *(She has become very coy and flirtatious now, an old dog playing old tricks)* You got jealous every time we went out any place and I even looked at another boy. There was never anything between Charlie and me; there never was.

DOC That was a long time ago . . .

LOLA Lots of other boys called me up for dates . . . Sammy Knight . . . Hand Biderman . . . Dutch McCoy.

DOC Sure, Baby. You were the "it" girl.

LOLA (*Pleading for his attention now*)   But I saved all my dates for *you*, didn't I, Doc?

DOC (*Trying to joke*)   As far as *I* know, Baby.

LOLA (*Hurt*)   Daddy, I did. You *got* to believe that. I never took a date with any other boy but you.

DOC (*A little weary and impatient*)   That's all forgotten now. (*Turns off radio*)

LOLA   How can you talk that way, Doc? That was the happiest time of our lives. I'll never forget it.

DOC (*Disapprovingly*)   Honey!

LOLA (*At the window*)   That was a nice spring. The trees were so heavy and green and the air smelled so sweet. Remember the walks we used to take, down to the old chapel, where it was so quiet and still?
(*Sits on couch*)

DOC   In the spring a young man's fancy turns . . . pretty fancy.

LOLA (*In the same tone of reverie*)   I was pretty then, wasn't I, Doc? Remember the first time you kissed me? You were scared as a young girl, I believe, Doc; you trembled so. (*She is being very soft and delicate. Caught in the reverie, he chokes a little and cannot answer*) We'd been going together all year and you were always so shy. Then for the first time you grabbed me and kissed me. Tears came to your eyes, Doc, and you said you'd love me forever and ever. Remember? You said . . . if I didn't marry you, you wanted to die . . . I remember 'cause it scared me for anyone to say a thing like that.

DOC (*In a repressed tone*)   Yes, Baby.

LOLA   And when the evening came on, we stretched out on the cool grass and you kissed me all night long.

DOC (*Opens doors*)   Baby, you've got to forget those things. That was twenty years ago.

LOLA   I'll soon be forty. Those years have just vanished—vanished into thin air.

DOC   Yes.

LOLA   Just disappeared—like Little Sheba. (*Pause*) Maybe you're sorry you married me now. You didn't know I was going to get old and fat and sloppy . . .

DOC   Oh, Baby!

LOLA   It's the truth. That's what I am. But I didn't know it, either. Are you sorry you married me, Doc?

DOC   Of course not.

LOLA   I mean, are you sorry you *had* to marry me?

DOC   *(Goes to porch)*   We were never going to talk about that, Baby.

LOLA   *(Following* DOC *out)*   You *were* the first one, Daddy, the *only* one. I'd just die if you didn't believe that.

DOC   *(Tenderly)*   I know, Baby.

LOLA   You were so nice and so proper, Doc; I thought nothing we could do together could ever be wrong—or make us unhappy. Do you think we did wrong, Doc?

DOC   *(Consoling)*   No, Baby, of course I don't.

LOLA   I don't think anyone knows about it except my folks, do you?

DOC   Of course not, Baby.

LOLA   *(Follows him in)*   I wish the baby had lived, Doc. I don't think that woman knew her business, do you, Doc?

DOC   I guess not.

LOLA   If we'd gone to a doctor, she would have lived, don't you think?

DOC   Perhaps.

LOLA   A doctor wouldn't have known we'd just got married, would he? Why were we so afraid?

DOC   *(Sits on couch)*   We were just kids. Kids don't know how to look after things.

LOLA   *(Sits on couch)*   If we'd had the baby she'd be a young girl now; then maybe you'd have *saved* your money, Doc, and she could be going to college—like Marie.

DOC   Baby, what's done is done.

LOLA   It must make you feel bad at times to think you had to give up being a doctor and to think you don't have any money like you used to.

DOC   No . . . no, Baby. We should never feel bad about what's past. What's in the past can't be helped. You . . . you've got to forget it and live for the present. If you can't forget the past, you stay in it and never get out. I might be a big M.D. today, instead of a chiropractor; we might have had a family to raise and be with us now; I might still have a lot of money if I'd used my head and invested it carefully, instead of gettin' drunk every night. We might have a nice house, and comforts, and friends. But we don't have any of those things. So what! We gotta keep on living, don't we? I can't stop just 'cause I made a few mistakes. I gotta keep goin' . . . somehow.

LOLA Sure, Daddy.

DOC *(Sighs and wipes brow)* I . . . I wish you wouldn't ask me questions like that, Baby. Let's not talk about it any more. I gotta keep goin', and not let things upset me, or . . . or . . . *I* saw enough at the City Hospital to keep me sober for a long time.

LOLA I'm sorry, Doc. I didn't mean to upset you.

DOC I'm not upset.

LOLA What time'll you be home tonight?

DOC 'Bout eleven o'clock.

LOLA I wish you didn't have to go tonight. I feel kinda lonesome.

DOC Ya, so am I, Baby, but some time soon, we'll go *out* together. I kinda hate to go to those night clubs and places since I stopped drinking, but some night I'll take you out to dinner.

LOLA Oh, will you, Daddy?

DOC We'll get dressed up and go to the Windermere and have a fine dinner and dance between courses.

LOLA *(Eagerly)* Let's do, Daddy. I got a little money saved up. I got about forty dollars out in the kitchen. We can take that if you need it.

DOC I'll have plenty of money the first of the month.

LOLA *(She has made a quick response to the change of mood, seeing a future evening of carefree fun)* What are we sitting round here so serious for? *(Turns to radio)* Let's have some music. (LOLA *gets a lively fox trot on the radio, dances with* DOC. *They begin dancing vigorously as though to dispense with the sadness of the preceding dialogue, but slowly it winds them and leaves* LOLA *panting)* We oughta go dancing . . . all the time, Docky . . . It'd be good for us. Maybe if I danced more often, I'd lose . . . some of . . . this fat. I remember . . . I used to be able to dance like

LOLA   I don't see any harm in it, Doc. I steamed it open and sealed it back.
(TURK *at switch in living room*) She'll never know the difference. I don't
see any harm in that, Doc.

DOC *(Gives up)*   O.K., Baby, if you don't see any harm in it, I guess I can't
explain it.
(Starts getting ready to go)

LOLA   I'm sorry, Doc. Honest, I'll never do it again. Will you forgive me?

DOC *(Giving her a peck of a kiss)*   I forgive you.

MARIE *(Comes back with book)*   Let's look like we're studying.

TURK   Biology? Hot dog!

LOLA *(After* MARIE *leaves her room)*   Now I feel better. Do you have to go
now?
(TURK *sits by* MARIE *on the couch*)

DOC   Yah.

LOLA   Before you go, why don't you show your tricks to Marie?

DOC *(Reluctantly)*   Not now.

LOLA   Oh, please do. They'd be crazy about them.

DOC *(With pride)*   O.K. *(Preens himself a little)* If you think they'd enjoy
them . . . (LOLA, *starting to living room, stops suddenly upon seeing*
MARIE *and* TURK *spooning behind a book. A broad, pleased smile breaks on
her face and she stands silently watching.* DOC *is at sink)* Well . . .
what's the matter, Baby?

LOLA *(In a soft voice)*   Oh . . . nothing . . . nothing . . . Doc.

DOC   Well, do you want me to show 'em my tricks or don't you?

LOLA *(Coming back to center kitchen; in a secretive voice with a little giggle)*   I guess they wouldn't be interested now.

DOC *(With injured pride. A little sore)*   Oh, very well.

LOLA   Come and look, Daddy.

DOC *(Shocked and angry)*   No!

LOLA   Just one little look. They're just kids, Daddy. It's sweet. *(Drags him
by arm)*

DOC *(Jerking loose)*   Stop it, Baby. I won't do it. It's not decent to snoop around spying on people like that. It's cheap and mischievous and mean.

LOLA *(This had never occurred to her)*   Is it?

DOC   Of course it is.

LOLA   I don't spy on Marie and Turk to be mischievous and mean.

DOC   Then why *do* you do it?

LOLA   You watch young people make love in the movies, don't you, Doc? There's nothing wrong with that. And I *know* Marie and I like her, and Turk's nice, too. They're both so young and pretty. Why shouldn't I watch them?

DOC   I give up.

LOLA   Well, why shouldn't I?

DOC   I don't know, Baby, but it's not nice.
(TURK *kisses* MARIE'S *ear*)

LOLA *(Plaintive)*   I think it's one of the nicest things I know.

MARIE   Let's go out on the porch.
(They steal out)

DOC   It's not right for Marie to do that, particularly since Bruce is coming. We shouldn't allow it.

LOLA   Oh, they don't do any harm, Doc. I think it's all right. (TURK *and* MARIE *go to porch*)

DOC   It's not all right. I don't know why you encourage that sort of thing.

LOLA   I don't encourage it.

DOC   You do, too. You like that fellow Turk. You said so. And I say he's no good. Marie's sweet and innocent; she doesn't understand guys like him. I think I oughta run him outa the house.

LOLA   Daddy, you wouldn't do that.

DOC *(Very heated)*   Then you talk to her and tell her how we feel.

LOLA   Hush, Daddy. They'll hear you.

DOC   I don't care if they do hear me.

LOLA *(To DOC at stove)*   Don't get upset, Daddy. Bruce is coming and Turk won't be around any longer. I promise you.

DOC   All right. I better go.

LOLA   I'll go with you, Doc. Just let me run up and get a sweater. Now wait for me.

DOC   Hurry, Baby.
(LOLA *goes upstairs.* DOC *is at platform when he hears* TURK *laugh on the porch.* DOC *sees whiskey bottle. Reaches for it and hears* MARIE *giggle. Turns away as* TURK *laughs again. Turns back to the bottle and hears* LOLA's *voice from upstairs*)

LOLA   I'll be there in a minute, Doc. (*Enters downstairs*) I'm all ready. (DOC *turns out kitchen lights and they go into living room*) I'm walking Doc down to the bus. (DOC *sees* TURK *with* LOLA's *picture. Takes it out of his hand, puts it on shelf as* LOLA *leads him out.* DOC *is offstage*) Then I'll go for a long walk in the moonlight. Have a good time.
(*She exits*)

MARIE   'Bye, Mrs. Delaney.
(*Exits*)

TURK   He hates my guts.
(*Goes to front door*)

MARIE   Oh, he does not.
(*Follows* TURK, *blocks his exit in door*)

TURK   Yes, he does. If you ask me, he's jealous.

MARIE   Jealous?

TURK   I've always thought he had a crush on you.

MARIE   Now, Turk, don't be silly. Doc is nice to me. It's just in a few little things he does, like fixing my breakfast, but he's nice to everyone.

TURK   He ever make a pass?

MARIE   No. He'd never get fresh.

TURK   He better not.

MARIE   Turk, don't be ridiculous. Doc's such a nice, quiet man; if he gets any fun out of being nice to me, why not?

TURK   He's got a wife of his own, hasn't he? Why doesn't he make a few passes at her?

MARIE   Things like that are none of our business.

TURK   O.K. How about a snuggle, lovely?

MARIE   *(A little prim and businesslike)*   No more for tonight, Turk.

TURK   Why's tonight different from any other night?

MARIE   I think we should make it a rule, every once in a while, just to sit and talk.
(Starts to sit on couch, but goes to chair)

TURK   *(Restless, sits on couch)*   O.K. What'll we talk about?

MARIE   Well . . . there's lotsa things.

TURK   O.K. Start in.

MARIE   A person doesn't start a conversation that way.

TURK   Start it any way you want to.

MARIE   Two people should have something to talk about, like politics or psychology or religion.

TURK   How 'bout sex?

MARIE   Turk!

TURK   *(Chases her around couch)*   Have you read the Kinsey Report, Miss Buckholder?

MARIE   I should say not.

TURK   How old were you when you had your first affair, Miss Buckholder? And did you ever have relations with your grandfather?

MARIE   Turk, stop it.

TURK   You wanted to talk about something; I was only trying to please. Let's have a kiss.

MARIE   Not tonight.

TURK   Who you savin' it up for?

MARIE   Don't talk that way.

TURK   *(Gets up, yawns)*   Well, thanks, Miss Buckholder, for a nice evening. It's been a most enjoyable talk.

MARIE   *(Anxious)*   Turk, where are you going?

TURK   I guess I'm a man of action, Baby.

MARIE   Turk, don't go.

TURK   Why not? I'm not doin' any good here.

MARIE   Don't go.

TURK   *(Returns and she touches him. They sit on couch)*   Now why didn't you think of this before? C'mon, let's get to work.

MARIE   Oh, Turk, this is all we ever do.

TURK   Are you complaining?

MARIE   *(Weakly)*   No.

TURK   Then what do you want to put on such a front for?

MARIE   It's not a front.

TURK   What else is it? *(Mimicking)* Oh, no, Turk. Not tonight, Turk. I want to talk about philosophy, Turk. *(Himself again)* When all the time you know that if I went outa here without givin' you a good lovin' up you'd be sore as hell . . . Wouldn't you?

MARIE   *(She has to admit to herself it's true; she chuckles)*   Oh . . . Turk . . .

TURK   It's true, isn't it?

MARIE   Maybe.

TURK   How about tonight, lovely; going to be lonesome?

MARIE   Turk, you're in training.

TURK   What of it? I can throw that old javelin any old time, *any* old time. C'mon, Baby, we've got by with it before, haven't we?

MARIE   I'm not so sure.

TURK   What do you mean?

MARIE   Sometimes I think Mrs. Delaney knows.

TURK   Well, bring her along. I'll take care of her, too, if it'll keep her quiet.

MARIE   *(A pretense of being shocked)*   Turk!

TURK   What makes you think so?

MARIE   Women just sense those things. She asks so many questions.

TURK   She ever *say* anything?

MARIE   No.

TURK   Now *you're* imagining things.

MARIE   Maybe.

TURK   Well, stop it.

MARIE   O.K.

TURK   *(Follows* MARIE*)*   Honey, I know I talk awful rough around you at times; I never was a very gentlemanly bastard, but you really don't mind it . . . do you? *(She only smiles mischievously)* Anyway, you know I'm nuts about you.

MARIE   *(Smug)*   Are you?
(Now they engage in a little rough-house, he cuffing her like an affection-ate bear, she responding with "Stop it," "Turk, that hurt," etc. And she slaps him playfully. Then they laugh together at their own pretense. Now LOLA *enters the back way very quietly, tiptoeing through the dark kitchen, standing by the doorway where she can peek at them. There is a quiet, satisfied smile on her face. She watches every move they make, alertly)*

TURK   Now, Miss Buckholder, what is your opinion of the psychodynamic pressure of living in the atomic age?

MARIE   *(Playfully)*   Turk, don't make fun of me.

TURK   Tonight?

MARIE   *(Her eyes dance as she puts him off just a little longer)*   Well.

TURK   Tonight will never come again. *(This is true. She smiles)* O.K.?

MARIE   Tonight will never come again. . . . *(They embrace and start to dance)* Let's go out somewhere first and have a few beers. We can't come back till they're asleep.

TURK   O.K.
(They dance slowly out the door. Then LOLA *moves quietly into the living room and out onto the porch. There she can be heard calling plaintively in a lost voice)*

LOLA   Little Sheba . . . Come back . . . Come back, Little Sheba. Come back.

CURTAIN

SCENE: *The next morning.* LOLA *and* DOC *are at breakfast again.* LOLA *is rambling on while* DOC *sits meditatively, his head down, his face in his hands.*

LOLA *(In a light, humorous way, as though the faults of youth were as blameless as the uncontrollable actions of a puppy. Chuckles)* Then they danced for a while and went out together, arm in arm. . . .

DOC *(Sitting at table, very nervous and tense)* I don't wanta hear any more about it, Baby.

LOLA What's the matter, Docky?

DOC Nothing.

LOLA You look like you didn't feel very good.

DOC I didn't sleep well last night.

LOLA You didn't take any of those sleeping pills, did you?

DOC No.

LOLA Well, don't. The doctors say they're terrible for you.

DOC I'll feel better after a while.

LOLA Of course you will.

DOC What time did Marie come in last night?

LOLA I don't know, Doc. I went to bed early and went right to sleep. Why?

DOC Oh . . . nothing.

LOLA You musta slept if you didn't hear her.

DOC I heard her; it was after midnight.

LOLA Then what did you ask me for?

DOC I wasn't sure it was her.

LOLA What do you mean?

DOC I thought I heard a man's voice.

LOLA Turk probably brought her inside the door.

DOC *(Troubled)* I thought I heard someone laughing. A man's laugh . . . I guess I was just hearing things.

LOLA Say your prayer?

DOC *(Gets up)* Yes.

LOLA Kiss me 'bye. *(He leans over and kisses her, then puts on his coat and starts to leave)* Do you think you could get home a little early? I want you to help me entertain Bruce. Marie said he'd be here about five-thirty. I'm going to have a lovely dinner: stuffed pork chops, twice-baked potatoes, and asparagus, and for dessert a big chocolate cake and maybe ice cream . . .

DOC Sounds fine.

LOLA So you get home and help me.

DOC O.K.
(DOC leaves kitchen and goes into living room. Again on the chair is MARIE'S scarf. He picks it up as before and fondles it. Then there is the sound of TURK's laughter, soft and barely audible. It sounds like the laugh of a sated Bacchus. DOC's body stiffens. It is a sickening fact he must face and it has been revealed to him in its ugliest light. The lyrical grace, the spiritual ideal of Ave Maria is shattered. He has been fighting the truth, maybe suspecting all along that he was deceiving himself. Now he looks as though he might vomit. All his blind confusion is inside him. With an immobile expression of blankness on his face, he stumbles into the table above the sofa)

LOLA *(Still in kitchen)* Haven't you gone yet, Docky?

DOC *(Dazed)* No . . . no, Baby.

LOLA *(In doorway)* Anything the matter?

DOC No . . . no. I'm all right now.
(Drops scarf, takes hat, exits. He has managed to sound perfectly natural. He braces himself and goes out. LOLA stands a moment, looking after him with a little curiosity. Then MRS. COFFMAN enters, sticks her head in back door)

MRS. COFFMAN Anybody home?

LOLA *(On platform)* 'Morning, Mrs. Coffman.

MRS. COFFMAN *(Inspecting the kitchen's new look)* So this is what you've been up to, Mrs. Delaney.

LOLA *(Proud)* Yes, I been busy.
(MARIE'S door opens and closes. MARIE sticks her head out of her bedroom door to see if the coast is clear, then sticks her head back in again to whisper to TURK that he can leave without being observed)

MRS. COFFMAN Busy? Good Lord, I never seen such activity. What got into you, lady?

LOLA Company tonight. I thought I'd fix things up a little.

MRS. COFFMAN You mean you done all this in one day?

LOLA *(With simple pride)* I said I been busy.

MRS. COFFMAN Dear God, you done your spring house-cleaning all in one day.
(TURK appears in living room)

LOLA *(Appreciating this)* I fixed up the living room a little, too.

MRS. COFFMAN I must see it. *(Goes into living room. TURK overhears her and ducks back into MARIE'S room, shutting the door behind himself and MARIE)* I declare! Overnight you turn the place into something really swanky.

LOLA Yes, and I bought a few new things, too.

MRS. COFFMAN Neat as a pin, and so warm and cozy. I take my hat off to you, Mrs. Delaney. I didn't know you had it in you. All these years, now, I been sayin' to myself, "That Mrs. Delaney is a good for nothing, sits around the house all day, and never so much as shakes a dust mop." I guess it just shows, we never really know what people are like.

LOLA I still got some coffee.

MRS. COFFMAN Not now, Mrs. Delaney. Seeing your house so clean makes me feel ashamed. I gotta get home and get to work.
(Goes to kitchen)

LOLA *(Follows)* I hafta get busy, too. I got to get out all the silver and china. I like to set the table early, so I can spend the rest of the day looking at it.
(Both laugh)

MRS. COFFMAN Good day, Mrs. Delaney.

(Exits. Hearing the screen door slam, MARIE *guards the kitchen door and* TURK *slips out the front. But neither has counted on* DOC'S *reappearance. After seeing that* TURK *is safe,* MARIE *blows a good-bye kiss to him and joins* LOLA *in the kitchen. But* DOC *is coming in the front door just as* TURK *starts to go out. There is a moment of blind embarrassment, during which* DOC *only looks stupefied and* TURK, *after mumbling an unintelligible apology, runs out. First* DOC *is mystified, trying to figure it all out. His face looks more and more troubled. Meanwhile,* MARIE *and* LOLA *are talking in the kitchen)*

MARIE　Boo!
(Sneaking up behind LOLA *at back porch)*

LOLA *(Jumping around)*　Heavens! You scared me, Marie. You up already?

MARIE　Yah.

LOLA　This is Saturday. You could sleep as late as you wanted.

MARIE *(Pouring a cup of coffee)*　I thought I'd get up early and help you.

LOLA　Honey, I'd sure appreciate it. You can put up the table in the living room, after you've had your breakfast. That's where we'll eat. Then you can help me set it.
*(*DOC *closes door)*

MARIE　O.K.

LOLA　Want a sweet roll?

MARIE　I don't think so. Turk and I had so much beer last night. He got kinda tight.

LOLA　He shouldn't do that, Marie.

MARIE *(Starts for living room)*　Just keep the coffee hot for me. I'll want another cup in a minute. *(Stops on seeing* DOC*)* Why, Dr. Delaney! I thought you'd gone.

DOC *(Trying to sustain his usual manner)*　Good morning, Marie.
(But not looking at her)

MARIE *(She immediately wonders)*　Why . . . why . . . how long have you been here, Doc?

DOC　Just got here, just this minute.

LOLA *(Comes in)*　That you, Daddy?

DOC　It's me.

LOLA What are you doing back?

DOC I . . . I just thought maybe I'd feel better . . . if I took a glass of soda water . . .

LOLA I'm afraid you're not well, Daddy.

DOC I'm all right.
(Starts for kitchen)

LOLA *(Helping* MARIE *with table)* The soda's on the drainboard. (DOC *goes to kitchen, fixes some soda, and stands a moment, just thinking. Then he sits sipping the soda, as though he were trying to make up his mind about something)* Marie, would you help me move the table? It'd be nice now if we had a dining room, wouldn't it? But if we had a dining room, I guess we wouldn't have you, Marie. It was my idea to turn the dining room into a bedroom and rent it. I thought of lots of things to do for extra money . . . a few years ago . . . when Doc was so . . . so sick.
*(They set up table—*LOLA *gets cloth from cabinet)*

MARIE This is a lovely tablecloth.

LOLA Irish linen. Doc's mother gave it to us when we got married. She gave us all our silver and china, too. The china's Havelin. I'm so proud of it. It's the most valuable possession we own. I just washed it. . . . Will you help me bring it in? *(Getting china from kitchen)* Doc was sortuva Mama's boy. He was an only child and his mother thought the sun rose and set in him. Didn't she, Docky? She brought Doc up like a real gentleman.

MARIE Where are the napkins?

LOLA Oh, I forgot them. They're so nice I keep them in my bureau drawer with my handkerchiefs. Come upstairs and we'll get them.
*(*LOLA *and* MARIE *go upstairs. Then* DOC *listens to be sure* LOLA *and* MARIE *are upstairs, looks cautiously at the whiskey bottle on pantry shelf but manages to resist several times. Finally he gives in to temptation, grabs bottle off shelf, then starts wondering how to get past* LOLA *with it. Finally, it occurs to him to wrap it inside his trench coat which he gets from pantry and carries over his arm.* LOLA *and* MARIE *are heard upstairs. They return to the living room and continue setting table as* DOC *enters from kitchen on his way out)*

LOLA *(Coming downstairs)* Did you ever notice how nice he keeps his fingernails? Not many men think of things like that. And he used to take his mother to church every Sunday.

MARIE *(At table)*   Oh, Doc's a real gentleman.

LOLA   Treats women like they were all beautiful angels. We went together a whole year before he even kissed me. (DOC *comes through the living room with coat and bottle, going to front door*) On your way back to the office now, Docky?

DOC *(His back to them)*   Yes.

LOLA   Aren't you going to kiss me good-bye before you go, Daddy? *(She goes to him and kisses him.* MARIE *catches* DOC'S *eye and smiles. Then she exits to her room, leaving door open)* Get home early as you can. I'll need you. We gotta give Bruce a royal welcome.

DOC   Yes, Baby.

LOLA   Feeling all right?

DOC   Yes.

LOLA *(In doorway,* DOC *is on porch)*   Take care of yourself.

DOC *(In a toneless voice)*   Good-bye.
   (He goes)

LOLA *(Coming back to table with pleased expression, which changes to a puzzled look, calls to* MARIE)   Now that's funny. Why did Doc take his raincoat? It's a beautiful day. There isn't a cloud in sight.

CURTAIN

SCENE: *It is now 5:30. The scene is the same as the preceding except that more finishing touches have been added and the two women, still primping the table, lighting the tapers, are dressed in their best.* LOLA *is arranging the centerpiece.*

LOLA *(Above table, fixing flowers)* I just love lilacs, don't you, Marie? *(Takes one and studies it)* Mrs. Coffman was nice; she let me have all I wanted. *(Looks at it very closely)* Aren't they pretty? And they smell so sweet. I think they're the nicest flower there is.

MARIE They don't last long.

LOLA *(Respectfully)* No. Just a few days. Mrs. Coffman's started blooming just day before yesterday.

MARIE By the first of the week they'll all be gone.

LOLA Vanish . . . they'll vanish into thin air. *(Gayer now)* Here, honey, we have them to spare *now*. Put this in your hair. There. (MARIE *does*) Mrs. Coffman's been so nice lately. I didn't use to like her. Now where could Doc be? He promised he'd get here early. He didn't even come home for lunch.

MARIE *(Gets two chairs from bedroom)* Mrs. Delaney, you're a peach to go to all this trouble.

LOLA *(Gets salt and pepper)* Shoot, I'm gettin' more fun out of it than you are. Do you think Bruce is going to like us?

MARIE If he doesn't, I'll never speak to him again.

LOLA *(Eagerly)* I'm just dying to meet him. But I feel sorta bad I never got to do anything nice for Turk.

MARIE *(Carefully prying)* Did . . . Doc ever say anything to you about Turk . . . and me?

LOLA   About Turk and you? No, honey. Why?

MARIE   I just wondered.

LOLA   What if Bruce finds out that you've been going with someone else?

MARIE   Bruce and I had a very businesslike understanding before I left for school that we weren't going to sit around lonely just because we were separated.

LOLA   Aren't you being kind of mean to Turk?

MARIE   I don't think so.

LOLA   How's he going to feel when Bruce comes?

MARIE   He may be sore for a little while, but he'll get over it.

LOLA   Won't he feel bad?

MARIE   He's had his eye on a pretty little Spanish girl in his history class for a long time. I like Turk, but he's not the marrying kind.

LOLA   No! Really?
(LOLA, *with a look of sad wonder on her face, sits on arm of couch. It's been a serious disillusionment*)

MARIE   What's the matter?

LOLA   I . . . I just felt kinda tired.
(*Sharp buzzing of doorbell.* MARIE *runs to answer it*)

MARIE   That must be Bruce. (*She skips to the mirror again, then to door*) Bruce!

BRUCE   How are you, sweetheart?

MARIE   Wonderful.

BRUCE   Did you get my wire?

MARIE   Sure.

BRUCE   You're looking swell.

MARIE   Thanks. What took you so long to get here?

BRUCE   Well, honey, I had to go to my hotel and take a bath.

MARIE   Bruce, this is Mrs. Delaney.

BRUCE   (*Now he gets the cozy quality out of his voice*)   How do you do, ma'am?

LOLA   How d'ya do?

BRUCE   Marie has said some very nice things about you in her letters.

MARIE   Mrs. Delaney has fixed the grandest dinner for us.

BRUCE   Now that was to be my treat. I have a big expense account now,
honey. I thought we could all go down to the hotel and have dinner
there, and celebrate first with a few cocktails.

LOLA   Oh, we can have cocktails, too. Excuse me, just a minute.
(She hurries to the kitchen and starts looking for the whiskey. BRUCE *kisses*
MARIE*)*

MARIE *(Whispers)*   Now, Bruce, she's been working on this dinner all day.
She even cleaned the house for you.

BRUCE *(With a surveying look)*   Did she?

MARIE   And Doc's joining us. You'll like Doc.

BRUCE   Honey, are we going to have to stay here the whole evening?

MARIE   We just can't eat and run. We'll get away as soon as we can.

BRUCE   I hope so. I got the raise, sweetheart. They're giving me new terri-
tory.
*(*LOLA *is frantic in the kitchen, having found the bottle missing. She hurries
back into the living room)*

LOLA   You kids are going to have to entertain yourselves awhile 'cause I'm
going to be busy in the kitchen. Why don't you turn on the radio,
Marie? Get some dance music. I'll shut the door so . . . so I won't
disturb you.
*(*LOLA *does so, then goes to the telephone)*

MARIE   Come and see my room, Bruce. I've fixed it up just darling. And
I've got your picture in the prettiest frame right on my dresser.
(They exit and their voices are heard from the bedroom while LOLA *is phon-
ing)*

LOLA *(At the phone)*   This is Mrs. Delaney. Is . . . Doc there? Well, then,
is Ed Anderson there? Well, would you give me Ed Anderson's telephone
number? You see, he sponsored Doc into the club and helped him . . .
you know . . . and . . . and I was a little worried tonight. . . . Oh,
thanks. Yes, I've got it. *(She writes down number)* Could you have Ed
Anderson call me if he comes in? Thank you. *(She hangs up. On her face
is a dismal expression of fear, anxiety and doubt. She searches flour bin,*

icebox, closet. Then she goes into the living room, calling to MARIE *and* BRUCE *as she comes)* I . . . I guess we'll go ahead without Doc, Marie.

MARIE *(Enters from her room)*　What's the matter with Doc, Mrs. Delaney?

LOLA　Well . . . he got held up at the office . . . just one of those things, you know. It's too bad. It would have to happen when I needed him most.

MARIE　Sure you don't need any help?

LOLA　Huh? Oh, no. I'll make out. Everything's ready. I tell you what I'm going to do. Three's a crowd, so I'm going to be the butler and serve the dinner to you two young lovebirds . . . *(The telephone rings)* Pardon me . . . pardon me just a minute. *(She rushes to phone, closing the door behind her)* Hello? Ed? Have you seen Doc? He went out this morning and hasn't come back. We're having company for dinner and he was supposed to be home early. . . . That's not all. This time we've had a quart of whiskey in the kitchen and Doc's never gone near it. I went to get it tonight. I was going to serve some cocktails. It was *gone.* Yes, I saw it there yesterday. No, I don't think so. . . . He said this morning he had an upset stomach but . . . Oh, would you? . . . Thank you, Mr. Anderson. Thank you a million times. And you let me know when you find out anything. Yes, I'll be here . . . yes. *(Hangs up and crosses back to living room)* Well, I guess we're all ready.

BRUCE　Aren't you going to look at your present?

MARIE　Oh, sure, let's get some scissors.
(Their voices continue in bedroom)

MARIE *(Enters with* BRUCE*)*　Mrs. Delaney, we think you should eat with us.

LOLA　Oh, no, honey, I'm not very hungry. Besides, this is the first time you've been together in months and I think you should be alone. Marie, why don't you light the candles? Then we'll have just the right atmosphere.
(She goes into kitchen, gets tomato-juice glasses from icebox while BRUCE *lights the candles)*

BRUCE　Do we have to eat by candlelight? I won't be able to see.
*(*LOLA *returns)*

LOLA   Now, Bruce, you sit here. *(He and* MARIE *sit)* Isn't that going to be cozy? Dinner for two. Sorry we won't have time for cocktails. Let's have a little music.

(She turns on the radio and a Viennese waltz swells up as the curtain falls with LOLA *looking at the young people eating)*

CURTAIN

SCENE: *Funereal atmosphere. It is about 5:30 the next morning. The sky is just beginning to get light outside, while inside the room the shadows still cling heavily to the corners. The remains of last night's dinner clutter the table in the living room. The candles have guttered down to stubs amid the dirty dinner plates, and the lilacs in the centerpiece have wilted.* LOLA *is sprawled on the davenport, sleeping. Slowly she awakens and regards the morning light. She gets up and looks about strangely, beginning to show despair for the situation she is in. She wears the same spiffy dress she had on the night before but it is wrinkled now, and her marcelled coiffure is awry. One silk stocking has twisted loose and falls around her ankle. When she is sufficiently awake to realize her situation, she rushes to the telephone and dials a number.*

LOLA *(At telephone. She sounds frantic)* Mr. Anderson? Mr. Anderson, this is Mrs. Delaney again. I'm sorry to call you so early, but I just *had* to. . . . Did you find Doc? . . . No, he's not home yet. I don't suppose he'll come home till he's drunk all he can hold and wants to sleep. . . . I don't know what else to think, Mr. Anderson. I'm scared, Mr. Anderson. I'm awful scared. Will you come right over? . . . Thanks, Mr. Anderson. *(She hangs up and goes to kitchen to make coffee. She finds some left from the night before, so turns on the fire to warm it up. She wanders around vaguely, trying to get her thoughts in order, jumping at every sound. Pours herself a cup of coffee, then takes it to living room, sits and sips it. Very quietly* DOC *enters through the back way into the kitchen. He carries a big bottle of whiskey which he carefully places back in the pantry, not making a sound, hangs up overcoat, then puts suitcoat on back of chair. Starts to go upstairs. But* LOLA *speaks)* Doc? That you, Doc?
(Then DOC *quietly walks in from kitchen. He is staggering drunk, but he is managing for a few minutes to appear as though he were perfectly sober and nothing had happened. His steps, however, are not too sure and his eyes are like blurred ink pots.* LOLA *is too frightened to talk. Her mouth is gaping and she is breathless with fear)*

DOC   Good morning, honey.

LOLA   Doc! You all right?

DOC   The morning paper here? I wanta see the morning paper.

LOLA   Doc, we don't get a morning paper. *You* know that.

DOC   Oh, then I suppose I'm drunk or something. That what you're trying to say?

LOLA   No, Doc . . .

DOC   Then give me the morning paper.

LOLA   *(Scampering to get last night's paper from console table)*   Sure, Doc. Here it is. Now you just sit there and be quiet.

DOC   *(Resistance rising)*   Why shouldn't I be quiet?

LOLA   Nothin', Doc . . .

DOC   *(Has trouble unfolding paper. He places it before his face in order not to be seen. But he is too blind even to see; he speaks mockingly)*   Nothing, Doc.

LOLA   *(Cautiously, after a few minutes' silence)*   Doc, are you all right?

DOC   Of course, I'm all right. Why shouldn't I be all right?

LOLA   Where you been?

DOC   What's it your business where I been? I been to London to see the Queen. What do you think of that? *(Apparently she doesn't know what to think of it)* Just let me alone. That's all I ask. I'm all right.

LOLA   *(Whimpering)*   Doc, what made you do it? You said you'd be home last night . . . 'cause we were having company. Bruce was here and I had a big dinner fixed . . . and you never came. What was the matter, Doc?

DOC   *(Mockingly)*   We had a big dinner for *Bruce*.

LOLA   Doc, it was for you, too.

DOC   Well . . . I don't want it.

LOLA   Don't get mad, Doc.

DOC   *(Threateningly)*   Where's Marie?

LOLA   I don't know, Doc. She didn't come in last night. She was out with Bruce.

DOC   *(Back to audience)*   I suppose you tucked them in bed together and peeked through the keyhole and applauded.

LOLA   *(Sickened)*   Doc, don't talk that way. Bruce is a nice boy. They're gonna get married.

DOC   He probably *has* to marry her, the poor bastard. Just 'cause she's pretty and he got amorous one day . . . Just like I had to marry *you.*

LOLA   Oh, Doc!

DOC   You and Marie are both a couple of sluts.

LOLA   Doc, please don't talk like that.

DOC   What are you good for? You can't even get up in the morning and cook my breakfast.

LOLA   *(Mumbling)*   I will, Doc. I will after this.

DOC   You won't even sweep the floors, till some bozo comes along to make love to Marie, and then you fix things up like Buckingham Palace or a Chinese whorehouse with perfume on the lampbulbs, and flowers, and the gold-trimmed china *my mother* gave us. We're not going to use these any more. My mother didn't buy those dishes for whores to eat off of. *(He jerks the cloth off the table, sending the dishes rattling to the floor)*

LOLA   Doc! Look what you done.

DOC   Look what I *did,* not *done.* I'm going to get me a drink. *(Goes to kitchen)*

LOLA   *(Follows to platform)*   Oh, no, Doc! You know what it does to you!

DOC   You're damn right I know what it does to me. It makes me willing to come home here and look at you, you two-ton old heifer. *(Takes a long swallow)* There! And pretty soon I'm going to have another, then another.

LOLA   *(With dread)*   Oh, Doc! (LOLA *takes phone.* DOC *sees this, rushes for the butcher-knife from kitchen-cabinet drawer. Not finding it, he gets a hatchet from the back porch)* Mr. Anderson? Come quick, Mr. Anderson. He's back. He's *back!* He's got a hatchet!

DOC   God damn you! Get away from that telephone. *(He chases her into living room where she gets the couch between them)* That's right, phone!

Tell the world I'm drunk. Tell the whole damn world. Scream your head off, you fat slut. Holler till all the neighbors think I'm beatin' hell outuv you. Where's Bruce now—under Marie's bed? You got all fresh and pretty for him, didn't you? Combed your hair for once—you even washed the back of your neck and put on a girdle. You were willing to harness all that fat into one bundle.

LOLA (*About to faint under the weight of the crushing accusations*) Doc, don't say any more . . . I'd rather you hit me with an ax, Doc. . . . Honest I would. But I can't stand to hear you talk like that.

DOC I oughta hack off all that fat, and then wait for Marie and chop off those pretty ankles she's always dancing around on . . . then start lookin' for Turk and fix him too.

LOLA Daddy, you're talking crazy!

DOC I'm making sense for the first time in my life. You didn't know I knew about it, did you? But I saw him coming outa there, I saw him. You knew about it all the time and thought you were hidin' something . . .

LOLA Daddy, I didn't know anything about it at all. Honest, Daddy.

DOC Then *you're* the one that's crazy, if you think I didn't know. You were running a regular house, weren't you? It's probably been going on for years, ever since we were married.
(*He lunges for her. She breaks for kitchen. They struggle in front of sink*)

LOLA Doc, it's not so; it's not so. You gotta believe me, Doc.

DOC You're lyin'. But none a that's gonna happen any more. I'm gonna fix you now, once and for all. . . .

LOLA Doc . . . don't do that to me. (LOLA, *in a frenzy of fear, clutches him around the neck holding arm with ax by his side*) Remember, Doc. It's *me*, Lola! You said I was the prettiest girl you ever saw. Remember, Doc! It's me! Lola!

DOC (*The memory has overpowered him. He collapses, slowly mumbling*) Lola . . . my pretty Lola.
(*He passes out on the floor.* LOLA *stands now, as though in a trance. Quietly* MRS. COFFMAN *comes creeping in through the back way*)

MRS. COFFMAN (*Calling softly*) Mrs. Delaney! (LOLA *doesn't even hear.* MRS. COFFMAN *comes in*) Mrs. Delaney! Here you are, lady. I heard screaming and I was frightened for you.

LOLA   I . . . I'll be all right . . . some men are comin' pretty soon; every-thing'll be all right.

MRS. COFFMAN   I'll stay until they get here.

LOLA *(Feeling a sudden need)*   Would you . . . would you *please*, Mrs. Coffman?
(Breaks into sobs)

MRS. COFFMAN   Of course, lady. *(Regarding* DOC) The doctor got "sick" again?

LOLA *(Mumbling)*   Some men . . . 'll be here pretty soon . . .

MRS. COFFMAN   I'll try to straighten things up before they get here. . . .
(She rights chair, hangs up telephone and picks up the ax, which she is holding when ED ANDERSON *and* ELMO HUSTON *enter unannounced. They are experienced AA's. Neatly dressed businessmen approaching middle age)*

ED   Pardon us for walking right in, Mrs. Delaney, but I didn't want to waste a second. *(Kneels by* DOC)

LOLA *(Weakly)*   It's all right. . . .
(Both men observe DOC *on the floor, and their expressions hold understand-ing mixed with a feeling of irony. There is even a slight smile of irony on* ED'S *face. They have developed the surgeon's objectivity)*

ED   Where is the hatchet? *(To* ELMO, *as though appraising* DOC'S *condition)* What do you think, Elmo?

ELMO   We can't leave him here if he's gonna play around with hatchets.

ED   Give me a hand, Elmo. We'll get him to sit up and then try to talk some sense into him. *(They struggle with the lumpy body,* DOC *grunting his resistance)* Come on, Doc, old boy. It's Ed and Elmo. We're going to take care of you. *(They seat him at table)*

DOC *(Through a thick fog)*   Lemme alone.

ED   Wake up. We're taking you away from here.

DOC   Lemme 'lone, God damn it.
(Falls forward, head on table)

ELMO *(To* MRS. COFFMAN)   Is there any coffee?

MRS. COFFMAN   I think so, I'll see.
(Goes to stove with cup from drainboard. Lights fire under coffee and waits for it to get heated)

ED   He's way beyond coffee.

ELMO   It'll help some. Get something hot into his stomach.

ED   If we could get him to eat. How 'bout some hot food, Doc?
  (DOC *gestures and they don't push the matter*)

ELMO   City Hospital, Ed?

ED   I guess that's what it will have to be.

LOLA   Where you going to take him?
  (ELMO *goes to phone; speaks quietly to City Hospital*)

ED   Don't know. Wanta talk to him first.

MRS. COFFMAN *(Coming in with the coffee)*   Here's the coffee.

ED *(Taking cup)*   Hold him, Elmo, while I make him swallow this.

ELMO   Come on, Doc, drink your coffee.
  (DOC *only blubbers*)

DOC *(After the coffee is down)*   Uh . . . what . . . what's goin' on here?

ED   It's me, Doc. Your old friend Ed. I got Elmo with me.

DOC *(Twisting his face painfully)*   Get out, both of you. Lemme 'lone.

ED *(With certainty)*   We're takin' you with us, Doc.

DOC   Hell you are. I'm all right. I just had a little slip. We all have
  slips. . . .

ED   Sometimes, Doc, but we gotta get over 'em.

DOC   I'll be O.K. Just gimme a day to sober up. I'll be as good as new.

ED   Remember the last time, Doc? You said you'd be all right in the
  morning and we found you with a broken collarbone. Come on.

DOC   Boys, I'll be all right. Now lemme alone.

ED   How much has he had, Mrs. Delaney?

LOLA   I don't know. He had a quart when he left here yesterday and he
  didn't get home till now.

ED   He's probably been through a *couple* of quarts. He's been dry for a
  long time. It's going to hit him pretty hard. Yah, he'll be a pretty sick
  man for a few days. *(Louder to* DOC, *as though he were talking to a deaf
  man)* Wanta go to the City Hospital, Doc?

DOC *(This has a sobering effect on him. He looks about him furtively for possible escape)*   No . . . no, boys. Don't take me there. That's a torture chamber. No, Ed. You wouldn't do that to me.

ED   They'll sober you up.

DOC   Ed, I been there; I've seen the place. That's where they take the crazy people. You can't do that to me, Ed.

ED   Well, *you're* crazy, aren't you? Goin' after your wife with a hatchet. *(They lift* DOC *to his feet.* DOC *looks with dismal pleading in his eyes at* LOLA, *who has her face in her hands)*

DOC *(So plaintive, a sob in his voice)*   Honey! Honey! (LOLA *can't look at him. Now* DOC *tries to make a getaway, bolting blindly into the living room before the two men catch him and hold him in front of living-room table)* Honey, don't let 'em take me there. They'll believe *you.* Tell 'em you won't *let* me take a drink.

LOLA   Isn't there any place else you could take him?

ED   Private sanitariums cost a lotta dough.

LOLA   I got forty dollars in the kitchen.

ED   That won't be near enough.

DOC   I'll be at the meeting tomorrow night sober as you are now.

ED *(To* LOLA)   All the king's horses couldn't keep him from takin' another drink now, Mrs. Delaney. He got himself into this; he's gotta sweat it out.

DOC   I won't go to the City Hospital. That's where they take the crazy people.
(Stumbles into chair)

ED *(Using all his patience now)*   Look, Doc. Elmo and I are your friends. You know that. Now if you don't come along peacefully, we're going to call the cops and you'll have to wear off this jag in the cooler. How'd you like that? (DOC *is as though stunned)* The important thing is for you to get sober.

DOC   I don't wanta go.

ED   The City Hospital or the City Jail. Take your choice. We're not going to leave you here. Come on, Elmo.
(They grab hold of him)

DOC (*Has collected himself and now given in*)   O.K., boys. Gimme another drink and I'll go.

LOLA   Oh, no, Doc.

ED   Might as well humor him, ma'am. Another few drinks couldn't make much difference now.
(MRS. COFFMAN *runs for bottle and glass in pantry and comes right back with them. She hands them to* LOLA) O.K., Doc, we're goin' to give you a drink. Take a good one; it's gonna be your last for a long, long time to come. (ED *takes the bottle, removes the cork and gives* DOC *a glass of whiskey.* DOC *takes his fill, straight, coming up once or twice for air. Then* ED *takes the glass from him and hands it to* LOLA. *To* LOLA) They'll keep him three or four days, Mrs. Delaney; then he'll be home again, good as new. (*Modestly*) I . . . I don't want to pry into personal affairs, ma'am . . . but he'll need you then, pretty bad . . . Come on, Doc. Let's go. (ED *has a hold of* DOC'S *coat sleeve trying to maneuver him. A faraway look is in* DOC'S *eyes, a dazed look containing panic and fear. He gets to his feet*)

DOC (*Struggling to sound reasonable*)   Just a minute, boys . . .

ED   What's the matter?

DOC   I . . . I wanta glass of water.

ED   You'll get a glass of water later. Come on.

DOC (*Beginning to twist a little in* ED'S *grasp*)   . . . a glass of water . . . that's all . . .
(*One furious, quick twist of his body and he eludes* ED)

ED   Quick, Elmo.
(ELMO *acts fast and they get* DOC *before he gets away. Then* DOC *struggles with all his might, kicking and screaming like a pampered child,* ED *and* ELMO *holding him tightly to usher him out*)

DOC (*As he is led out*)   Don't let 'em take me there. Don't take me there. Stop them, somebody. Stop them. That's where they take the crazy people. Oh, God, stop them, somebody. Stop them.
(LOLA *looks on blankly while* ED *and* ELMO *depart with* DOC. *Now there are several moments of deep silence*)

MRS. COFFMAN (*Clears up. Very softly*)   Is there anything more I can do for you now, Mrs. Delaney?

LOLA   I guess not.

MRS. COFFMAN *(Puts a hand on* LOLA's *shoulder)*   Get busy, lady. Get busy and forget it.

LOLA   Yes . . . I'll get busy right away. Thanks, Mrs. Coffman.

MRS. COFFMAN   I better go. I've got to make breakfast for the children. If you want me for anything, let me know.

LOLA   Yes . . . yes . . . good-bye, Mrs. Coffman.
(MRS. COFFMAN *exits.* LOLA *is too exhausted to move from the big chair. At first she can't even cry; then the tears come slowly, softly. In a few moments* BRUCE *and* MARIE *enter, bright and merry.* LOLA *turns her head slightly to regard them as creatures from another planet)*

MARIE *(Springing into room.* BRUCE *follows)*   Congratulate me, Mrs. Delaney.

LOLA   Huh?

MARIE   We're going to be married.

LOLA   Married? *(It barely registers)*

MARIE *(Showing ring)*   Here it is. My engagement ring.
(MARIE *and* BRUCE *are too engrossed in their own happiness to notice* LOLA's *stupor)*

LOLA   That's lovely . . . lovely.

MARIE   We've had the most wonderful time. We danced all night and then drove out to the lake and saw the sun rise.

LOLA   That's nice.

MARIE   We've made all our plans. I'm quitting school and flying back to Cincinnati with Bruce this afternoon. His mother has invited me to visit them before I go home. Isn't that wonderful?

LOLA   Yes . . . yes, indeed.

MARIE   Going to miss me?

LOLA   Yes, of course, Marie. We'll miss you very much . . . uh . . . congratulations.

MARIE   Thanks, Mrs. Delaney. *(Goes to bedroom door)* Come on, Bruce, help me get my stuff. *(To* LOLA*)* Mrs. Delaney, would you throw everything into a big box and send it to me at home? We haven't had breakfast yet. We're going down to the hotel and celebrate.

BRUCE I'm sorry we're in such a hurry, but we've got a taxi waiting.
(They go into room)

LOLA *(Goes to telephone, dials)* Long-distance? I want to talk to Green Valley two-two-three. Yes. This is Delmar one-eight-eight-seven.
(She hangs up. MARIE *comes from bedroom, followed by* BRUCE, *who carries suitcase)*

MARIE Mrs. Delaney, I sure hate to say good-bye to you. You've been so wonderful to me. But Bruce says I can come and visit you once in a while, didn't you, Bruce?

BRUCE Sure thing.

LOLA You're going?

MARIE We're going downtown and have our breakfast, then do a little shopping and catch our plane. And thanks for everything, Mrs. Delaney.

BRUCE It was very nice of you to have us to dinner.

LOLA Dinner? Oh, don't mention it.

MARIE *(To* LOLA*)* There isn't much time for good-bye now, but I just want you to know Bruce and I wish you the best of everything. You and Doc both. Tell Doc good-bye for me, will you, and remember I think you're both a coupla peaches.

BRUCE Hurry, honey.

MARIE 'Bye, Mrs. Delaney! *(She goes out)*

BRUCE 'Bye, Mrs. Delaney. Thanks for being nice to my girl.
(He goes out and off porch with MARIE*)*

LOLA *(Waves. The phone rings. She goes to it quickly)* Hello. Hello, Mom. It's Lola, Mom. How are you? Mom, Doc's sick again. Do you think Dad would let me come home for a while? I'm awfully unhappy, Mom. Do you think . . . just till I made up my mind? . . . All right. No, I guess it wouldn't do any good for you to come here . . . I . . . I'll let you know what I decide to do. That's all, Mom. Thanks. Tell Daddy hello.
(She hangs up)

CURTAIN

ACT TWO | Scene Four

SCENE: *It is morning, a week later. The house is neat again.* LOLA *is dusting in the living room as* MRS. COFFMAN *enters.*

MRS. COFFMAN   Mrs. Delaney! Good morning, Mrs. Delaney.

LOLA   Come in, Mrs. Coffman.

MRS. COFFMAN   *(Coming in)*   It's a fine day for the games. I've got a box lunch ready, and I'm taking all the kids to the Stadium. My boy's got a ticket for you, too. You better get dressed and come with us.

LOLA   Thanks, Mrs. Coffman, but I've got work to do.

MRS. COFFMAN   But it's a big day. The Spring Relays . . . All the athletes from the colleges are supposed to be there.

LOLA   Oh, yes. You know that boy, Turk, who used to come here to see Marie—he's one of the big stars.

MRS. COFFMAN   Is that so? Come on . . . do. We've got a ticket for you. . . .

LOLA   Oh, no, I have to stay here and clean up the house. Doc may be coming home today. I talked to him on the phone. He wasn't sure what time they'd let him out, but I wanta have the place all nice for him.

MRS. COFFMAN   Well, I'll tell you all about it when I come home. Everybody and his brother will be there.

LOLA   Have a good time.

MRS. COFFMAN   'Bye, Mrs. Delaney.

LOLA   'Bye.

(MRS. COFFMAN *leaves, and* LOLA *goes into kitchen. The* MAILMAN *comes onto porch and leaves a letter, but* LOLA *doesn't even know he's there. Then the* MILKMAN *knocks on the kitchen door*)

LOLA   Come in.

MILKMAN   (*Entering with armful of bottles, etc.*)   I see you checked the list, lady. You've got a lot of extras.

LOLA   Ya—I think my husband's coming home.

MILKMAN   (*He puts the supplies on table, then pulls out magazine*)   Remember, I told you my picture was going to appear in *Strength and Health.* (*Showing her magazine*) Well, see that pile of muscles? That's me.

LOLA   My goodness. You got your picture in a magazine.

MILKMAN   Yes, ma'am. See what it says about my chest development? For the greatest self-improvement in a three months' period.

LOLA   Goodness sakes. You'll be famous, won't you?

MILKMAN   If I keep busy on these bar-bells. I'm working now for "muscular separation."

LOLA   That's nice.

MILKMAN   (*Cheerily*)   Well, good day, ma'am.

LOLA   You forgot your magazine.

MILKMAN   That's for you.
(*Exits. LOLA puts away the supplies in the icebox. Then DOC comes in the front door, carrying the little suitcase she previously packed for him. His quiet manner and his serious demeanor are the same as before. LOLA is shocked by his sudden appearance. She jumps and can't help showing her fright*)

LOLA   Docky!
(*Without thinking, she assumes an attitude of fear. DOC observes this and it obviously pains him*)

DOC   Good morning, honey.
(*Pause*)

LOLA   (*On platform*)   Are . . . are you all right, Doc?

DOC   Yes, I'm all right. (*An awkward pause. Then DOC tries to reassure her*) Honest, I'm all right, honey. Please don't stand there like that . . . like I was gonna . . . gonna . . .

LOLA   (*Tries to relax*)   I'm sorry, Doc.

DOC How you been?

LOLA Oh, I been all right, Doc. Fine.

DOC Any news?

LOLA I told you about Marie—over the phone.

DOC Yah.

LOLA He was a very nice boy, Doc. Very nice.

DOC That's good. I hope they'll be happy.

LOLA *(Trying to sound bright)* She said . . . maybe she'd come back and visit us some time. That's what she *said.*

DOC *(Pause)* It . . . it's good to be home.

LOLA Is it, Daddy?

DOC Yah.
  (Beginning to choke up, just a little)

LOLA Did everything go all right . . . I mean . . . did they treat you well and . . .

DOC *(Now loses control of his feelings. Tears in his eyes, he all but lunges at her, gripping her arms, drilling his head into her bosom)* Honey, don't ever leave me. *Please* don't ever leave me. If you do, they'd have to keep me down at that place all the time. I don't know what I said to you or what I did, I can't remember hardly anything. But please forgive me . . . please . . . please . . . And I'll try to make everything up.

LOLA *(There is surprise on her face and new contentment. She becomes almost angelic in demeanor. Tenderly she places a soft hand on his head)* Daddy! Why, of course I'll never leave you. *(A smile of satisfaction)* You're all I've got. You're all I ever had.
  (Very tenderly he kisses her)

DOC *(Collecting himself now.* LOLA *sits beside* DOC*)* I . . . I feel better . . . already.

LOLA *(Almost gay)* So do I. Have you had your breakfast?

DOC No. The food there was terrible. When they told me I could go this morning, I decided to wait and fix myself breakfast here.

LOLA *(Happily)* Come on out in the kitchen and I'll get you a nice big breakfast. I'll scramble some eggs and . . . You see I've got the place all cleaned up just the way you like it. (DOC *goes to kitchen*) Now you sit down here and I'll get your fruit juice. *(He sits and she gets fruit juice from refrigerator)* I've got bacon this morning, too. My, it's expensive now. And I'll light the oven and make you some toast, and here's some orange marmalade, and . . .

DOC *(With a new feeling of control)*   Fruit juice. I'll need lots of fruit juice for a while. The doctor said it would restore the vitamins. You see, that damn whiskey kills all the vitamins in your system, eats up all the sugar in your kidneys. They came around every morning and shot vitamins in my arm. Oh, it didn't hurt. And the doctor told me to drink a quart of fruit juice every day. And you better get some candy bars for me at the grocery this morning. Doctor said to eat lots of candy, try to replace the sugar.

LOLA   I'll do that, Doc. Here's another glass of this pineapple juice now. I'll get some candy bars first thing.

DOC   The doctor said I should have a hobby. Said I should go out more. That's all that's wrong with me. I thought maybe I'd go hunting once in a while.

LOLA   Yes, Doc. And bring home lots of good things to eat.

DOC   I'll get a big bird dog, too. Would you like a sad-looking old bird dog around the house?

LOLA   Of course, I would. *(All her life and energy have been restored)* You know what, Doc? I had another dream last night.

DOC   About Little Sheba?

LOLA   Oh, it was about everyone and everything. *(In a raptured tone. She gets bacon from icebox and starts to cook it)* Marie and I were going to the Olympics back in our old high school stadium. There were thousands of people there. There was Turk out in the center of the field throwing the javelin. Every time he threw it, the crowd would roar . . . and you know who the man in charge was? It was my father. Isn't that funny? . . . But Turk kept changing into someone else all the time. And then my father disqualified him. So he had to sit on the sidelines . . . and guess who took his place, Daddy? You! You came trotting out there on the field just as big as you please . . .

DOC *(Smilingly)*   How did I do, Baby?

LOLA   Fine. You picked the javelin up real careful, like it was awful heavy. But you threw it, Daddy, clear, *clear* up into the sky. And it never came down again. (DOC *looks very pleased with himself.* LOLA *goes on*) Then it started to rain. And I couldn't find Little Sheba. I almost went crazy looking for her and there were so many people, I didn't even know where to look. And you were waiting to take me home. And we walked and walked through the slush and mud, and people were hurrying all around us and . . . and . . . (*Leaves stove and sits. Sentimental tears come to her eyes*) But this part is sad, Daddy. All of a sudden I saw Little Sheba . . . she was lying in the middle of the field . . . dead. . . . It made me cry, Doc. No one paid any attention . . . I cried and cried. It made me feel so bad, Doc. That sweet little puppy . . . her curly white fur all smeared with mud, and no one to stop and take care of her . . .

DOC   Why couldn't *you*?

LOLA   I wanted to, but you wouldn't let me. You kept saying, "We can't stay here, honey; we gotta go on. We gotta go on." (*Pause*) Now, isn't that strange?

DOC   Dreams are funny.

LOLA   I don't think Little Sheba's ever coming back, Doc. I'm not going to call her any more.

DOC   Not much point in it, Baby. I guess she's gone for good.

LOLA   I'll fix your eggs.
(*She gets up, embraces* DOC, *and goes to stove.* DOC *remains at table sipping his fruit juice*)

THE CURTAIN COMES SLOWLY DOWN

Picnic

PICNIC *was produced by* The Theatre Guild *and Joshua Logan, at the Music Box Theatre, New York City, on February 19, 1953, with the following cast:*

HELEN POTTS	*Ruth McDevitt*
HAL CARTER	*Ralph Meeker*
MILLIE OWENS	*Kim Stanley*
BOMBER	*Morris Miller*
MADGE OWENS	*Janice Rule*
FLO OWENS	*Peggy Concklin*
ROSEMARY SYDNEY	*Eileen Heckart*
ALAN SEYMOUR	*Paul Newman*
IRMA KRONKITE	*Reta Shaw*
CHRISTINE SCHOENWALDER	*Elizabeth Wilson*
HOWARD BEVANS	*Arthur O'Connell*

DIRECTED BY Joshua Logan
SCENERY AND LIGHTING BY Jo Mielziner

Scenes

The action of the play takes place in a small Kansas town in the yard shared by Flo Owens and Helen Potts.

ACT ONE	Early morning, Labor Day.
ACT TWO	Late the same afternoon.
ACT THREE	SCENE I. Very early the following morning.
	SCENE II. A few hours later.

ACT ONE

SCENE: *The action of the play is laid on the porches and in the yards of two small houses that sit close beside each other in a small Kansas town. The house at the right belongs to* MRS. FLORA OWENS, *a widow lady of about forty who lives there with her two young daughters,* MADGE *and* MILLIE. *The audience sees only a section of the house, from the doorstep and the front door extending to the back door, a porch lining all of the house that we see.*

The house at the left is inhabited by MRS. HELEN POTTS, *another but older widow lady who lives with her aged and invalid mother. Just the back of her house is visible, with steps leading up to the back door. Down farther is a woodshed, attached to the house by the roof. The space between woodshed and house forms a narrow passageway leading to the rest of* MRS. POTTS' *property. The yard between the houses is used interchangeably by members of both houses for visiting and relaxation.*

Both houses are humble dwellings built with no other pretension than to provide comfortable shelter for their occupants. The ladies cannot always afford to keep their houses painted, but they work hard to maintain a tidy appearance, keeping the yards clean, watching the flower beds, supplying colorful slip covers for the porch furniture.

Behind the houses is a stretch of picket fence with a gateway leading from the sidewalk into the yard between the houses. Beyond the fence, in the distance, is the panorama of a typical small Midwestern town, including a grain elevator, a railway station, a great silo and a church steeple, all blessed from above by a high sky of innocent blue.

The curtain rises on an empty, sunlit stage. It is early morning in late summer, Labor Day, and autumn has just begun to edge the green landscape with a rim of brown. Dew is still on the landscape and mist rises from the earth in the distance. MRS. POTTS *appears on her back porch, at left. She is a merry, dumpy little woman close to sixty. She comes down the steps and stands before the woodshed, waiting for* HAL CARTER *to follow.* HAL *comes out carrying a basket of trash on his shoulder, an exceedingly handsome, husky youth dressed in T-shirt, dungarees and cowboy boots. In a past era he would have been called a vagabond, but* HAL *today is usually referred to as a bum.* MRS. POTTS *speaks to him.*

MRS. POTTS You just had a big breakfast. Wouldn't you like to rest a while before you go to work?

HAL *(Managing to sound cheerful)* Work's good for my digestion, ma'am.

MRS. POTTS Now, stop being embarrassed because you asked for breakfast.

HAL I never did it before.

MRS. POTTS What's the difference? We all have misfortune part of the time.

HAL Seems to me, ma'am, like I have it *lots* of the time.
(Then they laugh together. MRS. POTTS *leads him off through the passageway. In a moment,* MILLIE OWENS *bursts out of the kitchen door of the house, right. She is a wiry kid of sixteen, boisterous and assertive, but likable when one begins to understand that she is trying to disguise her basic shyness. Her secret habit is to come outside after breakfast and enjoy her morning cigarette where her mother will not see her. She is just lighting up when* BOMBER, *the newsboy, appears at the back gate and slings a paper noisily against the house. This gives* MILLIE *a chance to assail him)*

MILLIE Hey, crazy, wanta knock the house down?

BOMBER *(A tough kid about* MILLIE'S *age)* I don't hear you.

MILLIE If you ever break a window, you'll hear me.

BOMBER Go back to bed.

MILLIE Go blow your nose.

BOMBER *(With a look at the upper window of the house which presumably marks* MADGE'S *room)* Go back to bed and tell your pretty sister to come out. It's no fun lookin' at you. *(*MILLIE *ignores him.* BOMBER *doesn't intend to let her)* I'm talkin' to *you,* goonface!

MILLIE *(Jumping to her feet and tearing into* BOMBER *with flying fists)* You take that back, you ornery bastard. You take that back.

BOMBER *(Laughing, easily warding off her blows)* Listen to goonface! She cusses just like a man.

MILLIE *(Goes after him with doubled fists)* I'll kill you, you ornery bastard! I'll *kill* you!

BOMBER *(Dodging her fists)* Lookit Mrs. Tar-zan! Lookit Mrs. Tar-zan!

MADGE *(*MADGE *comes out of the back door. She is an unusually beautiful girl of eighteen, who seems to take her beauty very much for granted. She wears* *sandals and a simple wash dress. She has just shampooed her hair and is now scrubbing her head with a towel)*   Who's making so much noise?

BOMBER *(With a shy grin)*   Hi, Madge!

MADGE   Hi, Bomber.

BOMBER   I hope I didn't wake you, Madge, or bother you or anything.

MADGE   Nothing bothers me.

BOMBER *(Warming up)*   Hey, Madge, a bunch of us guys are chippin' in on a hot rod—radio and everything. I get it every Friday night.

MADGE   I'm not one of those girls that jump in a hot rod every time you boys turn a corner and honk. If a boy wants a date with me, he can come to the door like a gentleman and ask if I'm in.

MILLIE   Alan Seymour sends her flowers every time they go out.

BOMBER *(To MADGE)*   I can't send you flowers, baby—but I can *send* you!

MILLIE   Listen to him braggin'.

BOMBER *(Persisting)*   Lemme pick you up some night after Seymour brings you home.

MADGE *(A trifle haughty)*   That wouldn't be fair to Alan. We go steady.

MILLIE   Don't you know what "steady" means, stupid?

BOMBER   I seen you riding around in his Cadillac like you was a duchess. Why do good-looking girls have to be so stuck on themselves?

MADGE *(Jumps up, furious)*   I'm not stuck on myself! You take that back, Bomber Gutzel!

BOMBER *(Still persisting)*   Lemme pick you up some night! Please! (MADGE *walks away to evade him but* BOMBER *is close behind her)* We'll get some cans of beer and go down to the river road and listen to music on the radio.
(HAL CARTER *has come on from right and put a rake in the woodshed. He observes the scene between* MADGE *and* BOMBER)

MILLIE *(Laughing at BOMBER)*   Wouldn't that be romantic!

BOMBER *(Grabbing MADGE's arm)*   C'mon, Madge, give a guy a break!

HAL *(To BOMBER)*   On your way, lover boy!

BOMBER *(Turning)*   Who're *you*?

HAL   What's that matter? I'm bigger'n you are.
   (BOMBER *looks at* HAL, *feels a little inadequate, and starts off*)

MILLIE   (*Calling after* BOMBER)   Go peddle your papers!
   (*Gives* BOMBER *a raspberry as he disappears with papers*)

HAL   (*To* MILLIE)   Got a smoke, kid? (MILLIE *gives* HAL *a cigarette, wondering*
   who he is) Thanks, kid.

MILLIE   You workin' for Mrs. Potts?

HAL   Doin' a few jobs in the yard.

MILLIE   She give you breakfast?

HAL   (*Embarrassed about it*)   Yah.

MADGE   Millie! Mind your business.

HAL   (*Turning to* MADGE, *his face lighting*)   Hi.

MADGE   Hi.
   (MADGE *and* HAL *stand looking at each other, awkward and self-conscious.*
   FLO, *the mother, comes out almost immediately, as though she had sensed*
   HAL'S *presence.* FLO *carries a sewing basket in one arm and a party dress*
   over the other. She is a rather impatient little woman who has worked hard
   for ten years or more to serve as both father and mother to her girls. One
   must feel that underneath a certain hardness in her character there is a
   deep love and concern for the girls. She regards HAL *suspiciously*)

FLO   Young man, this is *my* house. Is there something you want?

HAL   Just loafin', ma'am.

FLO   This is a busy day for us. We have no time to loaf.
   (*There is a quick glance between* HAL *and* FLO, *as though each sized up the*
   other as a potential threat)

HAL   You the mother?

FLO   Yes. You better run along now.

HAL   Like you say, lady. It's your house.
   (*With a shrug of the shoulders, he saunters off stage*)

FLO   Has Helen Potts taken in another tramp?

MADGE   I don't see why he's a tramp just because Mrs. Potts gave him
   breakfast.

FLO   I'm going to speak to her about the way she takes in every Tom, Dick and Harry!

MADGE   He wasn't doing any harm.

FLO   I bet he'd like to. (*Sits on the porch and begins sewing on party dress. To* MADGE) Have you called Alan this morning?

MADGE   I haven't had time.

MILLIE   He's coming by pretty soon to take us swimming.

FLO (*To* MADGE)   Tell him they're expecting a big crowd at the park this evening, so he'd better use his father's influence at the City Hall to reserve a table. Oh, and tell him to get one down by the river, close to a Dutch oven.

MADGE   He'll think I'm being bossy.

FLO   Alan is the kind of man who doesn't mind if a woman's bossy.
    (*A* train *whistle in the distance.* MADGE *listens*)

MADGE   Whenever I hear that train coming to town, I always get a little feeling of excitement—in here.
    (*Hugging her stomach*)

MILLIE   Whenever I hear it, I tell myself I'm going to get on it some day and go to New York.

FLO   That train just goes as far as Tulsa.

MILLIE   In Tulsa I could catch another train.

MADGE   I always wonder, maybe some wonderful person is getting off here, just by accident, and he'll come into the dime store for something and see me behind the counter, and he'll study me very strangely and then decide I'm just the person they're looking for in Washington for an important job in the Espionage Department. (*She is carried away*) Or maybe he wants me for some great medical experiment that'll save the whole human race.

FLO   Things like that don't happen in dime stores. (*Changing the subject*) Millie, would you take the milk inside?

MILLIE (*As she exits into kitchen with milk*)   Awwww.

FLO (*After a moment*)   Did you and Alan have a good time on your date last night?

MADGE   Uh-huh.

FLO   What'd you do?

MADGE   We went over to his house and he played some of his classical records.

FLO *(After a pause)*   Then what'd you do?

MADGE   Drove over to Cherryvale and had some barbecue.

FLO *(A hard question to ask)*   Madge, does Alan ever—make love?

MADGE   When we drive over to Cherryvale we always park the car by the river and get real romantic.

FLO   Do you let him kiss you? After all, you've been going together all summer.

MADGE   Of course I let him.

FLO   Does he ever want to go beyond kissing?

MADGE *(Embarrassed)*   Mom!

FLO   I'm your mother, for heaven's sake! These things have to be talked about. Does he?

MADGE   Well—yes.

FLO   Does Alan get mad if you—won't?

MADGE   No.

FLO *(To herself, puzzled)*   He doesn't . . .

MADGE   Alan's not like *most* boys. He doesn't wanta do anything he'd be sorry for.

FLO   Do *you* like it when he kisses you?

MADGE   Yes.

FLO   You don't sound very enthusiastic.

MADGE   What do you expect me to do—pass out every time Alan puts his arm around me?

FLO   No, you don't have to pass out. *(Gives* MADGE *the dress she has been sewing on)* Here. Hold this dress up in front of you. *(She continues)* It'd be awfully nice to be married to Alan. You'd live in comfort the rest of your life, with charge accounts at all the stores, automobiles and trips. You'd be invited by all his friends to parties in their homes and at the country club.

MADGE *(A confession)* Mom, I don't feel right with those people.

FLO Why not? You're as good as they are.

MADGE I know, Mom, but all of Alan's friends talk about college and trips to Europe. I feel left out.

FLO You'll get over those feelings in time. Alan will be going back to school in a few weeks. You better get busy.

MADGE Busy what?

FLO A pretty girl doesn't have long—just a few years. Then she's the equal of kings and she can walk out of a shanty like this and live in a palace with a doting husband who'll spend his life making her happy.

MADGE *(To herself)* I know.

FLO Because once, *once* she was young and pretty. If she loses her chance then, she might as well throw all her prettiness away.
(Giving MADGE *the dress)*

MADGE *(Holding the dress before her as* FLO *checks length)* I'm only eighteen.

FLO And next summer you'll be nineteen, and then twenty, and then twenty-one, and then the years'll start going by so fast you'll lose count of them. First thing you know, you'll be forty, still selling candy at the dime store.

MADGE You don't have to get morbid.

MILLIE *(Comes out with sketch book, see* MADGE *holding dress before her)* Everyone around here gets to dress up and go places except me.

MADGE Alan said he'd try to find you a date for the picnic tonight.

MILLIE I don't want Alan asking any of these crazy boys in town to take me anywhere.

MADGE Beggars can't be choosers!

MILLIE You shut up.

FLO Madge, that was mean. There'll be dancing at the pavilion tonight. Millie should have a date, too.

MADGE If she wants a date, why doesn't she dress up and act decent?

MILLIE 'Cause I'm gonna dress and act the way I want to, and if you don't like it you know what you can do!

MADGE   Always complaining because she doesn't have any friends, but she smells so bad people don't want to be near her!

FLO   Girls, don't fight.

MILLIE   *(Ignoring* FLO*)*   La-de-da! Madge is the pretty one—but she's so dumb they almost had to burn the schoolhouse down to get *her* out of it!
(She mimics MADGE*)*

MADGE   That's not so!

MILLIE   Oh, isn't it? You never would have graduated if it hadn't been for Jumpin' Jeeter.

FLO   *(Trying at least to keep up with the scrap)*   Who's Jumpin' Jeeter?

MILLIE   Teaches history. Kids call him Jumpin' Jeeter 'cause he's so *jumpy* with all the pretty girls in his classes. He was flunking Madge till she went in his room and cried, and said . . . *(Resorting again to mimicry)* "I just don't know what I'll do if I don't pass history!"

MADGE   Mom, she's making that up.

MILLIE   Like fun I am! You couldn't even pass Miss Sydney's course in shorthand and you have to work in the dime store!

MADGE   *(The girls know each other's most sensitive spots)*   You *are* a goon!

FLO   *(Giving up)*   Oh, girls!

MILLIE   *(Furious)*   Madge, you slut! You take that back or I'll kill you!
(She goes after MADGE, *who screams and runs onto the porch)*

FLO   Girls! What will the neighbors say!
*(*MILLIE *gets hold of* MADGE'S *hair and yanks.* FLO *has to intercede)*

MILLIE   No one can call me goon and get by with it!

FLO   You called her worse names!

MILLIE   It doesn't hurt what names I call her! She's pretty, so names don't bother her at all! She's pretty, so nothing else matters.
(She storms inside)

FLO   Poor Millie!

MADGE   *(Raging at the injustice)*   All I ever hear is "poor Millie," and poor Millie won herself a scholarship for four whole years of college!

FLO   A girl like Millie can need confidence in other ways.
  (*This quiets* MADGE. *There is a silence*)

MADGE   (*Subdued*)   Mom, do you love Millie more than me?

FLO   Of course not!

MADGE   Sometimes you act like you did.

FLO   (*With warmth, trying to effect an understanding*)   You were the first
  born. Your father thought the sun rose and set in you. He used to carry
  you on his shoulder for all the neighborhood to see. But things were
  different when Millie came.

MADGE   How?

FLO   (*With misgivings*)   They were just—different. Your father wasn't home
  much. The night Millie was born he was with a bunch of his wild friends
  at the roadhouse.

MADGE   I loved Dad.

FLO   (*A little bitterly*)   Oh, everyone loved your father.

MADGE   Did you?

FLO   (*After a long pause of summing up*)   Some women are humiliated to
  love a man.

MADGE   Why?

FLO   (*Thinking as she speaks*)   Because—a woman is weak to begin with, I
  suppose, and sometimes—her love for him makes her feel—almost helpless. And maybe she fights him—'cause her love makes her seem so
  dependent.
  (*There is another pause.* MADGE *ruminates*)

MADGE   Mom, what good is it to be pretty?

FLO   What a question!

MADGE   I mean it.

FLO   Well—pretty things are rare in this life.

MADGE   But what good are they?

FLO   Well—pretty things—like flowers and sunsets and rubies—and pretty
  girls, too—they're like billboards telling us life is good.

MADGE   But where do *I* come in?

FLO   What do you mean?

MADGE   Maybe I get tired being looked at.

FLO   Madge!

MADGE   Well, maybe I do!

FLO   Don't talk so selfish!

MADGE   I don't care if I *am* selfish. It's no good just being pretty. It's no good!

HAL   *(Comes running on from passageway)*   Ma'am, is it all right if I start a fire?

FLO   *(Jumps to see HAL)*   What?

HAL   The nice lady, she said it's a hot enough day already and maybe you'd object.

FLO   *(Matter-of-factly)*   I guess we can stand it.

HAL   Thank you, ma'am.
      (HAL runs off)

FLO   *(Looking after him)*   He just moves right in whether you want him to or not!

MADGE   I knew you wouldn't like him when I first saw him.

FLO   Do *you?*

MADGE   I don't like him or dislike him. I just wonder what he's like.
      (ROSEMARY SYDNEY makes a sudden, somewhat cavalier entrance out of the front door. She is a roomer, probably as old as FLO but would never admit it. Her hair is plastered to her head with wave-set and she wears a flowered kimono)

ROSEMARY   Anyone mind if an old-maid schoolteacher joins their company?

FLO   Sit down, Rosemary.

ROSEMARY   Mail come yet?

FLO   No mail today. It's Labor Day.

ROSEMARY   I forgot. I thought I might be gettin' a letter from that man I met at the high-school picnic last spring. *(A bawdy laugh)* Been wantin' to marry me ever since. A nice fellow and a peck of fun, but I don't have time for any of 'em when they start gettin' serious on me.

FLO You schoolteachers are mighty independent!
(MILLIE *wanders out of kitchen, reading a book*)

ROSEMARY Shoot! I lived this long without a man. I don't see what's to keep me from getting *on* without one.

FLO What about Howard?

ROSEMARY Howard's just a friend-boy—not a boy friend. (MADGE *and* MILLIE *giggle at this.* ROSEMARY *sniffs the air*) I smell smoke.

FLO Helen Potts is having her leaves burned. Smells kind of good, doesn't it?

ROSEMARY (*Seeing* HAL *offstage*) Who's the young man?

FLO Just another no-good Helen Potts took in.

ROSEMARY (*Very concerned*) Mrs. Owens, he's working over there with his shirt off. I don't think that's right in the presence of ladies.

FLO (*As* MILLIE *runs to look*) Get away from there, Millie!

MILLIE (*Returning to doorstep*) Gee whiz! I go swimming every day and the boys don't have on half as much as he does now.

FLO Swimming's different!

MILLIE Madge, can I use your manicure set, just for kicks?

MADGE If you promise not to get it messy.
(MILLIE *picks up the set and begins to experiment*)

FLO (*Looking off at* HAL) Look at him showing off!

ROSEMARY (*Turning away with propriety*) Who does he think is interested?
(*She massages her face*)

FLO (*To* ROSEMARY) What's that you're rubbing in?

ROSEMARY Ponsella Three-Way Tissue Cream. Makes a good base for your make-up.

FLO There was an article in *The Reader's Digest* about some woman who got skin poisoning from using all those face creams.

ROSEMARY Harriett Bristol—she's the American history teacher—she got ahold of some of that beauty clay last winter and it darn near took her skin off. All we girls thought she had leprosy!
(*She manages one more glance back at* HAL)

MILLIE *(Laboring over her manicure)* Madge, how do you do your right hand?

MADGE If you were nicer to people, maybe people would do something nice for *you* some time.

ROSEMARY You got a beau, Millie?

MILLIE No!

ROSEMARY You can't kid me! Girls don't paint their fingernails unless they think some boy is gonna take notice.

FLO Madge, will you try this dress on now, dear?
   (MADGE goes inside with the dress)

MRS. POTTS *(Appears on her back porch, carrying a bundle of wet laundry)* Flo!

FLO *(Calling back, a noise like an owl)* Hoooo!

MRS. POTTS Are you going to be using the clothesline this morning?

FLO I don't think so.

MRS. POTTS' MOTHER *(An aged and quivering voice that still retains its command, issuing from the upper window of the house, left)* Helen! Helen!

MRS. POTTS *(Calling back)* I'm hanging out the clothes, Mama. I'll be right back.
   (She goes busily off stage through the passageway)

FLO *(Confidentially to ROSEMARY)* Poor Helen! She told me sometimes she has to get up *three* times a night to take her mother to the bathroom.

ROSEMARY Why doesn't she put her in an old ladies' home?

FLO None of 'em will take her. She's too mean.

ROSEMARY She must be mean—if that story is true.

FLO It *is* true! Helen and the Potts boy *ran off* and got married. Helen's mother caught her that very day and had the marriage annulled!

ROSEMARY *(With a shaking of her head)* She's Mrs. Potts in name only.

FLO Sometimes I think she keeps the boy's name just to defy the old lady.
   (ALAN'S car is heard approaching. It stops and the car door slams)

MILLIE *(Putting down her book)* Hi, Alan! *(Jumps up, starts inside)* Oh, boy! I'm gonna get my suit!

FLO (*Calling after* MILLIE) See if Madge is decent. (ALAN *comes on down-stage, right*) Good morning, Alan!

ALAN Morning, Mrs. Owens . . . Miss Sydney.
(ROSEMARY *doesn't bother to speak, usually affecting indifference to men*)

MRS. POTTS (*Coming back on from the passageway*) Have you girls seen the handsome young man I've got working for me?

ROSEMARY I think it's a disgrace, his parading around, naked as an Indian.

MRS. POTTS (*Protectingly*) I *told* him to take his shirt off.

FLO Helen Potts, I wish you'd stop taking in all sorts of riffraff!

MRS. POTTS He isn't riffraff. He's been to several colleges.

FLO College—and he begs for breakfast!

MRS. POTTS He's working for his breakfast! Alan, he said he knew you at the university.

ALAN (*With no idea whom she's talking about*) Who?

MILLIE (*Coming out the front door*) We going swimming, Alan?

ALAN You bet.

FLO Alan, why don't you go up and see Madge? Just call from the bottom of the stairs.

ALAN (*Goes inside, calling*) Hey, Delilah!

FLO (*Seeing that* MILLIE *is about to follow* ALAN *inside*) Millie!
(MILLIE *gets the idea that* MADGE *and* ALAN *are to be left alone. She sulks*)

ROSEMARY (*To* FLO, *confidentially*) Do you think Alan's going to marry Madge?

FLO (*She's usually a very truthful woman*) I hadn't thought much about it.

MRS. POTTS (*After a moment, drying her neck with handkerchief*) It's so hot and still this time of year. When it gets this way I'd welcome a good strong wind.

FLO I'd rather wipe my brow than get blown away.

MRS. POTTS (*Looking off at* HAL, *full of smiling admiration*) Look at him lift that big old washtub like it was so much tissue paper!

MRS. POTTS' MOTHER (*Offstage, again*) Helen! Helen!

MRS. POTTS (*Patient but firm*) I'm visiting Flo, Mama. You're all right. You don't need me.

FLO What did you feed him?

MRS. POTTS Biscuits.

FLO You went to all that trouble?

MRS. POTTS He was *so* hungry. I gave him ham and eggs and all the hot coffee he could drink. Then he saw a piece of cherry pie in the icebox and he wanted that, too!

ROSEMARY (*Laughs bawdily*) Sounds to me like Mrs. Potts had herself a new boy friend!

MRS. POTTS (*Rising, feeling injured*) I don't think that's very funny.

FLO Helen, come on. Sit down.

ROSEMARY Shoot, Mrs. Potts, I'm just a tease.

FLO Sit down, Helen.

MRS. POTTS (*Still touchy*) I *could* sit on my own porch, but I hate for the neighbors to see me there all alone.
(MADGE *and* ALAN *come out together,* MADGE *in her new dress. They march out hand in hand in a mock ceremony as though they were marching down the aisle*)

ROSEMARY (*Consolingly*) Mrs. Potts, if I said anything to offend you . . .

FLO (*Signals* ROSEMARY *to be quiet, points to* MADGE *and* ALAN) Bride and groom! Look, everybody! Bride and groom! (*To* MADGE) How does it feel, Madge? (*Laughs at her unconscious joke*) I mean the dress.

MADGE (*Crossing to her mother*) I love it, Mom, except it's a little tight in places.

MRS. POTTS (*All eyes of admiration*) Isn't Madge the pretty one!

ALAN (*Turning to* MILLIE) What are you reading, Millie?

MILLIE *The Ballad of the Sad Café* by Carson McCullers. It's wonderful!

ROSEMARY (*Shocked*) Good Lord, Mrs. Owens, you let your daughter read filthy books like that?

FLO Filthy?

ROSEMARY Everyone in it is some sort of degenerate!

MILLIE That's not so!

ROSEMARY The D.A.R.'s had it banned from the public library.

MRS. POTTS *(Eliminating herself from the argument)* I don't read much.

FLO Millie, give me that book!

MILLIE *(Tenaciously)* No!

ALAN Mrs. Owens, I don't wanta interfere, but that book is on the reading list at college. For the course in the modern novel.

FLO *(Full of confusion)* Oh, dear! What's a person to believe?
(ALAN's *word about such matters is apparently final*)

ROSEMARY Well, those college professors don't have any morals!
(MILLIE *and* ALAN *shake hands*)

FLO Where Millie comes by her tastes, I'll never know.

MADGE *(As* FLO *inspects her dress)* Some of the pictures she has over her bed *scare* me.

MILLIE Those pictures are by Picasso, and he's a great artist.

MADGE A woman with seven eyes. Very pretty.

MILLIE *(Delivering her ultimatum)* Pictures don't have to be *pretty!*
(A *sudden explosion from* MRS. POTTS' *backyard. The women are startled*)

FLO Helen!

MRS. POTTS *(Jumping up, alarmed)* I'll go see what it is.

FLO Stay here! He must have had a gun!

VOICE OFF STAGE Helen! Helen!

FLO *(Grabbing* MRS. POTTS' *arm)* Don't go over there, Helen! Your mother's old. She has to go soon anyway!

MRS. POTTS *(Running off stage)* Pshaw! I'm not afraid.

ALAN *(Looking off at* HAL) Who did that guy say he was?
(No one hears ALAN)

MRS. POTTS *(Coming back and facing* FLO) I was a bad girl.

FLO What *is* it, Helen?

MRS. POTTS I threw the *new* bottle of cleaning fluid into the trash.

FLO   You're the limit! Come on, Madge, let's finish that dress. (FLO *and*
MADGE *go into the house.* ROSEMARY *looks at her watch and then goes into
the house also*)

MRS. POTTS   Come help me, Millie. The young man ran into the clothesline.
(*She and* MILLIE *hurry off stage.* ALAN *stands alone, trying to identify* HAL,
who comes on from MRS. POTTS'. HAL *is bare-chested now, wearing his
T-shirt wrapped about his neck.* ALAN *finally recognizes him and is
overjoyed at seeing him*)

ALAN   Where did *you* come from?

HAL   (*Loud and hearty*)   Kid!

ALAN   Hal Carter!

HAL   I was comin' over to see you a little later.

ALAN   (*Recalling some intimate roughhouse greeting from their college
days*)   How's the old outboard motor?

HAL   (*With the eagerness of starting a game*)   Want a ride?

ALAN   (*Springing to* HAL, *clasping his legs around* HAL'S *waist, hanging by one
hand wrapped about* HAL'S *neck, as though riding some sort of imagined
machine*)   Gassed up? (*With his fingers, he twists* HAL'S *nose as if it were
a starter.* HAL *makes the sputtering noise of an outboard motor and swings*
ALAN *about the stage,* ALAN *holding on like a bronco-buster. They laugh
uproariously together*) Ahoy, brothers! Who's winkin', blinkin', and
stinkin'?
(ALAN *drops to the ground, both of them still laughing uproariously with
the recall of carefree college days*)

HAL   That used to wake the whole damn fraternity!

ALAN   The last time I saw you, you were on your way to Hollywood to
become a movie hero.

HAL   (*With a shrug of his shoulders*)   Oh, that!

ALAN   What do you mean, "Oh, that"? Isn't that what I loaned you the
hundred bucks for?

HAL   Sure, Seymour.

ALAN   Well, what happened?

HAL *(He'd rather the subject had not been brought up)* Things just didn't work out.

ALAN I tried to warn you, Hal. Every year some talent scout promised screen tests to all the athletes.

HAL Oh, I got the test okay! I was about to have a big career. They were gonna call me Brush Carter. How d'ya like that?

ALAN Yeah?

HAL Yah! They took a lotta pictures of me with my shirt off. Real rugged. Then they dressed me up like the Foreign Legion. Then they put me in a pair of tights—and they gave me a big hat with a plume, and had me makin' with the sword play. *(Pantomimes a duel)* Touché, mug! *(Returning the sword to its scabbard)* It was real crazy!

ALAN *(A little skeptical)* Did they give you any lines to read?

HAL Yah, that part went okay. It was my teeth.

ALAN Your teeth?

HAL Yah! Out there, you gotta have a certain kind of teeth or they can't use you. Don't ask me why. This babe said they'd have to pull all my teeth and give me new ones, so naturally . . .

ALAN Wait a minute. What babe?

HAL The babe that got me the test. She wasn't a babe exactly. She was kinda beat up—but not bad. *(He sees ALAN's critical eye)* Jesus, Seymour, a guy's gotta get along somehow.

ALAN Uh-huh. What are you doing here?

HAL *(A little hurt)* Aren't you glad to see me?

ALAN Sure, but fill me in.

HAL Well—after I left Hollywood I took a job on a ranch in Nevada. You'da been proud of me, Seymour. In bed every night at ten, up every morning at six. No liquor—no babes. I saved up two hundred bucks!

ALAN *(Holding out a hand)* Oh! I'll take half.

HAL Gee, Seymour, I wish I had it, but I got rolled.

ALAN Rolled? *You?*

HAL *(He looks to see that no one can overhear)* Yeah, I was gonna hitchhike to Texas to get in a big oil deal. I got as far as Phoenix when two babes pull up in this big yellow convertible. And one of these dames slams on the brakes and hollers, "Get in, stud!" So I got in. Seymour, it was crazy. They had a shakerful of martinis right there in the car!

MRS. POTTS *(Appears on her porch, followed by* MILLIE. MRS. POTTS *carries a cake)* Oh, talking over old times? Millie helped me ice the cake.

HAL Any more work, ma'am?

MRS. POTTS No. I feel I've been more than paid for the breakfast.

HAL S'pose there's any place I could wash up?

MILLIE We got a shower in the basement. Come on, I'll show you.

ALAN *(Holding* HAL*)* He'll be there in a minute. (MRS. POTTS *and* MILLIE *exit into the* OWENS' *house)* O.K., so they had a shakerful of martinis!

HAL And one of these babes was smokin' the weed!

ALAN *(With vicarious excitement)* Nothing like that ever happens to me! Go on!

HAL Seymour, you wouldn't believe it, the things those two babes started doin' to me.

ALAN Were they good-looking?

HAL What do you care?

ALAN Makes the story more interesting. Tell me what happened.

HAL Well, you know *me*, Seymour. I'm an agreeable guy.

ALAN Sure.

HAL So when they parked in front of this tourist cabin, I said, "Okay, girls, if I gotta pay for the ride, this is the easiest way I know." *(He shrugs)* But, gee, they musta thought I was Superman.

ALAN You mean—*both* of them?

HAL Sure.

ALAN Golly!

HAL Then I said, "Okay, girls, the party's over—let's get goin'." Then this dame on the weed, she sticks a gun in my back. She says, "This party's goin' on till *we* say it's over, Buck!" You'da thought she was Humphrey Bogart!

ALAN Then what happened?

HAL Finally I passed out! And when I woke up, the dames was gone and so was my two hundred bucks! I went to the police and they wouldn't believe me—they said my whole story was wishful thinking! How d'ya like *that!*

ALAN *(Thinking it over)* Mmmm.

HAL Women are gettin' desperate, Seymour.

ALAN *Are* they?

HAL Well, that did it. Jesus, Seymour, what's a poor bastard like me ever gonna do?

ALAN You don't sound like you had such a hard time.

HAL I got thinking of you, Seymour, at school—how you always had things under control.

ALAN Me?

HAL Yah. Never cut classes—understood the lectures—took notes! (ALAN *laughs)* What's so funny?

ALAN The hero of the campus, and he envied me!

HAL Yah! Big hero, between the goal posts. You're the only guy in the whole fraternity ever treated me like a human being.

ALAN *(With feeling for* HAL) I know.

HAL Those other snob bastards always watchin' to see which fork I used.

ALAN You've got an inferiority complex. You imagined those things.

HAL In a pig's eye!

ALAN *(Delicately)* What do you hear about your father?

HAL *(Grave)* It finally happened . . . before I left for Hollywood.

ALAN What?

HAL *(With a solemn hurt)* He went on his last bender. The police scraped him up off the sidewalk. He died in jail.

ALAN *(Moved)* Gee, I'm sorry to hear that, Hal.

HAL The old lady wouldn't even come across with the dough for the funeral. They had to bury him in Pauper's Row.

ALAN What happened to the filling station?

HAL He left it to me in his will, but the old lady was gonna have him declared insane so she could take over. I let her have it. Who cares?

ALAN *(Rather depressed by* HAL'S *story)* Gee, Hal, I just can't believe people really do things like that.

HAL Don't let *my* stories cloud up your rosy glasses.

ALAN Why didn't you come to see me, when you got to town?

HAL I didn't want to walk into your palatial mansion lookin' like a bum. I wanted to get some breakfast in my belly and pick up a little change.

ALAN That wouldn't have made any difference.

HAL I was hoping maybe you and your old man, between you, might fix me up with a job.

ALAN What kind of a job, Hal?

HAL What kinda jobs you got?

ALAN What kind of job did you have in mind?

HAL *(This is his favorite fantasy)* Oh, something in a nice office where I can wear a tie and have a sweet little secretary and talk over the telephone about enterprises and things. *(As* ALAN *walks away skeptically)* I've always had the feeling, if I just had the chance, I could set the world on fire.

ALAN Lots of guys have that feeling, Hal.

HAL *(With some desperation)* I gotta get some place in this world, Seymour. I *got* to.

ALAN *(With a hand on* HAL'S *shoulder)* Take it easy.

HAL This is a free country, and I got just as much rights as the next fellow. Why can't I get along?

ALAN Don't worry, Hal. I'll help you out as much as I can. (MRS. POTTS *comes out the* OWENS' *back door)* Sinclair is hiring new men, aren't they, Mrs. Potts?

MRS. POTTS Yes, Alan. Carey Hamilton needs a hundred new men for the pipeline.

HAL *(Had dared to hope for more)* Pipeline?

ALAN If you wanta be president of the company, Hal, I guess you'll just have to work hard and be patient.

HAL *(Clenching his fists together, so eager is he for patience)* Yah. That's something I gotta learn. Patience!
(He hurries inside the OWENS' *back door now)*

MRS. POTTS   I feel sorry for young men today.

ROSEMARY *(Coming out the front door, very proud of the new outfit she is wearing, a fall suit and an elaborate hat)* Is this a private party I'm crashin'?

MRS. POTTS *(With some awe of* ROSEMARY'S *finery)* My, you're dressed up!

ROSEMARY   'S my new fall outfit. Got it in Kansas City. Paid twenty-two-fifty for the hat.

MRS. POTTS   You schoolteachers do have nice things.

ROSEMARY   And don't have to ask anybody when we wanta get 'em, either.

FLO *(Coming out back door with* MADGE) Be here for lunch today, Rosemary?

ROSEMARY   No. There's a welcome-home party down at the hotel. Lunch and bridge for the new girls on the faculty.

MADGE   Mom, can't I go swimming, too?

FLO   Who'll fix lunch? I've got a million things to do.

MADGE   It wouldn't kill Millie if she ever did any cooking.

FLO   No, but it might kill the rest of us.
(Now we hear the voices of IRMA KRONKITE *and* CHRISTINE SCHOENWALDER, *who are coming by for* ROSEMARY. *They think it playful to call from a distance)*

IRMA   Rosemary! Let's get going, girl! *(As they come into sight,* IRMA *turns to* CHRISTINE) You'll love Rosemary Sydney. She's a peck of fun! Says the craziest things.

ROSEMARY *(With playful suspiciousness)* What're you saying about me, Irma Kronkite?
(They run to hug each other like eager sisters who had not met in a decade)

IRMA   Rosemary Sydney!

ROSEMARY   Irma Kronkite! How was your vacation?

IRMA   I worked like a slave. But I had fun, too. I don't care if I *never* get that Masters. I'm not going to be a slave *all* my life.

CHRISTINE *(Shyly)*   She's been telling me about all the wicked times she had in New York—and *not* at Teachers College, if I may add.

IRMA *(To* ROSEMARY*)*   Kid, this is Christine Schoenwalder, taking Mabel Fremont's place in feminine hygiene. (ROSEMARY *and* CHRISTINE *shake hands)* Been a hot summer, Mrs. Owens?

FLO   The worst I can remember.

MRS. POTTS *(As* ROSEMARY *brings* CHRISTINE *up on porch)*   Delighted to know you, Christine. Welcome back, Irma.

IRMA   Are you working now, Madge?

MADGE   Yes.

FLO *(Taking over for* MADGE*)*   Yes, Madge has been working downtown this summer—just to keep busy. *(Now* HAL *and* MILLIE *burst out the kitchen door, engaged in a noisy and furious mock fist-fight.* HAL *is still bare-chested, his T-shirt still around his neck, and the sight of him is something of a shock to the ladies)* Why, when did he . . .

ALAN *(Seizing* HAL *for an introduction)*   Mrs. Owens, this is my friend, Hal Carter. Hal is a fraternity brother.

MRS. POTTS *(Nudging* FLO*)*   What did I tell you, Flo?

FLO *(Stunned)*   Fraternity brother! Really? *(Making the best of it)* Any friend of Alan's is a friend of ours.
(She offers HAL *her hand)*

HAL   Glad to make your acquaintance, ma'am.

ALAN *(Embarrassed for him)*   Hal, don't you have a shirt?

HAL   It's all sweaty, Seymour.
(ALAN *nudges him.* HAL *realizes he has said the wrong thing and reluctantly puts on the T-shirt)*

ROSEMARY *(Collecting* IRMA *and* CHRISTINE*)*   Girls, we better get a hustle on.

CHRISTINE *(To* IRMA*)*   Tell them about what happened in New York, kid.

IRMA *(The center of attention)*   I went to the Stork Club!

ROSEMARY   How did *you* get to the Stork Club?

IRMA   See, there was this fellow in my educational statistics class . . .

ROSEMARY *(Continuing the joke)*   I *knew* there was a *man* in it.

IRMA   Now, girl! It was nothing serious. He was just a good sport, that's all. We made a bet that the one who made the lowest grade on the *final* had to take the other to the Stork Club—and *I* lost!
(The teachers go off noisily laughing, as FLO *and* MRS. POTTS *watch them)*

ALAN *(Calling to* HAL, *at back of stage playing with* MILLIE)   Wanta go swimming, Hal? I've got extra trunks in the car.

HAL   Why not?

MRS. POTTS *(In a private voice)*   Flo, let's ask the young man on the picnic. He'd be a date for Millie.

FLO   That's right, but . . .

MRS. POTTS *(Taking it upon herself)*   Young man, Flo and I are having a picnic for the young people. You come, too, and be an escort for Millie.

HAL   Picnic?

MRS. POTTS   Yes.

HAL   I don't think it's right, me bargin' in this way.

MRS. POTTS   Nonsense. A picnic's no fun without lots and lots of young people.

ALAN *(Bringing* HAL *down center)*   Hal, I want you to meet Madge.

MADGE   Oh, we've met already. That is, we *saw* each other.

HAL   Yah, we saw each other.

ALAN *(To* MADGE)   Hal sees every pretty girl.

MADGE *(Pretending to protest)*   Alan.

ALAN   Well, you're the prettiest girl in town, aren't you? *(To* HAL)   The Chamber of Commerce voted her Queen of Neewollah last year.

HAL   I don't dig.

MILLIE   She was Queen of Neewollah. Neewollah is Halloween spelled backwards.

MRS. POTTS *(Joining in)*   Every year they have a big coronation ceremony in Memorial Hall, with all kinds of artistic singing and dancing.

MILLIE   Madge had to sit through the whole ceremony till they put a crown on her head.

HAL *(Impressed)*   Yah?

MADGE I got awfully tired.

MILLIE The Kansas City *Star* ran color pictures in their Sunday magazine.

MADGE Everyone expected me to get real conceited, but I didn't.

HAL You didn't?

MILLIE It'd be pretty hard to get conceited about *those* pictures.

MADGE *(Humorously)* The color got blurred and my mouth was printed right in the middle of my forehead.

HAL *(Sympathetic)* Gee, that's too bad.

MADGE *(Philosophically)* Things like that are bound to happen.

MILLIE *(To HAL)* I'll race you to the car.

HAL *(Starting off with MILLIE)* Isn't your sister goin' with us?

MILLIE Madge has to cook lunch.

HAL Do you mean *she cooks?*

MILLIE Sure! Madge cooks and sews and does all those things that women do.
(They race off, MILLIE getting a head start through the gate and HAL scaling the fence to get ahead of her)

FLO *(In a concerned voice)* Alan!

ALAN Yes?

FLO How did a boy like him get into college?

ALAN On a football scholarship. He made a spectacular record in a little high school down in Arkansas.

FLO But a fraternity! Don't those boys have a little more . . . breeding?

ALAN I guess they're *supposed* to, but fraternities like to pledge big athletes —for the publicity. And Hal could have been All-American . . .

MRS. POTTS *(Delighted)* All-American!

ALAN . . . if he'd only studied.

FLO But how did the other boys feel about him?

ALAN *(Reluctantly)* They didn't like him, Mrs. Owens. They were pretty rough on him. Every time he came into a room, the other fellows seemed to *bristle*. I didn't like him either, at first. Then we shared a room and I got to know him better. Hal's really a nice guy. About the best friend I ever had.

FLO *(More to the point)* Is he wild?

ALAN Oh—not really. He just . . .

FLO Does he drink?

ALAN A little. *(Trying to minimize)* Mrs. Owens, Hal pays attention to me. I'll see he behaves.

FLO I wouldn't want anything to happen to Millie.

MADGE Millie can take care of herself. You pamper her.

FLO Maybe I do. Come on, Helen. *(As she and MRS. POTTS go in through the back door)* Oh, dear, why can't things be simple?

ALAN *(After FLO and MRS. POTTS leave)* Madge, I'm sorry I have to go back to school this fall. It's Dad's idea.

MADGE I thought it was.

ALAN Really, Madge, Dad likes you very much. I'm sure he does. *(But ALAN himself doesn't sound convinced)*

MADGE Well—he's always very polite.

ALAN I'll miss you, Madge.

MADGE There'll be lots of pretty girls at college.

ALAN Honestly, Madge, my entire four years I never found a girl I liked.

MADGE I don't believe that.

ALAN It's true. They're all so affected, if you wanted a date with them you had to call them a month in advance.

MADGE Really?

ALAN Madge, it's hard to say, but I honestly never believed that a girl like you could care for me.

MADGE *(Touched)* Alan . . .

ALAN I—I hope you do care for me, Madge. *(He kisses her)*

HAL *(Comes back on stage somewhat apologetically. He is worried about something and tries to get ALAN's attention)* Hey, Seymour . . .

ALAN *(Annoyed)*   What's the matter, Hal? Can't you stand to see anyone else kiss a pretty girl?

HAL   What the hell, Seymour!

ALAN *(An excuse to be angry)*   Hal, will you watch your language!

MADGE   Alan! It's all right.

HAL   I'm sorry.
     (Beckons ALAN *to him)*

ALAN *(Crossing to him)*   What's the trouble?
     (MADGE *walks away, sensing that* HAL *wants to talk privately)*

HAL   Look, Seymour, I—I never been on a picnic.

ALAN   What're you talking about? Everybody's been on a picnic.

HAL   Not me. When I was a kid, I was too busy shooting craps or stealing milk bottles.

ALAN   Well, there's a first time for everything.

HAL   I wasn't brought up proper like *you*. I won't know how to act around all these *women*.

ALAN   Women aren't anything new in *your* life.

HAL   But these are—*nice* women. What if I say the wrong word or maybe my stomach growls? I feel *funny*.

ALAN   You're a psycho!

HAL   O.K., but if I do anything wrong, you gotta try to overlook it.
     (He runs off stage. ALAN *laughs. Then* ALAN *returns to* MADGE)

ALAN   We'll be by about five, Madge.

MADGE   O.K.

ALAN *(Beside her, tenderly)*   Madge, after we have supper tonight maybe you and I can get away from the others and take a boat out on the river.

MADGE   All right, Alan.

ALAN   I want to see if you look *real* in the moonlight.

MADGE   Alan! Don't say that!

ALAN   Why? I don't care if you're real or not. You're the prettiest girl I ever saw.

MADGE   Just the same, I'm real.
   (As ALAN starts to kiss her, the noise of an automobile horn is heard)

HAL   *(Hollering lustily from offstage)*   Hey, Seymour—get the lead outa
   your pants!
   *(ALAN goes off, irritated. MADGE watches them as they drive away. She waves
   to them)*

FLO   *(Inside)*   Madge! Come on inside now.

MADGE   All right, Mom.
   *(As she starts in, there is a train whistle in the distance. MADGE hears it
   and stands listening)*

CURTAIN

ACT TWO

SCENE: *It is late afternoon, the same day. The sun is beginning to set and fills the atmosphere with radiant orange. When the curtain goes up,* MILLIE *is on the porch alone. She has permitted herself to "dress up" and wears a becoming, feminine dress in which she cannot help feeling a little strange. She is quite attractive. Piano music can be heard offstage, somewhere past* MRS. POTTS' *house, and* MILLIE *stands listening to it for a moment. Then she begins to sway to the music and in a moment is dancing a strange, impromptu dance over the porch and yard. The music stops suddenly and* MILLIE'S *mood is broken. She rushes upstage and calls off, left.*

MILLIE   Don't quit now, Ernie! *(She cannot hear* ERNIE'S *reply)* Huh? *(*MADGE *enters from kitchen.* MILLIE *turns to* MADGE*)* Ernie's waiting for the rest of the band to practice. They're going to play out at the park tonight.

MADGE   *(Crossing to center and sitting on chair)*   I don't know why you couldn't have helped us in the kitchen.

MILLIE   *(Lightly, giving her version of the sophisticated belle)*   I had to dress for the ball.

MADGE   I had to make the potato salad and stuff the eggs and make three dozen bread-and-butter sandwiches.

MILLIE   *(In a very affected accent)*   I had to *bathe*—and dust my limbs with powder—and slip into my frock . . .

MADGE   Did you clean out the bathtub?

MILLIE   Yes, I cleaned out the bathtub. *(She becomes very self-conscious)* Madge, how do I look? Now tell me the truth.

MADGE   You look very pretty.

MILLIE   I feel sorta funny.

MADGE   You can have the dress if you want it.

MILLIE   Thanks. *(A pause)* Madge, how do you talk to boys?

MADGE   Why, you just talk, silly.

MILLIE   How d'ya think of things to say?

MADGE   I don't know. You just say whatever comes into your head.

MILLIE   Supposing nothing ever comes into my head?

MADGE   You talked with him all right this morning.

MILLIE   But now I've got a *date* with him, and it's *different!*

MADGE   You're crazy.

MILLIE   I think he's a big show-off. You should have seen him this morning
on the high diving board. He did real graceful swan dives, and a two and
a half gainer, and a back flip—and kids stood around clapping. He just
ate it up.

MADGE   *(Her mind elsewhere)*   I think I'll paint my toenails tonight and
wear sandals.

MILLIE   And he was braggin' all afternoon how he used to be a deep-sea
diver off Catalina Island.

MADGE   Honest?

MILLIE   And he says he used to make hundreds of dollars doin' parachute
jumps out of a balloon. Do you believe it?

MADGE   I don't see why not.

MILLIE   You never hear Alan bragging that way.

MADGE   Alan never jumped out of a balloon.

MILLIE   Madge, I think he's girl crazy.

MADGE   You think every boy you see is something horrible.

MILLIE   Alan took us into the Hi Ho for Cokes and there was a gang of girls
in the back booth—Juanita Badger and her gang. (MADGE *groans at hearing this name*) When they saw him, they started giggling and tee-heeing
and saying all sorts of crazy things. Then Juanita Badger comes up to me
and whispers, "He's the cutest thing I ever saw." Is he, Madge?

MADGE   *(Not willing to go overboard)*   I certainly wouldn't say he was "the
cutest thing I ever *saw*."

MILLIE   Juanita Badger's an old floozy. She sits in the back row at the
movie so the guys that come in will see her and sit with her. One time

she and Rubberneck Krauss were asked by the management to leave—and they weren't just kissin', either!

MADGE *(Proudly)*   I never even speak to Juanita Badger.

MILLIE   Madge, do you think he'll like me?

MADGE   Why ask me all these questions? You're supposed to be the smart one.

MILLIE   I don't really care. I just wonder.

FLO *(Coming out of kitchen)*   Now I tell myself I've got two beautiful daughters.

MILLIE *(Embarrassed)*   Be quiet, Mom!

FLO   Doesn't Millie look pretty, Madge?

MADGE   When she isn't picking her nose.

FLO   Madge! *(To* MILLIE*)* She doesn't want anyone to be pretty but her.

MILLIE   You're just saying I'm pretty because you're my mom. People we love are always pretty, but people who're pretty to begin with, everybody loves *them*.

FLO   Run over and show Helen Potts how nice you look.

MILLIE *(In a wild parody of herself)*   Here comes Millie Owens, the great beauty of all time! Be prepared to swoon when you see her!
(She climbs up over the side of MRS. POTTS' *porch and disappears)*

FLO *(Sits on chair on porch)*   Whatever possessed me to let Helen Potts ask that young hoodlum to take Millie on the picnic?

MADGE   Hal?

FLO   Yes, Hal, or whatever his name is. He left every towel in the bathroom black as dirt. He left the seat up, too.

MADGE   It's not going to hurt anyone just to be nice to him.

FLO   If there's any drinking tonight, you put a stop to it.

MADGE   I'm not going to be a wet blanket.

FLO   If the boys feel they have to have a few drinks, there's nothing you can do about it, but you can keep Millie from taking any.

MADGE   She wouldn't pay any attention to me.

FLO *(Changing the subject)* You better be getting dressed. And don't spend the whole evening admiring yourself in the mirror.

MADGE Mom, don't make fun of me.

FLO You shouldn't object to being kidded if it's well meant.

MADGE It seems like—when I'm looking in the mirror that's the only way I can prove to myself I'm alive.

FLO Madge! You puzzle me.
(The three schoolteachers come on, downstage right, making a rather tired return from their festivity. After their high-spirited exit in Act One, their present mood seems glum, as though they had expected from the homecoming some fulfillment that had not been realized)

IRMA We've brought home your wayward girl, Mrs. Owens!

FLO *(Turning from* MADGE*)* Hello, girls! Have a nice party?

IRMA It wasn't a real party. Each girl paid for her own lunch. Then we played bridge all afternoon. *(Confidentially, to* ROSEMARY*)* I get tired playing bridge.

FLO Food's good at the hotel, isn't it?

IRMA Not very. But they serve it to you nice, with honest-to-goodness napkins. Lord, I hate paper napkins!

CHRISTINE I had a French-fried pork chop and it was mostly fat. What'd you girls have?

ROSEMARY I had the stuffed peppers.

IRMA I had the Southern-fried chicken.

CHRISTINE Linda Sue Breckenridge had pot roast of veal and there was only one little hunk of meat in it. All we girls at her table made her call the waiter and complain.

ROSEMARY Well, I should hope so!

IRMA Good for you! *(There is a pause)* I thought by this time someone might have noticed my new dress.

ROSEMARY I was going to say something, kid, and then I . . . uh . . .

IRMA Remember that satin-back crepe I had last year?

ROSEMARY Don't tell me!

IRMA   Mama remodeled it for me while I was at Columbia. I feel like I had a brand-new outfit. *(Smarting)* But nobody said anything all afternoon!

CHRISTINE   It's—chic.

IRMA *(This soothes* IRMA *a bit and she beams. But now there is an awkward pause wherein no one can think of any more to say)*   Well—we better run along, Christine. Rosemary has a date. *(To* ROSEMARY*)* We'll come by for you in the morning. Don't be late.
(She goes upstage and waits at the gate for CHRISTINE*)*

CHRISTINE *(Crossing to* ROSEMARY*)*   Girl, I want to tell you, in one afternoon I feel I've known you my whole life.

ROSEMARY *(With assurance of devotion)*   I look upon you as an old friend already.

CHRISTINE *(Overjoyed)*   Aw . . .

ROSEMARY *(As* CHRISTINE *and* IRMA *go off)*   Good-bye, girls!

FLO *(To* ROSEMARY*)*   What time's Howard coming by?

ROSEMARY   Any minute now.

MADGE   Mom, is there any hot water?

FLO   You'll have to see.

MADGE *(Crosses to door, then turns to* ROSEMARY*)*   Miss Sydney, would you mind terribly if I used some of your Shalimar?

ROSEMARY   Help yourself!

MADGE   Thanks.
(She goes inside)

ROSEMARY   Madge thinks too much about the boys, Mrs. Owens.

FLO *(Disbelieving)*   Madge?
(The conversation is stopped by the excited entrance of MRS. POTTS *from her house. She is followed by* MILLIE, *who carries another cake)*

MRS. POTTS   It's a *miracle*, that's what it is! I never knew Millie could look so pretty. It's just like a movie I saw once with Betty Grable—or was it Lana Turner? Anyway, she played the part of a secretary to some very important businessman. She wore glasses and did her hair real plain and men didn't pay any attention to her at all. Then one day she took off her glasses and her boss wanted to marry her right away! Now all the boys are going to fall in love with Millie!

ROSEMARY Millie have a date tonight?

FLO Yes, I'm sorry to say.

MRS. POTTS Why, Flo!

ROSEMARY Who is he, Millie? Tell your Aunt Rosemary.

MILLIE Hal.

ROSEMARY Who?

FLO The young man over at Helen's turned out to be a friend of Alan's.

ROSEMARY Oh, *him!*
  (MILLIE *exits into kitchen*)

FLO Helen, have you gone to the trouble of baking another cake?

MRS. POTTS An old lady like me, if she wants any attention from the young men on a picnic, all she can do is bake a cake!

FLO (*Rather reproving*) Helen Potts!

MRS. POTTS I feel sort of excited, Flo. I think we plan picnics just to give ourselves an excuse—to let something thrilling happen in our lives.

FLO Such as what?

MRS. POTTS I don't know.

MADGE (*Bursting out the door*) Mom, Millie makes me furious! Every time she takes a bath, she fills the whole tub. There isn't any hot water at all.

FLO You should have thought of it earlier.

ROSEMARY (*Hears* HOWARD'S *car drive up and stop*) It's him! It's him!

MRS. POTTS Who? Oh, it's Howard. Hello, Howard!

ROSEMARY (*Sitting down again*) If he's been drinking, I'm not going out with him.

HOWARD (*As he comes on through gate*) Howdy, ladies.
  (HOWARD *is a small, thin man, rapidly approaching middle age. A small-town businessman, he wears a permanent smile of greeting which, most of the time, is pretty sincere*)

FLO Hello, Howard.

HOWARD You sure look nice, Rosemary.

ROSEMARY *(Her tone of voice must tell a man she is independent of him)*   Seems to me you might have left your coat on.

HOWARD   Still too darn hot, even if it is September. Good evening, Madge.

MADGE   Hi, Howard.

FLO   How are things over in Cherryvale, Howard?

HOWARD   Good business. Back to school and everybody buying.

FLO   When business is good, it's good for everyone.

MILLIE *(Comes out of kitchen, stands shyly behind HOWARD)*   Hi, Howard!

HOWARD *(Turning around, making a discovery)*   Hey, Millie's a good-lookin' kid. I never realized it before.

MILLIE *(Crossing to FLO, apprehensive)*   Mom, what time did the fellows say they'd be here?

FLO   At five-thirty. You've asked me a dozen times. *(There is a sound of approaching automobiles, and FLO looks off stage, right)* Alan's brought *both* cars!
  (MILLIE runs into the house)

MRS. POTTS *(To FLO)*   Some day *you'll* be riding around in that big Cadillac, ladybug.

ALAN *(Coming on from right)*   Everyone ready?

FLO   Come sit down, Alan.

ROSEMARY *(Like a champion hostess)*   The more the merrier!

ALAN   I brought both cars. I thought we'd let Hal and Millie bring the baskets out in the Ford. Hal's parking it now. *(To MADGE, who is sitting up on MRS. POTTS' porch railing)* Hello, Beautiful!

MADGE   Hello, Alan!

ALAN *(Calling off stage)*   Come on, Hal.

FLO   Is he a careful driver, Alan?
  (This question does not get answered. HAL comes running on, tugging uncomfortably at the shoulders of his jacket and hollering in a voice that once filled the locker rooms)

HAL   Hey, Seymour! Hey, I'm a big man, Seymour. I'm a lot huskier than you are. I can't wear your jacket.

ALAN Then take it off.

MRS. POTTS Yes. I like to see a man comfortable.

HAL *(With a broad smile of total confidence)* I never could wear another fellow's clothes. See, I'm pretty big through the shoulders. *(He demonstrates the fact)* I should have all my clothes tailor-made.
(He now swings his arms in appreciation of their new freedom. MRS. POTTS *is admiring, the other women speculative)*

ALAN *(Wanting to get over the formalities)* Hey—uh—Hercules, you've met Mrs. Owens . . .

HAL Sure!
(FLO nods at him)

ALAN . . . and I believe you met Mrs. Potts this morning.

HAL *(Throwing his arms around her)* Oh, she's my best girl!

MRS. POTTS *(Giggling like a girl)* I baked a Lady Baltimore cake!

HAL *(Expansively, as though making an announcement of public interest)* This little lady, she took pity on me when I was practically starving. I ran into some hard luck when I was travelin'. Some characters robbed me of every cent I had.

ALAN *(Interrupting)* And—er—this is Rosemary Sydney, Hal. Miss Sydney teaches shorthand and typing in the local high school.

ROSEMARY *(Offering her hand)* Yes, I'm an old-maid schoolteacher.

HAL *(With unnecessary earnestness)* I have every respect for schoolteachers, ma'am. It's a lotta hard work and not much pay.
(ROSEMARY cannot decide whether or not this is a compliment)

ALAN And this is Howard Bevans, Hal. Mr. Bevans is a friend of Miss Sydney.

HOWARD *(As they shake hands)* I run a little shop over in Cherryvale. Notions, novelties and school supplies. You and Alan drive over some time and get acquainted.
(MILLIE enters and stands on the porch, pretending to be nonchalant and at ease)

HAL *(To HOWARD, earnestly)* Sir, we'll come over as soon as we can fit it into our schedule. *(He spies MILLIE)* Hey, kid! *(He does an elaborate imitation of a swan dive and lands beside her on the porch)* You got a little more tan today, didn't you? *(He turns to the others)* You folks shoulda seen Millie this morning. She did a fine jackknife off the high diving board!

MILLIE *(Breaking away, sitting on steps)*   Cut it out!

HAL   What'sa matter, kid? Think I'm snowin' you under? *(Back to the whole group)* I wouldn't admit this to many people, but she does a jackknife almost as good as me! *(Realizes that this sounds bragging so goes on to explain)* You see, I was diving champion on the West Coast, so I know what I'm talking about!
(He laughs to reassure himself and sits beside MILLIE on doorstep)

FLO *(After a moment)*   Madge, you should be getting dressed.

ALAN   Go on upstairs and get beautiful for us.

MADGE   Mom, can I wear my new dress?

FLO   No. I made you that dress to save for dances this fall. *(The attention returns now to HAL, and MADGE continues to sit, unnoticed, watching him)*

ROSEMARY *(To HAL)*   Where'd you get those boots?

HAL   I guess maybe I should apologize for the way I look. But you see, those characters I told you about made off with all my clothes, too.

MRS. POTTS   What a pity!

HAL   You see, I didn't want you folks to think you were associatin' with a bum.
(He laughs uncomfortably)

MRS. POTTS *(Intuitively, she says what is needed to save his ego)*   Clothes don't make the man.

HAL   That's what I tell myself, ma'am.

FLO   Is your mother taken care of, Helen?

MRS. POTTS   Yes, Flo. I've got a baby sitter for her.
(All laugh)

FLO   Then let's start packing the baskets.
(She goes into kitchen. MRS. POTTS starts after her, but HAL's story holds her and she sits down again)

HAL *(Continuing his explanation to Rosemary)*   See, ma'am, my old man left me these boots when he died.

ROSEMARY *(Impishly)*   That all he left you—just a pair of boots?

HAL   He said, "Son, the man of the house needs a pair of boots 'cause he's
gotta do a lot of kickin'.
                    "Your wages all are spent.
                    The landlord wants his rent.
                    You go to your woman for solace,
                    And she fills you fulla torment."
(HAL *smiles and explains proudly*) That's a little poem he made up. He
says, "Son, there'll be times when the only thing you got to be proud of
is the fact you're a man. So wear your boots so people can hear you
comin', and keep your fists doubled up so they'll know you mean business when you get there." (*He laughs*) My old man, he was a corker!

ALAN   (*Laughing*)   Hal's always so shy of people before he meets them.
Then you can't keep him still!
(*Suddenly* HAL's *eye catches* MADGE, *perched on* MRS. POTTS' *porch*)

HAL   Hi!

MADGE   Hi!
(*Now they both look away from each other, a little guiltily*)

HOWARD   What line of business you in, son?

HAL   (*He begins to expand with importance*)   I'm about to enter the oil
business, sir.
(*He sits on the chair, center stage*)

HOWARD   Oh!

HAL   You see, while my old man was no aristocratic millionaire or anything,
he had some very important friends who were very big men—in their
own way. One of them wanted me to take a position with this oil company down in Texas, but . . .

ALAN   (*Matter-of-factly*)   Dad and I have found a place for Hal on the
pipeline.

HAL   Gee, Seymour, I think you oughta let *me* tell the story.

ALAN   (*Knowing he might as well let* HAL *go on*)   Sorry, Hal.

HAL   (*With devout earnestness to all*)   You see, I've decided to start in from
the very bottom, 'cause that way I'll learn things lots better—even if I
don't make much money for a while.

MRS. POTTS   (*Comes through again*)   Money isn't everything.

HAL   That's what I tell myself, ma'am. Money isn't everything. I've learned that much. And I sure do appreciate Alan and his old . . . *(Thinks a moment and substitutes* father *for* man*) father* . . . giving me this opportunity.

MRS. POTTS   I think that's wonderful.
(She has every faith in him)

HOWARD   It's a good business town. A young man can go far.

HAL   Sir! I intend to go *far.*

ROSEMARY *(Her two-bits' worth)*   A young man, coming to town, he's gotta be a good mixer.

MRS. POTTS   Wouldn't it be nice if he could join the country club and play golf?

ALAN   He won't be able to afford that.

ROSEMARY   The bowling team's a rowdy gang.

MRS. POTTS   And there's a young men's Bible class at the Baptist Church.
*(*HAL's *head has been spinning with these plans for his future. Now he reassures them)*

HAL   Oh, I'm gonna join clubs and go to church and do all those things.

FLO *(Coming out of the kitchen)*   Madge! Are you still here?

MADGE *(Running across to the front door of her own house)*   If everyone will pardon me, I'll get dressed.
(She goes inside)

FLO   It's about time.

ALAN *(Calling after* MADGE*)*   Hurry it up, will you, Delilah?

MILLIE   You oughta see the way Madge primps. She uses about six kinds of face cream and dusts herself all over with powder, and rubs perfume underneath her ears to make her real mysterious. It takes her half an hour just to get her lipstick on. She won't be ready for hours.

FLO   Come on, Helen. Alan, we'll need a man to help us chip the ice and put the baskets in the car.
*(*MRS. POTTS *goes inside)*

HAL *(Generously)*   I'll help you, ma'am.

FLO *(She simply cannot accept him)*   No, thank you. Alan won't mind.

ALAN *(To* HAL *as he leaves)*   Mind your manners, Hal.
(He and FLO *start in)*

MILLIE *(Uncertain how to proceed with* HAL *on her own, she runs to* FLO*)*
Mom!

FLO   Millie, show the young man your drawings.

MILLIE *(To* HAL*)*   Wanta see my art?

HAL   You mean to tell me you can draw pictures?

MILLIE *(Gets her sketch book and shows it to* HAL. FLO *and* ALAN *go inside)*   That's Mrs. Potts.

HAL *(Impressed)*   Looks just like her.

MILLIE   I just love Mrs. Potts. When I go to heaven, I expect everyone to be just like her.

HAL   Hey, kid, wanta draw me?

MILLIE   Well, I'll try.

HAL   I had a job as a model once. *(Strikes a pose)* How's this? (MILLIE *shakes her head)* Here's another. *(Sits on stump in another pose)* Okay?

MILLIE   Why don't you just try to look natural?

HAL   Gee, that's hard.
(But he shakes himself into a natural pose finally. MILLIE *starts sketching him.* ROSEMARY *and* HOWARD *sit together on the doorstep. The sun now is beginning to set, filling the stage with an orange glow that seems almost aflame)*

ROSEMARY *(Grabs* HOWARD'S *arm)*   Look at that sunset, Howard!

HOWARD   Pretty, isn't it?

ROSEMARY   That's the most flaming sunset I ever did see.

HOWARD   If you painted it in a picture, no one'd believe you.

ROSEMARY   It's like the daytime didn't want to end, isn't it?

HOWARD *(Not fully aware of what she means)*   Oh—I don't know.

ROSEMARY   Like the daytime didn't wanta end, like it was gonna put up a big scrap and maybe set the world on fire—to keep the nighttime from creepin' on.

HOWARD   Rosemary . . . you're a poet.

HAL (*As* MILLIE *sketches him he begins to relax and reflect on his life*)   You know, there comes a time in every man's life when he's gotta settle down. A little town like this, this is the place to settle down in, where people are easygoin' and sincere.

ROSEMARY   No, Howard, I don't think there ought to be any drinking, while Millie's here.

HAL (*Turns at the mention of drink*)   What's that?

ROSEMARY   We were just talkin'.

HAL (*Back to* MILLIE)   What'd you do this afternoon, kid?

MILLIE   Read a book.

HAL (*Impressed*)   You mean, you read a *whole* book in one afternoon?

MILLIE   Sure. Hold still.

HAL   I'm a son of a gun. What was it about?

MILLIE   There wasn't much story. It's just the way you feel when you read it—kind of warm inside and sad and amused—all at the same time.

HAL   Yeah—sure. (*After a moment*) I wish I had more time to read books. (*Proudly*) That's what I'm gonna do when I settle down. I'm gonna read all the better books—and listen to all the better music. A man owes it to himself. (MILLIE *continues sketching*) I used to go with a girl who read books. She joined the Book-of-the-Month Club and they had her readin' books all the time! She wouldn't any more finish one book than they'd send her another!

ROSEMARY (*As* HOWARD *walks off*)   Howard, where you goin'?

HOWARD   I'll be right back, honey.
(ROSEMARY *follows him to gate and watches him while he is off stage*)

HAL (*As* MILLIE *hands him the sketch*)   Is that *me*? (*Admiring it*) I sure do admire people who are artistic. Can I keep it?

MILLIE   Sure. (*Shyly*) I write poetry, too. I've written poems I've never shown to a living soul.

HAL   Kid, I think you must be some sort of a genius.

ROSEMARY (*Calling off to* HOWARD)   Howard, leave that bottle right where it is!

HAL (*Jumps at the word* bottle)   Did she say "bottle"?

ROSEMARY *(Coming down to* HAL) He's been down to the hotel, buying bootleg whiskey off those good-for-nothing porters!

HOWARD *(Coming back, holding out a bottle)* Young man, maybe you'd like a swig of this.

HAL Hot damn!
(He takes a drink)

ROSEMARY Howard, put that away.

HOWARD Millie's not gonna be shocked if she sees someone take a drink. Are you, Millie?

MILLIE Gosh, no!

ROSEMARY What if someone'd come by and tell the School Board? I'd lose my job quick as you can say Jack Robinson.

HOWARD Who's gonna see you, honey? Everyone in town's at the park, havin' a picnic.

ROSEMARY I don't care. Liquor's against the law in this state, and a person oughta abide by the law. *(To* HAL) Isn't that what you say, young fellow?

HAL *(Eager to agree)* Oh, sure! A person oughta abide by the law.

HOWARD Here, honey, have one.

ROSEMARY No, Howard, I'm not gonna touch a drop.

HOWARD Come on, honey, have one little drink just for *me.*

ROSEMARY *(Beginning to melt)* Howard, you oughta be ashamed of yourself.

HOWARD *(Innocent)* I don't see why.

ROSEMARY I guess I know why you want me to take a drink.

HOWARD Now, honey, that's not so. I just think you should have a good time like the rest of us. *(To* HAL) Schoolteachers gotta right to live. Isn't that what you say, young fella?

HAL Sure, schoolteachers got a right to live.

ROSEMARY *(Taking the bottle)* Now, Millie, don't you tell any of the kids at school.

MILLIE What do you take me for?

ROSEMARY *(Looking around her)* Anyone coming?

HOWARD   Coast is clear.

ROSEMARY *(Takes a hearty drink, and makes a lugubrious face)*   Whew! I want some water!

HOWARD   Millie, why don't you run in the house and get us some?

ROSEMARY   Mrs. Owens'd suspect something. I'll get a drink from the hydrant!
(She runs off to MRS. POTTS' *yard)*

HOWARD   Millie, my girl, I'd like to offer *you* one, but I s'pose your old lady'd raise Ned.

MILLIE   What Mom don't know won't hurt her!
(She reaches for the bottle)

HAL *(Grabs the bottle first)*   No, kid. You lay off the stuff!
(He takes another drink)

ROSEMARY *(Calling from offstage)*   Howard, come help me! I see a snake!

HOWARD   You go, Millie. She don't see no snake. (MILLIE *goes off. As* HAL *takes another drink, he sees a light go on in* MADGE'S *window.* HOWARD *follows* HAL'S *gaze)* Look at her there, powdering her arms. You know, every time I come over here I look forward just to seein' her. I tell myself, "Bevans, old boy, you can look at that all you want, but you couldn't touch it with a ten-foot pole."

HAL *(With some awe of her)*   She's the kind of girl a guy's gotta *respect.*

HOWARD   Look at her, putting lipstick on that cute kisser. Seems to me, when the good Lord made a girl as pretty as she is, he did it for a reason, and it's about time she found out what that reason is. *(He gets an idea)* Look, son, if you're agonizin', I know a couple of girls down at the hotel.

HAL   Thanks, but I've given up that sorta thing.

HOWARD   I think that's a very fine attitude.

HAL   Besides, I never had to pay for it.

ROSEMARY *(Entering, followed by* MILLIE)   Lord, I thought I was going to faint!

MILLIE *(Laughing at* ROSEMARY'S *excitability)*   It was just a piece of garden hose.

ROSEMARY *(Regarding the two men suspiciously)*   What're you two talking about?

HOWARD Talkin' about the weather, honey. Talkin' about the weather.

ROSEMARY I bet.

MILLIE *(Seeing* MADGE *in the window)* Hey, Madge, why don't you charge admission?
*(*MADGE'S *curtains close)*

ROSEMARY Shoot! When I was a girl I was just as good-looking as she is!

HOWARD Of course you were, honey.

ROSEMARY *(Taking the bottle)* I had boys callin' me all the time. But if my father had ever caught me showing off in front of the window he'd have tanned me with a razor strap. *(Takes a drink)* 'Cause I was brought up strict by a God-fearing man.
(Takes another)

MILLIE *(Music has started in the background)* Hey, hit it, Ernie! *(Explaining to* HAL*)* It's Ernie Higgins and his Happiness Boys. They play at all the dances around here.

ROSEMARY *(Beginning to sway rapturously)* Lord, I like that music! Come dance with me, Howard.

HOWARD Honey, I'm no good at dancin'.

ROSEMARY That's just what you menfolks tell yourselves to get out of it. *(Turns to* MILLIE*)* Come dance with me, Millie!
(She pulls MILLIE *up onto the porch and they push the chairs out of the way)*

MILLIE I gotta lead! I gotta lead.
*(*ROSEMARY *and* MILLIE *dance together in a trim, automatic way that keeps time to the music but little else. Both women seem to show a little arrogance in dancing together, as though boasting to the men of their independence. Their rhythm is accurate but uninspired.* HOWARD *and* HAL *watch, laughing)*

HOWARD S'posin' Hal and I did that.

ROSEMARY Go ahead for all I care. (HOWARD *turns to* HAL *and, laughing, they start dancing together,* HAL *giving his own version of a coy female.* ROSEMARY *is irritated by this)* Stop it!

HOWARD I thought we were doin' very nicely.
*(*ROSEMARY *grabs* HOWARD *and pulls him up on the porch)*

HAL Come and dance with me, Millie!

MILLIE   Well—I never danced with boys. I always have to lead.

HAL   Just relax and do the steps I do. Come on and try.
(They dance together but MILLIE *has an awkward feeling of uncertainty that shows in her dancing.* HOWARD, *dancing with* ROSEMARY, *has been cutting up)*

ROSEMARY   Quit clowning, Howard, and dance with me.

HOWARD   Honey, you don't get any fun out of dancing with *me.*

ROSEMARY   The band's playin'. You gotta dance with *someone.*
(They resume an uncertain toddle)

MILLIE *(To* HAL*)*   Am I too bad?

HAL   Naw! You just need a little practice.

ROSEMARY *(While dancing)*   Lord, I love to dance. At school, kids all called me the Dancin' Fool. Went somewhere dancin' every night!

MRS. POTTS *(Coming out of kitchen, she sits and watches the dancers.* FLO *and* ALAN *appear and stand in doorway watching)*   I can't stay in the kitchen while there's dancing!

HAL *(Stops the dancing to deliver the needed instructions)*   Now look, kid, you gotta remember *I'm* the man, and you gotta do the steps *I* do.

MILLIE   I keep wantin' to do the steps I make up myself.

HAL   The man's gotta take the lead, kid, as long as he's able. *(They resume dancing)*

MRS. POTTS   You're doing fine, Millie!

MILLIE *(As she is whirled around)*   I feel like Rita Hayworth!
*(*FLO *and* ALAN *go into the house)*

ROSEMARY *(Her youth returns in reverie)*   One night I went dancin' at a big Valentine party. I danced so hard I swooned! That's when they called me the Dancin' Fool.

HAL *(Stops dancing for a moment)*   I'll show you a new step, kid. I learned this in L. A. Try it.
(He nimbly executes a somewhat more intricate step)

MRS. POTTS   Isn't he graceful?

MILLIE   Gee, that looks hard.

HAL   Takes a little time. Give it a try!
(MILLIE *tries to do it, but it is too much for her*)

MILLIE *(Giving up)*   I'm sorry, I just can't seem to get it.

HAL   Watch close, kid. If you learn this step you'll be the sharpest kid in town. See?
(He continues his demonstration)

MILLIE *(Observing but baffled)*   Yah—but . . .

HAL   Real loose, see? You give it a little of this—and give it a little of that.
(He snaps his fingers, keeping a nimble, sensitive response to the rhythm)

MILLIE   Gee, I wish *I* could do that.
(Now the music changes to a slower, more sensuous rhythm. HAL *and* MILLIE *stop dancing and listen)*

ROSEMARY *(Who has been watching* HAL *enviously)*   That's the way to dance, Howard! That's the way.
*(*HAL *begins to dance to the slower rhythm and* MILLIE *tries to follow him. Now* MADGE *comes out the front door, wearing her new dress. Although the dress is indeed "too fussy" for a picnic, she is ravishing. She stands watching* HAL *and* MILLIE*)*

HOWARD *(Drifting from* ROSEMARY*)*   You sure look pretty, Madge.

MADGE   Thank you, Howard.

HOWARD   Would you like a little dance?
(She accepts, and they dance together on the porch. ROSEMARY *is dancing by herself on the porch, upstage, and does not notice them)*

MRS. POTTS *(Seeing* MADGE *and* HOWARD *dancing)*   More dancers! We've turned the backyard into a ballroom!

ROSEMARY *(Snatching* HOWARD *from* MADGE*)*   Thought you couldn't dance.
*(*MADGE *goes down into the yard and watches* HAL *and* MILLIE*)*

MRS. POTTS *(To* MADGE*)*   The young man is teaching Millie a new step.

MADGE   Oh, that's fun. I've been trying to teach it to Alan.
(She tries the step herself and does it as well as HAL*)*

MRS. POTTS   Look, everyone! Madge does it, too!

HAL *(Turns around and sees* MADGE *dancing)*   Hey!
(Some distance apart, snapping their fingers to the rhythm, their bodies respond without touching. Then they dance slowly toward each other and

HAL *takes her in his arms. The dance has something of the nature of a primitive rite that would mate the two young people. The others watch rather solemnly)*

MRS. POTTS *(Finally)*   It's like they were *made* to dance together, isn't it? *(This remark breaks the spell.* MILLIE *moves to* MRS. POTTS' *steps and sits quietly in the background, beginning to inspect the bottle of whiskey)*

ROSEMARY *(Impatiently to* HOWARD)   Can't *you* dance that way?

HOWARD   Golly, honey, I'm a businessman.

ROSEMARY *(Dances by herself, kicking her legs in the air.* MILLIE *takes an occasional drink from the whiskey bottle during the following scene, unobserved by the others)*   I danced so hard one night, I swooned! Right in the center of the ballroom!

HOWARD *(Amused and observing)*   Rosemary's got pretty legs, hasn't she?

ROSEMARY *(This strikes her as hilarious)*   That's just like you men, can't talk about anything but women's legs.

HOWARD *(A little offended to be misinterpreted)*   I just noticed they had a nice shape.

ROSEMARY *(Laughing uproariously)*   How would you like it if we women went around talkin' 'bout *your* legs all the time?

HOWARD *(Ready to be a sport, stands and lifts his trousers to his knees)*   All right! There's *my* legs if you wanta talk about them.

ROSEMARY *(She explodes with laughter)*   Never saw anything so ugly. Men's big hairy legs! (ROSEMARY *goes over to* HAL, *yanking him from* MADGE *possessively)* Young man, let's see your legs.

HAL *(Not knowing what to make of his seizure)*   Huh?

ROSEMARY   We passed a new rule here tonight. Every man here's gotta show his legs.

HAL   Ma'am, I got on boots.

HOWARD   Let the young man alone, Rosemary. He's dancin' with Madge.

ROSEMARY   Now it's his turn to dance with *me*. *(To* HAL) I may be an old-maid schoolteacher, but *I* can keep up with you. Ride 'em cowboy! *(A little tight, stimulated by* HAL'S *physical presence, she abandons convention and grabs* HAL *closely to her, plastering a cheek next to his and holding her hips fast against him. One can sense that* HAL *is embarrassed and repelled)*

HAL *(Wanting to object)*   Ma'am, I . . .

ROSEMARY   I used to have a boy friend was a cowboy. Met him in Colorado when I went out there to get over a case of flu. He was in love with me, 'cause I was an older woman and had some sense. Took me up in the mountains one night and made love. Wanted me to marry him right there on the mountain top. Said God'd be our preacher, the moon our best man. Ever hear such talk?

HAL *(Trying to get away)*   Ma'am, I'd like another li'l drink now.

ROSEMARY *(Jerking him closer to her)*   Dance with me, young man. Dance with me. I can keep up with you. You know what? You remind me of one of those ancient statues. There was one in the school library until last year. He was a Roman gladiator. All he had on was a shield. *(She gives a bawdy laugh)* A shield over his arm. That was all he had on. All we girls felt insulted, havin' to walk past that statue every time we went to the library. We got up a petition and made the principal do something about it. *(She laughs hilariously during her narration)* You know what he did? He got the school janitor to fix things right. He got a chisel and made that statue decent. *(Another bawdy laugh)* Lord, those ancient people were depraved.

HAL *(He seldom has been made so uncomfortable)*   Ma'am, I guess I just don't feel like dancin'.

ROSEMARY *(Sobering from her story, grabs for* HAL, *catching him by the shirt)*   Where you goin'?

HAL   Ma'am, I . . .

ROSEMARY *(Commanding him imploringly)*   Dance with me, young man. Dance with me.

HAL   I . . . I . . .
(He pulls loose from her grasp, but her hand, still clutching, tears off a strip of his shirt as he gets away. HOWARD *intervenes)*

HOWARD   He wants to dance with Madge, Rosemary. Let 'em alone. They're young people.

ROSEMARY *(In a hollow voice)*   Young? What do you mean, they're *young?*

MILLIE *(A sick groan from the background)*   Oh, I'm sick.

MRS. POTTS Millie!

MILLIE I wanna die.
(*All eyes are on* MILLIE *now as she runs over to the kitchen door*)

MADGE Millie!

HOWARD What'd the little dickens do? Get herself tight?

HAL Take it easy, kid.

ROSEMARY (*She has problems of her own. She gropes blindly across the stage, suffering what has been a deep humiliation*) I suppose that's something wonderful—they're *young.*

MADGE (*Going to* MILLIE) Let's go inside, Millie.

MILLIE (*Turning on* MADGE *viciously*) I *hate* you!

MADGE (*Hurt*) Millie!

MILLIE (*Sobbing*) Madge is the pretty one—Madge is the pretty one.
(MILLIE *dashes inside the kitchen door,* MRS. POTTS *behind her*)

MADGE (*To herself*) What did she have to do that for?

HOWARD (*Examining the bottle*) She must have had several good snifters.

ROSEMARY (*Pointing a finger at* HAL. *She has found vengeance*) It's all *his* fault, Howard.

HOWARD Now, honey . . .

ROSEMARY (*To* HAL, *defiantly and accusingly*) Millie was your date. You shoulda been looking after her. But you were too busy making eyes at Madge.

HOWARD Honey . . .

ROSEMARY And you're no better than he is, Madge. You should be ashamed.

FLO (*Flies out on the porch in a fury*) Who fed whiskey to my Millie?

ROSEMARY (*Pointing fanatically at* HAL) He did, Mrs. Owens! It's all his fault!
(FLO *glares at* HAL)

HOWARD (*Trying to straighten things out*) Mrs. Owens, it was this way . . .

FLO My Millie is too young to be drinking whiskey!

ROSEMARY   Oh, he'd have fed her whiskey and taken his pleasure with the child and then skedaddled!

HOWARD *(Trying to bring them to reason)*   Now listen, everyone. Let's . . .

ROSEMARY   I know what I'm doing, Howard! And I don't need any advice from *you. (Back at* HAL) You been stomping around here in those boots like you owned the place, thinking every woman you saw was gonna fall madly in love. But here's one woman didn't pay you any mind.

HOWARD   The boy hasn't done anything, Mrs. Owens!

ROSEMARY *(Facing* HAL, *drawing closer with each accusation)*   Aristocratic millionaire, my foot! You wouldn't know an aristocratic millionaire if he spit on you. Braggin' about your father, and I bet he wasn't any better'n you are.
(HAL *is as though paralyzed.* HOWARD *still tries to reason with* FLO)

HOWARD   None of us saw Millie drink the whiskey.

ROSEMARY *(Closer to* HAL)   You think just 'cause you're a man, you can walk in here and make off with whatever you like. You think just 'cause you're young you can push other people aside and not pay them any mind. You think just 'cause you're strong you can show your muscles and nobody'll know what a pitiful specimen you are. But you won't stay young forever, didja ever thinka that? What'll become of you then? You'll end your life in the gutter and it'll serve you right, 'cause the gutter's where you came from and the gutter's where you belong.
(She has thrust her face into HAL'S and is spitting her final words at him before HOWARD finally grabs her, almost as though to protect her from herself, and holds her arms at her sides, pulling her away)

HOWARD   Rosemary, shut your damn mouth.
(HAL *withdraws to the far edge of the porch, no one paying any attention to him now, his reaction to the attack still a mystery)*

MRS. POTTS *(Comes out of kitchen)*   Millie's going to be perfectly all right, Flo. Alan held her head and let her be sick. She's going to be perfectly all right, now.

FLO *(A general announcement, clear and firm)*   I want it understood by everyone that there's to be no more drinking on this picnic.

HOWARD   It was all my fault, Mrs. Owens. My fault.
(ALAN *escorts a sober* MILLIE *out on the porch)*

MRS. POTTS   Here's Millie now, good as new. And we're all going on the picnic and forget it.

ALAN *(Quick to accuse* HAL)   Hal, what's happened?
(HAL *does not respond*)

FLO *(To* ALAN)   Millie will come with *us*, Alan.

ALAN   Sure, Mrs. Owens. Hal, I told you not to drink!
(HAL *is still silent*)

FLO   Madge, why did you wear your new dress?

MADGE *(As though mystified at herself)*   I don't know. I just put it on.

FLO   Go upstairs and change, this minute. I mean it! You come later with Rosemary and Howard!
(MADGE *runs inside*)

MRS. POTTS   Let's hurry. All the tables will be taken.

ALAN   Mr. Bevans, tell Madge I'll see her out there. Hal, the baskets are all in the Ford. Get goin'.
(HAL *doesn't move.* ALAN *hurries off*)

FLO   Millie, darling, are you feeling better?
(FLO *and* MILLIE *go off through alley, right*)

MRS. POTTS *(To* HAL)   Young man, you can follow us and find the way.
(MRS. POTTS *follows the others off. We hear the Cadillac drive off.* HAL *is sitting silent and beaten on the edge of the porch.* HOWARD *and* ROSEMARY *are on the lawn by* MRS. POTTS' *house*)

HOWARD   He's just a boy, Rosemary. You talked awful.

ROSEMARY   What made me do it, Howard? What made me act that way?

HOWARD   You gotta remember, men have got feelings, too—same as women. *(To* HAL) Don't pay any attention to her, young man. She didn't mean a thing.

ROSEMARY *(Has gone up to the gate)*   I don't want to go on the picnic, Howard. This is my last night of vacation and I want to have a good time.

HOWARD   We'll go for a ride, honey.

ROSEMARY   I want to drive into the sunset, Howard! I want to drive into the sunset!
(*She runs off toward the car,* HOWARD *following.* HOWARD'S *car drives away.*

HAL *sits on the porch, defeated.* MADGE *soon comes out in another dress. She comes out very quietly and he shows no recognition of her presence. She sits on a bench on the porch and finally speaks in a soft voice)*

MADGE   You're a wonderful dancer . . .

HAL *(Hardly audible)*   Thanks.

MADGE   . . . and I can tell a lot about a boy by dancing with him. Some boys, even though they're very smart, or very successful in some other way, when they take a girl in their arms to dance, they're sort of awkward and a girl feels sort of uncomfortable.

HAL *(He keeps his head down, his face in his hands)*   Yah.

MADGE   But when you took me in your arms—to dance—I had the most relaxed feeling, that you knew what you were doing, and I could follow every step of the way.

HAL   Look, baby, I'm in a pretty bad mood.
(He stands suddenly and walks away from her, his hands thrust into his pockets. He is uncomfortable to be near her, for he is trembling with insult and rage)

MADGE   You mustn't pay any attention to Miss Sydney. (HAL *is silent)* Women like her make me mad at the whole female sex.

HAL   Look, baby, why don't you beat it?

MADGE *(She is aware of the depth of his feelings)*   What's the matter?

HAL *(Gives up and begins to shudder, his shoulders heaving as he fights to keep from bawling)*   What's the use, baby? I'm a bum. She saw through me like a goddamn X-ray machine. There's just no place in the world for a guy like me.

MADGE   There's got to be.

HAL *(With self-derision)*   Yah?

MADGE   Of course. You're young, and—you're very entertaining. I mean—you say all sorts of witty things, and I just loved listening to you talk. And you're strong and—you're very good-looking. I bet Miss Sydney thought so, too, or she wouldn't have said those things.

HAL   Look, baby, lemme level with you. When I was fourteen, I spent a year in the reform school. How ya like that?

MADGE   Honest?

HAL   Yah!

MADGE   What for?

HAL   For stealin' another guy's motorcycle. Yah! I *stole* it. I stole it 'cause I wanted to get on the damn thing and go so far away, so fast, that no one'd ever catch up with me.

MADGE   I think—lots of boys feel that way at times.

HAL   Then my old lady went to the authorities. (*He mimics his "old lady"*) "I've done everything I can with the boy. I can't do anything more." So off I go to the goddamn reform school.

MADGE (*With all the feeling she has*)   Gee!

HAL   Finally some welfare league hauls me out and the old lady's sorry to see me back. Yah! she's got herself a new boy friend and I'm in the way.

MADGE   It's awful when parents don't get along.

HAL   I never told that to another soul, not even Seymour.

MADGE (*At a loss*)   I—I wish there was something I could say—or *do*.

HAL   Well—that's the Hal Carter story, but no one's ever gonna make a movie of it.

MADGE (*To herself*)   Most people would be awfully shocked.

HAL (*Looking at her, then turning away cynically*)   There you are, baby. If you wanta faint—or get sick—or run in the house and lock the doors— go ahead. I ain't stoppin' you. (*There is a silence. Then* MADGE, *suddenly and impulsively, takes his face in her hands and kisses him. Then she returns her hands to her lap and feels embarrassed.* HAL *looks at her in amazement*) Baby! What'd you do?

MADGE   I . . . I'm proud you told me.

HAL (*With humble appreciation*)   Baby!

MADGE   I . . . I get so tired of being told I'm pretty.

HAL (*Folding her in his arms caressingly*)   Baby, baby, baby.

MADGE (*Resisting him, jumping to her feet*)   Don't. We have to go. We have all the baskets in our car and they'll be waiting. (HAL *gets up and walks slowly to her, their eyes fastened and* MADGE *feeling a little thrill of excitement as he draws nearer*) Really—we have to be going. (HAL *takes her in his arms and kisses her passionately. Then* MADGE *utters his name in a voice of resignation)* Hal!

HAL   Just be quiet, baby.

MADGE   Really . . . We have to go. They'll be waiting.

HAL   *(Picking her up in his arms and starting off. His voice is deep and firm)*   We're not goin' on no goddamn picnic.

CURTAIN

SCENE: *It is after midnight. A great harvest moon shines in the sky, a deep, murky blue. The moon is swollen and full and casts a pale light on the scene below. Soon we hear* HOWARD'S *Chevrolet chugging to a stop by the house, then* HOWARD *and* ROSEMARY *come on,* ROSEMARY *first. Wearily, a groggy depression having set in, she makes her way to the doorstep and drops there, sitting limp. She seems preoccupied at first and her responses to* HOWARD *are mere grunts.*

HOWARD   Here we are, honey. Right back where we started from.

ROSEMARY *(Her mind elsewhere)*   Uhh.

HOWARD   You were awful nice to me tonight, Rosemary.

ROSEMARY   Uhh.

HOWARD   Do you think Mrs. Owens suspects anything?

ROSEMARY   I don't care if she does.

HOWARD   A businessman's gotta be careful of talk. And after all, you're a schoolteacher. *(Fumbling to get away)* Well, I better be gettin' back to Cherryvale. I gotta open up the store in the morning. Good night, Rosemary.

ROSEMARY   Uhh.

HOWARD *(He pecks at her cheek with a kiss)*   Good night. Maybe I should say, good morning.
(He starts off)

ROSEMARY *(Just coming to)*   Where you goin', Howard?

HOWARD   Honey, I gotta get home.

ROSEMARY   You can't go off without me.

HOWARD   Honey, talk sense.

ROSEMARY   You can't go off without me. Not after tonight. *That's* sense.

HOWARD   *(A little nervous)*   Honey, be reasonable.

ROSEMARY   Take me with you.

HOWARD   What'd people say?

ROSEMARY   *(Almost vicious)*   To *hell* with what people'd say!

HOWARD   *(Shocked)*   Honey!

ROSEMARY   What'd people say if I thumbed my nose at them? What'd people say if I walked down the street and showed 'em my pink panties? What do I care what people say?

HOWARD   Honey, you're not yourself tonight.

ROSEMARY   Yes, I am. I'm more myself than I ever was. Take me with you, Howard. If you don't I don't know what I'll do with myself. I mean it.

HOWARD   Now look, honey, you better go upstairs and get some sleep. You gotta start school in the morning. We'll talk all this over Saturday.

ROSEMARY   Maybe you won't be back Saturday. Maybe you won't be back ever again.

HOWARD   Rosemary, you know better than that.

ROSEMARY   Then what's the next thing in store for me? To be nice to the next man, then the next—till there's no one left to care whether I'm nice to him or not. Till I'm ready for the grave and don't have anyone to take me there.

HOWARD   *(In an attempt to be consoling)*   Now, Rosemary!

ROSEMARY   You can't let that happen to me, Howard. I won't let you.

HOWARD   I don't understand. When we first started going together, you were the best sport I ever saw, always good for a laugh.

ROSEMARY   *(In a hollow voice)*   I can't laugh any more.

HOWARD   We'll talk it over Saturday.

ROSEMARY   We'll talk it over *now*.

HOWARD   *(Squirming)*   Well—honey—I . . .

ROSEMARY   You said you were gonna marry me, Howard. You said when I got back from my vacation, you'd be waitin' with the preacher.

HOWARD   Honey, I've had an awful busy summer and . . .

ROSEMARY   Where's the preacher, Howard? Where is he?

HOWARD *(Walking away from her)*   Honey, I'm forty-two years old. A person forms certain ways of livin', then one day it's too late to change.

ROSEMARY *(Grabbing his arm and holding him)*   Come back here, Howard. I'm no spring chicken either. Maybe I'm a little older than you think *I* am. I've formed my ways too. But they can be changed. They *gotta* be changed. It's no good livin' like this, in rented rooms, meetin' a bunch of old maids for supper every night, then comin' back home alone.

HOWARD   *I* know how it is, Rosemary. My life's no bed of roses either.

ROSEMARY   Then why don't you do something about it?

HOWARD   I figure—there's some bad things about every life.

ROSEMARY   There's too much bad about mine. Each year, I keep tellin' myself, is the last. Something'll happen. Then nothing ever does—except I get a little crazier all the time.

HOWARD *(Hopelessly)*   Well . . .

ROSEMARY   A *well's* a hole in the ground, Howard. Be careful you don't fall in.

HOWARD   I wasn't tryin' to be funny.

ROSEMARY   . . . and all this time you just been leadin' me on.

HOWARD *(Defensive)*   Rosemary, that's not *so!* I've not been leading you *on.*

ROSEMARY   I'd like to know what else you call it.

HOWARD   Well—can't we talk about it Saturday? I'm dead tired and I got a busy week ahead, and . . .

ROSEMARY *(She grips him by the arm and looks straight into his eyes)*   You gotta marry me, Howard.

HOWARD *(Tortured)*   Well—honey, I can't marry you *now.*

ROSEMARY   You can be over here in the morning.

HOWARD   Sometimes you're unreasonable.

ROSEMARY   You gotta marry me.

HOWARD   What'll you do about your job?

ROSEMARY   Alvah Jackson can take my place till they get someone new from the agency.

HOWARD   I'll have to pay Fred Jenkins to take care of the store for a few days.

ROSEMARY   Then get him.

HOWARD   Well . . .

ROSEMARY   I'll be waitin' for you in the morning, Howard.

HOWARD   *(After a few moments' troubled thought)*   No.

ROSEMARY   *(A muffled cry)*   Howard!

HOWARD   I'm not gonna marry anyone that says, "You gotta marry me, Howard." I'm not gonna. *(He is silent.* ROSEMARY *weeps pathetic tears. Slowly* HOWARD *reconsiders)* If a woman wants me to marry her—she can at least say "please."

ROSEMARY   *(Beaten and humble)*   *Please* marry me, Howard.

HOWARD   Well—you got to give me time to think it over.

ROSEMARY   *(Desperate)*   Oh, God! Please marry me, Howard. Please . . . *(She sinks to her knees)* Please . . . please . . . .

HOWARD   *(Embarrassed by her suffering humility)*   Rosemary . . . I . . . I gotta have some time to think it over. You go to bed now and get some rest. I'll drive over in the morning and maybe we can talk it over before you go to school. I . . .

ROSEMARY   You're not just tryin' to get out of it, Howard?

HOWARD   I'll be over in the morning, honey.

ROSEMARY   Honest?

HOWARD   Yah. I gotta go to the courthouse anyway. We'll talk it over then.

ROSEMARY   Oh, God, please marry me, Howard. Please.

HOWARD   *(Trying to get away)*   Go to bed, honey. I'll see you in the morning.

ROSEMARY   Please, Howard!

HOWARD   I'll see you in the morning. Good night, Rosemary. *(Starting off)*

ROSEMARY   *(In a meek voice)*   Please!

HOWARD   Good night, Rosemary.

ROSEMARY *(After he is gone)*   Please.
(ROSEMARY *stands alone on the doorstep. We hear the sound of* HOWARD'S *car start up and drive off, chugging away in the distance.* ROSEMARY *is drained of energy. She pulls herself together and goes into the house. The stage is empty for several moments. Then* MADGE *runs on from the back, right. Her face is in her hands. She is sobbing.* HAL *follows fast behind. He reaches her just as she gets to the door, and grabs her by the wrist. She resists him furiously)*

HAL   Baby . . . you're not sorry, are you?
(There is a silence. MADGE *sobs)*

MADGE   Let me go.

HAL   Please, baby. If I thought I'd done anything to make you unhappy, I . . . I'd almost wanta die.

MADGE   I . . . I'm so ashamed.

HAL   Don't say that, baby.

MADGE   I didn't even know what was happening, and then . . . all of a sudden, it seems like my whole life was changed.

HAL   *(With bitter self-disparagement)*   I oughta be taken out and hung. I'm just a no-good bum. That schoolteacher was right. I oughta be in the gutter.

MADGE   Don't talk that way.

HAL   Times like this, I hate myself, baby.

MADGE   I guess . . . it's no more your fault than mine.

HAL   Sometimes I do pretty impulsive things. (MADGE *starts inside)* Will I see you tomorrow?

MADGE   I don't know.

HAL   Gee, I almost forgot. I start a new job tomorrow.

MADGE   I have to be at the dime store at nine.

HAL   What time you through?

MADGE   Five.

HAL   Maybe I could see you then, huh? Maybe I could come by and . . .

MADGE   I've got a date with Alan—if he'll still speak to me.

HAL *(A new pain)*   Jesus, I'd forgot all about Seymour.

MADGE   So had I.

HAL   I can't go back to his house. What'll I do?

MADGE   Maybe Mrs. Potts could . . .

HAL   I'll take the car back to where we were, stretch out in the front seat and get a little sleep. *(He thinks a moment)* Baby, how you gonna handle your old lady?

MADGE *(With a slight tremor)*   I . . . I don't know.

HAL *(In a funk again)*   Jesus, I ought to be shot at sunrise.

MADGE   I . . . I'll think of something to tell her.

HAL *(Awkward)*   Well—good night.

MADGE   Good night.
      (She starts again)

HAL   Baby—would you kiss me good night . . . maybe? Just one more time.

MADGE   I don't think I better.

HAL   Please!

MADGE   It . . . It'd just start things all over again. Things I better forget.

HAL   Pretty please!

MADGE   Promise not to hold me?

HAL   I'll keep my hands to my side. Swear to God!

MADGE   Well . . . *(Slowly she goes toward him, takes his face in her hands and kisses him. The kiss lasts. HAL's hands become nervous and finally find their way around her. Their passion is revived. Then MADGE utters a little shriek, tears herself away from HAL and runs into the house, sobbing)* Don't. You *promised.* I never wanta see you again. I might as well be dead.
      (She runs inside the front door, leaving HAL behind to despise himself. He beats his fists together, kicks the earth with his heel, and starts off, hating the day he was born)

ACT THREE | Scene Two

SCENE: *It is very early the next morning.* MILLIE *sits on the doorstep smoking a cigarette. She wears a fresh wash dress in honor of the first day of school.* FLO *breaks out of the front door. She is a frantic woman.* MILLIE *puts out her cigarette quickly.* FLO *has not even taken the time to dress. She wears an old robe over her nightdress. She speaks to* MILLIE.

FLO Were you awake when Madge got in?

MILLIE No.

FLO Did she say anything to you this morning?

MILLIE No.

FLO Dear God! I couldn't get two words out of her last night, she was crying so hard. Now she's got the door locked.

MILLIE I bet I know what happened.

FLO *(Sharply)* You don't know anything, Millie Owens. And if anyone says anything to you, you just . . . *(Now she sniffs the air)* Have you been smoking?

MRS. POTTS *(Coming down her back steps)* Did Madge tell you what happened?

FLO The next time you take in tramps, Helen Potts, I'll thank you to keep them on your own side of the yard.

MRS. POTTS Is Madge all right?

FLO Of course she's all right. She got out of the car and left that hoodlum alone. That's what she did.

MRS. POTTS Have you heard from Alan?

FLO He said he'd be over this morning.

MRS. POTTS Where's the young man?

FLO   I know where he should be! He should be in the penitentiary, and that's where he's going if he shows up around here again!

ROSEMARY *(Sticking her head out front door)*   Has anyone seen Howard?

FLO *(Surprised)*   Howard? Why, no, Rosemary!

ROSEMARY *(Nervous and uncertain)*   He said he might be over this morning. Mrs. Owens, I'm storing my summer clothes in the attic. Could someone help me?

FLO   We're busy, Rosemary.

MRS. POTTS   I'll help you, Rosemary.
(She looks at FLO, then goes up on porch)

ROSEMARY   Thanks, Mrs. Potts.
(Goes inside)

FLO *(To MRS. POTTS)*   She's been running around like a chicken with its head off all morning. Something's *up!* (MRS. POTTS *goes inside.* FLO *turns to* MILLIE) You keep watch for Alan.
(FLO goes inside. Now we hear the morning voices of IRMA and CHRISTINE, coming by for ROSEMARY)

IRMA   Girl, I hope Rosemary is ready. I promised the principal that I'd be there early to help with registration.

CHRISTINE   How do I look, Irma?

IRMA   It's a cute dress. Let me fix it in the back.
(IRMA adjusts the hang of the dress as CHRISTINE stands patiently)

CHRISTINE   I think a teacher should dress up first day of school, to give the students a good first impression.

IRMA *(Going up on the porch)*   Good morning, Millie!

MILLIE   Hi.

IRMA   Is Rosemary ready?

MILLIE   Go on up if you want to.

CHRISTINE *(To MILLIE)*   We missed seeing Madge on the picnic last night.

MILLIE   So did a lot of other people.

IRMA *(Gives CHRISTINE a significant look)*   Come on, Christine. I bet we have to get that sleepy girl out of bed.
(They go inside front door. BOMBER rides on, gets off his bicycle, throws a

paper on MRS. POTTS' *steps, then on* FLO'S *back porch. Then he climbs up on* MRS. POTTS' *porch so he can look across into* MADGE'S *room)*

BOMBER   Hey, Madge! Wanta go dancin'? Let me be next, Madge!

MILLIE   You shut up, crazy.

BOMBER   My brother seen 'em parked under the bridge. Alan Seymour was lookin' for 'em all over town. She always put on a lot of airs, but I knew she liked guys.
(He sees ALAN *approaching from beyond the* OWENS' *house, and leaves quickly)*

MILLIE   Some day I'm really gonna kill that ornery bastard. *(She turns and sees* ALAN)

ALAN   Could I see Madge?

MILLIE   I'll call her, Alan. *(Calls up to* MADGE'S *window)* Madge! Alan's here! *(Back to* ALAN) She prob'ly has to dress.

ALAN   I'll wait.

MILLIE   *(She sits on the stump and turns to him very shyly)*   I . . . I always liked you, Alan. Didn't you know it?

ALAN   *(With some surprise)*   *Like* me?

MILLIE   *(Nods her head)*   It's awfully hard to show someone you like them, isn't it?

ALAN   *(With just a little bitterness)*   It's easy for *some* people.

MILLIE   It makes you feel like such a sap. I don't know why.

ALAN   *(Rather touched)*   I . . . I'm glad you like me, Millie.

MILLIE   *(One can sense her loneliness)*   I don't expect you to do anything about it. I just wanted to tell you.
*(*HOWARD *comes bustling on through the gate, very upset. He addresses* MILLIE)*

HOWARD   Could I see Rosemary?

MILLIE   My gosh, Howard, what are you doing here?

HOWARD   I think she's expecting me.

MILLIE   You better holler at the bottom of the stairs—*(*HOWARD *is about to go in the door, but turns back at this)* all the others are up there, too.

HOWARD *(He looks very grave)* The others?

MILLIE Mrs. Potts and Miss Kronkite and Miss Schoenwalder.

HOWARD Golly, I gotta see her alone.

ROSEMARY *(Calling from inside)* Howard! *(Inside, to all the women)* It's Howard! He's here!

HOWARD *(Knowing he is stuck)* Golly!
(We hear a joyful babble of women's voices from inside. HOWARD gives one last pitiful look at MILLIE, then goes in. MILLIE follows him in and ALAN is left alone in the yard. After a moment, MADGE comes out the kitchen door. She wears a simple dress, and her whole being appears chastened. She is inscrutable in her expression)

MADGE Hello, Alan.

ALAN *(Very moved by seeing her)* Madge!

MADGE I'm sorry about last night.

ALAN Madge, whatever happened—it wasn't your fault. I know what Hal's like when he's drinking. But I've got Hal taken care of now! He won't be bothering you again!

MADGE Honest?

ALAN At school I spent half of my life getting him out of jams. I knew he'd had a few tough breaks, and I always tried to be sorry for the guy. But this is the thanks I get.

MADGE *(Still noncommittal)* Where is he now?

ALAN Don't worry about Hal! I'll take it on myself now to offer you his official good-bye!

MADGE *(One still cannot decipher her feelings)* Is he gone?

FLO *(Running out kitchen door. She is dressed now)* Alan, I didn't know you were here!
(Now we hear shouts from inside the house. MILLIE comes out, throwing rice over her shoulder at all the others, who are laughing and shouting so that we only hear bits of the following)

MRS. POTTS Here comes the bride! Here comes the bride!

IRMA May all your troubles be little ones!

CHRISTINE You're getting a wonderful girl, Howard Bevans!

IRMA   Rosemary is getting a fine man!

CHRISTINE   They don't come any better'n Rosemary!

MRS. POTTS   Be happy!

IRMA   May all your troubles be little ones!

MRS. POTTS   Be happy forever and ever!
(Now they are all out on the porch and we see that HOWARD *carries two suitcases. His face has an expression of complete confusion.* ROSEMARY *wears a fussy going-away outfit)*

IRMA *(To* ROSEMARY)   Girl, are you wearing something old?

ROSEMARY   An old pair of nylons but they're as good as new.

CHRISTINE   And that's a brand-new outfit she's got on. Rosemary, are you wearing something blue? I don't see it!

ROSEMARY *(Daringly)*   And you're not gonna! *(They all laugh, and* ROSEMARY *begins a personal inventory)* Something borrowed! I don't have anything to borrow!
(Now we see HAL'S *head appear from the edge of the woodshed. He watches for a moment when he can be sure of not being observed, then darts into the shed)*

FLO   Madge, you give Rosemary something to borrow. It'll mean good luck for you. Go on, Madge! *(She takes* ALAN'S *arm and pulls him toward the steps with her)* Rosemary, Madge has something for you to borrow!

MADGE *(Crossing to the group by steps)*   You can borrow my handkerchief, Miss Sydney.

ROSEMARY   Thank you, Madge. *(She takes the handkerchief)* Isn't Madge pretty, girls?

IRMA *and* CHRISTINE   Oh, yes! Yes, indeed!
*(*MADGE *turns and leaves the group, going toward* MRS. POTTS' *house)*

ROSEMARY *(During the above)*   She's modest! A girl as pretty as Madge can sail through life without a care! *(*ALAN *turns from the group to join* MADGE. FLO *then turns and crosses toward* MADGE. ROSEMARY *follows* FLO*)* Mrs. Owens, I left my hot-water bottle in the closet and my curlers are in the bathroom. You and the girls can have them. I stored the rest of my things in the attic. Howard and I'll come and get 'em after we settle down. Cherryvale's not so far away. We can be good friends, same as before. (HAL *sticks his head through woodshed door and catches* MADGE'S *eye.* MADGE *is startled*)

FLO I hate to mention it now, Rosemary, but you didn't give us much notice. Do you know anyone I could rent the room to?

IRMA *(To* ROSEMARY*)* Didn't you tell her about Linda Sue Breckenridge?

ROSEMARY Oh, yes! Linda Sue Breckenridge—she's the sewing teacher!

IRMA *(A positive affirmation to them all)* And she's a darling girl!

ROSEMARY She and Mrs. Bendix had a fight. Mrs. Bendix wanted to charge her twenty cents for her orange juice in the morning and none of us girls ever paid more'n fifteen. Did we, girls?

IRMA *and* CHRISTINE *(In stanch support)* No! Never! I certainly never did!

ROSEMARY Irma, you tell Linda Sue to get in touch with Mrs. Owens.

IRMA I'll do that very thing.

FLO Thank you, Rosemary.

HOWARD Rosemary, we still got to pick up the license . . .

ROSEMARY *(To* IRMA *and* CHRISTINE, *all of them blubbering)* Good-bye, girls! We've had some awfully jolly times together!
(IRMA, CHRISTINE *and* ROSEMARY *embrace*)

HOWARD *(A little restless)* Come on, honey!
(ALAN *takes the suitcases from* HOWARD)

HOWARD *(To* ALAN*)* A man's gotta settle down some time.

ALAN Of course.

HOWARD And folks'd rather do business with a married man!

ROSEMARY *(To* MADGE *and* ALAN*)* I hope both of you are going to be as happy as Howard and I will be. *(Turns to* MRS. POTTS*)* You've been a wonderful friend, Mrs. Potts!

MRS. POTTS I wish you all sorts of happiness, Rosemary.

ROSEMARY Good-bye, Millie. You're going to be a famous author some day and I'll be proud I knew you.

MILLIE Thanks, Miss Sydney.

HOWARD *(To* ROSEMARY*)* All set?

ROSEMARY   All set and rarin' to go! (*A sudden thought*) Where we goin'?

HOWARD (*After an awkward pause*)   Well . . . I got a cousin who runs a
tourist camp in the Ozarks. He and his wife could put us up for free.

ROSEMARY   Oh, I love the Ozarks!
(*She grabs* HOWARD'S *arm and pulls him off stage.* ALAN *carries the suitcases
off stage.* IRMA, CHRISTINE, MRS. POTTS *and* MILLIE *follow them, all throwing
rice and calling after them*)

ALL (*As they go off*)
                        The Ozarks are lovely this time of year!
                        Be happy!
                        May all your troubles be little ones!
                        You're getting a wonderful girl!
                        You're getting a wonderful man!

FLO (*Alone with* MADGE)   Madge, what happened last night? You haven't
told me a word.

MADGE   Let me alone, Mom.

ROSEMARY (*Offstage*)   Mrs. Owens, aren't you going to tell us good-bye?

FLO (*Exasperated*)   Oh, dear! I've been saying good-bye to her all morning.

ALAN (*Appearing in gateway*)   Mrs. Owens, Miss Sydney wants to give you
her house keys.

MRS. POTTS (*Behind* ALAN)   Come on, Flo!

FLO (*Hurrying off*)   I'm coming. I'm coming.
(*She follows* ALAN *and* MRS. POTTS *to join the noisy shivaree in the background. Now* HAL *appears from the woodshed. His clothes are drenched and
cling plastered to his body. He is barefoot and there is blood on his T-shirt.
He stands before* MADGE)

HAL   Baby!

MADGE (*Backing from him*)   You shouldn't have come here.

HAL   Look, baby, I'm in a jam.

MADGE   Serves you right.

HAL   Seymour's old man put the cops on my tail. Accused me of stealin'
the car. I had to knock one of the bastards cold and swim the river to get
away. If they ever catch up with me, it'll be too bad.

MADGE *(Things are in a slightly different light now)*   You were born to get in trouble.

HAL   Baby, I just *had* to say good-bye.

MADGE *(Still not giving away her feelings)*   Where you going?

HAL   The freight train's by pretty soon. I'll hop a ride. I done it lotsa times before.

MADGE   What're you gonna do?

HAL   I got some friends in Tulsa. I can always get a job hoppin' bells at the Hotel Mayo. Jesus, I hate to say good-bye.

MADGE *(Not knowing what her precise feelings are)*   Well . . . I don't know what else there is to do.

HAL   Are you still mad, baby?

MADGE *(Evasively)*   I . . . I never knew a boy like you.
    (The shivaree is quieting down now, and HOWARD *and* ROSEMARY *can be heard driving off as the others call.* FLO *returns, stopping in the gateway, seeing* HAL*)*

FLO   Madge!
    (Now ALAN *comes running on)*

ALAN *(Incensed)*   Hal, what're you doing here?
    *(*MRS. POTTS *and* MILLIE *come on, followed by* IRMA *and* CHRISTINE*)*

MRS. POTTS   It's the young man!

HAL   Look, Seymour, I didn't swipe your lousy car. Get that straight!

ALAN   You better get out of town if you know what's good for you.

HAL   I'll go when I'm ready.

MRS. POTTS   Go? I thought you were going to stay here and settle down.

HAL   No'm. I'm not gonna settle down.

ALAN *(Tearing into* HAL *savagely)*   You'll go *now.* What do you take me for?

HAL *(Holding* ALAN *off, not wanting a fight)*   Look, kid, I don't wanta fight with *you.* You're the only friend I ever had.

ALAN   We're not friends any more. I'm not scared of you. (ALAN *plows into* HAL, *but* HAL *is far beyond him in strength and physical alertness. He fastens* ALAN'S *arms quickly behind him and brings him to the ground.* IRMA *and* CHRISTINE *watch excitedly from the gateway.* MRS. POTTS *is apprehensive.* ALAN *cries out in pain)* Let me go, you goddamn tramp! Let me go!

FLO *(To* HAL*)*   Take your hands off him, this minute.
(But ALAN *has to admit he is mastered.* HAL *releases him and* ALAN *retires to* MRS. POTTS' *back doorstep, sitting there, holding his hands over his face, feeling the deepest humiliation. A train whistle is heard in the distance.* HAL *hurries to* MADGE'S *side)*

HAL *(To* MADGE*)*   Baby, aren't you gonna say good-bye?

FLO *(To* IRMA *and* CHRISTINE*)*   You better run along, girls. This is no side show we're running.
(They depart in a huff)

MADGE *(Keeping her head down, not wanting to look at* HAL*)*   . . . Good-bye . . .

HAL   Please don't be mad, baby. You were sittin' there beside me lookin' so pretty, sayin' all those sweet things, and I . . . I thought you liked me, too, baby. Honest I did.

MADGE   It's all right. I'm not mad.

HAL   Thanks. Thanks a lot.

FLO *(Like a barking terrier)*   Young man, if you don't leave here this second, I'm going to call the police and have you put where you belong.
*(MADGE *and* HAL *do not even hear)*

MADGE   And I . . . I *did* like you . . . the first time I saw you.

FLO *(Incensed)*   Madge!

HAL *(Beaming)*   Honest? (MADGE *nods)* I kinda thought you did.
(All has been worth it now for HAL*.* MILLIE *watches skeptically from doorstep.* MRS. POTTS *looks on lovingly from the back.* FLO *at times concerns herself with* ALAN, *then with trying to get rid of* HAL*)*

FLO   Madge, I want you inside the house this minute.
*(MADGE *doesn't move)*

HAL   Look, baby, I never said it before. I never could. It made me feel like such a freak, but I . . .

MADGE   What?

HAL   I'm nuts about you, baby. I mean it.

MADGE   You make love to lots of girls . . .

HAL   A few.

MADGE   . . . just like you made love to me last night.

HAL   Not like last night, baby. Last night was . . . (*Gropes for the word*) *inspired.*

MADGE   Honest?

HAL   The way you sat there, knowin' just how I felt. The way you held my hand and talked.

MADGE   I couldn't stand to hear Miss Sydney treat you that way. After all, you're a man.

HAL   And you're a woman, baby, whether you know it or not. You're a real, live woman.
(*A police siren is heard stirring up the distance.* FLO, MRS. POTTS *and* MILLIE *are alarmed*)

MILLIE   Hey, it's the cops.

MRS. POTTS   I'll know how to take care of them.
(MRS. POTTS *hurries off, right,* MILLIE *watching.* HAL *and* MADGE *have not moved. They stand looking into each other's eyes. Then* HAL *speaks*)

HAL   Do—do you love me?

MADGE   (*Tears forming in her eyes*)   What good is it if I do?

HAL   I'm a poor bastard, baby. I've gotta claim the things in this life that're mine. Kiss me good-bye. (*He grabs her and kisses her*) Come with me, baby. They gimme a room in the basement of the hotel. It's kinda crummy but we could share it till we found something better.

FLO   (*Outraged*)   Madge! Are you out of your senses?

MADGE   I couldn't.
(*The train whistles in the distance*)

FLO   Young man, you'd better get on that train as fast as you can.

HAL   (*To* MADGE)   When you hear that train pull outa town and know I'm on it, your little heart's gonna be busted, 'cause you love me, God damn it! You love me, you love me, you love me.
(*He stamps one final kiss on her lips, then runs off to catch his train.* MADGE *falls in a heap when he releases her.* FLO *is quick to console* MADGE)

FLO   Get up, girl.

MADGE   Oh, Mom!

FLO   Why did this have to happen to you?

MADGE   I *do* love him! I *do!*

FLO   Hush, girl. Hush. The neighbors are on their porches, watching.

MADGE   I never knew what the feeling was. Why didn't someone tell me?

MILLIE *(Peering off at the back)*   He made it. He got on the train.

MADGE *(A cry of deep regret)*   Now I'll never see him again.

FLO   Madge, believe me, that's for the best.

MADGE   Why? Why?

FLO   At least you didn't marry him.

MADGE *(A wail of anguish)*   Oh, Mom, what can you do with the love you feel? Where is there you can take it?

FLO *(Beaten and defeated)*   I . . . I never found out.
    (MADGE *goes into the house, crying.* MRS. POTTS *returns, carrying* HAL'S *boots. She puts them on the porch)*

MRS. POTTS   The police found these on the river bank.

ALAN *(On* MRS. POTTS' *steps, rises)*   Girls have always liked Hal. Months after he'd left the fraternity, they still called. "Is Hal there?" "Does anyone know where Hal's gone?" Their voices always sounded so forlorn.

FLO   Alan, come to dinner tonight. I'm having sweet-potato pie and all the things you like.

ALAN   I'll be gone, Mrs. Owens.

FLO   Gone?

ALAN   Dad's been wanting me to take him up to Michigan on a fishing trip. I've been stalling him, but now I . . .

FLO   You'll be back before you go to school, won't you?

ALAN   I'll be back Christmas, Mrs. Owens.

FLO   Christmas! Alan, go inside and say good-bye to Madge!

ALAN *(Recalling his past love)*   Madge is beautiful. It made me feel so proud—just to *look* at her—and tell myself she's mine.

FLO   See her one more time, Alan!

ALAN *(His mind is made up)*   No! I'll be home Christmas. I'll run over then and—say hello.
(He runs off)

FLO *(A cry of loss)*   Alan!

MRS. POTTS *(Consolingly)*   He'll be back, Flo. He'll be back.

MILLIE *(Waving good-bye)*   Good-bye, Alan!

FLO *(Getting life started again)*   You better get ready for school, Millie.

MILLIE *(Going to doorstep, rather sad)*   Gee, I almost forgot.
(She goes inside. FLO turns to MRS. POTTS)

FLO   You—you liked the young man, didn't you, Helen? Admit it.

MRS. POTTS   Yes, I did.

FLO *(Belittlingly)*   Hmm.

MRS. POTTS   With just Mama and me in the house, I'd got so used to things as they were, everything so prim, occasionally a hairpin on the floor, the geranium in the window, the smell of Mama's medicines . . .

FLO   I'll keep things as they are in *my* house, thank you.

MRS. POTTS   Not when a man is there, Flo. He walked through the door and suddenly everything was different. He clomped through the tiny rooms like he was still in the great outdoors, he talked in a booming voice that shook the ceiling. Everything he did reminded me there was a man in the house, and it seemed good.

FLO *(Skeptically)*   Did it?

MRS. POTTS   And that reminded *me* . . . I'm a woman, and that seemed good, too.
(Now MILLIE comes swaggering out the front door, carrying her schoolbooks)

MILLIE *(Disparagingly)*   Madge is in love with that crazy guy. She's in there crying her eyes out.

FLO   Mind your business and go to school.

MILLIE   I'm never gonna fall in love. Not me.

MRS. POTTS   Wait till you're a little older before you say that, Millie-girl.

MILLIE   I'm old enough already. Madge can *stay* in this jerkwater town and marry some ornery guy and raise a lot of dirty kids. When I graduate from college I'm going to New York, and write novels that'll shock people right out of their senses.

MRS. POTTS   You're a talented girl, Millie.

MILLIE *(Victoriously)*   I'll be so great and famous—I'll never have to fall in love.

A BOY'S VOICE *(From offstage, heckling MILLIE)*   Hey, goongirl!

MILLIE *(Spotting him in the distance)*   It's Poopdeck McCullough. He thinks he's so smart.

BOY'S VOICE   Hey, goongirl! Come kiss me. I wanna be sick.

MILLIE *(Her anger roused)*   If he thinks he can get by with that, he's crazy. *(She finds a stick with which to chastise her offender)*

FLO   Millie! Millie! You're a grown girl now.
(MILLIE thinks better of it, drops the stick and starts off)

MILLIE   See you this evening.
(She goes off)

FLO *(Wanting reassurance)*   Alan *will* be back, don't you think so, Helen?

MRS. POTTS   Of course he'll be back, Flo. He'll be back at Christmas time and take her to the dance at the country club, and they'll get married and live happily ever after.

FLO   I hope so.
(Suddenly MADGE comes out the front door. She wears a hat and carries a small cardboard suitcase. There is a look of firm decision on her face. She walks straight to the gateway)

FLO *(Stunned)*   Madge!

MADGE   I'm going to Tulsa, Mom.

MRS. POTTS *(To herself)*   For heaven's sake.

MADGE   Please don't get mad. I'm not doing it to be spiteful.

FLO *(Holding her head)*   As I live and breathe!

MADGE   I know how you feel, but I don't know what else to do.

FLO *(Anxiously)*   Now look, Madge, Alan's coming back Christmas. He'll take you to the dance at the club. I'll make another new dress for you, and . . .

MADGE   I'm going, Mom.

FLO *(Frantic)*   Madge! Listen to what I've got to say . . .

MADGE   My bus leaves in a few minutes.

FLO   He's no good. He'll never be able to support you. When he does have a job, he'll spend all his money on booze. After a while, there'll be other women.

MADGE   I've thought of all those things.

MRS. POTTS   You don't love someone 'cause he's perfect, Flo.

FLO   Oh, God!

BOYS' VOICES *(In the distance)*   Hey, Madge! Hey, beautiful! You're the one for me!

MRS. POTTS   Who are those boys?

MADGE   Some of the gang, in their hot rod. *(Kisses* MRS. POTTS*)* Good-bye, Mrs. Potts. I'll miss you almost as much as Mom.

FLO *(Tugging at* MADGE, *trying to take the suitcase from her)*   Madge, now listen to me. I can't let you . . .

MADGE   It's no use, Mom. I'm going. Don't worry. I've got ten dollars I was saving for a pair of pumps, and I saw ads in the Tulsa *World.* There's lots of jobs as waitresses. Tell Millie good-bye for me, Mom. Tell her I never meant it all those times I said I hated her.

FLO *(Wailing)*   Madge . . . Madge . . .

MADGE   Tell her I've always been very proud to have such a smart sister. *(She runs off now,* FLO *still tugging at her, then giving up and standing by the gatepost, watching* MADGE *in the distance)*

FLO   Helen, could I stop her?

MRS. POTTS   Could anyone have stopped you, Flo?
    *(*FLO *gives* MRS. POTTS *a look of realization)*

BOYS' VOICES   Hey, Madge! You're the one for me!

FLO *(Still watching* MADGE *in the distance)*   She's so young. There are so many things I meant to tell her, and never got around to it.

MRS. POTTS   Let her learn them for herself, Flo.

MRS. POTTS' MOTHER   Helen! Helen!

MRS. POTTS   Be patient, Mama.
(*Starts up the stairs to her back porch.* FLO *still stands in the gateway,
watching in the distance*)

CURTAIN

Bus Stop

BUS STOP *was first presented by Robert Whitehead and Roger L. Stevens at The Music Box, New York City, on March 2, 1955, with the following cast:*

ELMA DUCKWORTH	*Phyllis Love*
GRACE	*Elaine Stritch*
WILL MASTERS	*Lou Polan*
CHERIE	*Kim Stanley*
DR. GERALD LYMAN	*Anthony Ross*
CARL	*Patrick McVey*
VIRGIL BLESSING	*Crahan Denton*
BO DECKER	*Albert Salmi*

DIRECTED BY Harold Clurman
SETTING BY Boris Aronson
COSTUMES AND LIGHTING BY Paul Morrison

Scenes

The action of the play takes place in a street-corner restaurant in a small town about thirty miles west of Kansas City.

ACT
ONE | A night in early March. 1:00 A.M.

ACT
TWO | A few minutes later.

ACT
THREE | Early morning. About 5:00 A.M.

SCENE: *The entire play is set inside a street-corner restaurant in a small Kansas town about thirty miles west of Kansas City. The restaurant serves also as an occasional rest stop for the bus lines in the area. It is a dingy establishment with few modern improvements: scenic calendars and pretty-girl posters decorate the soiled walls, and illumination comes from two badly shaded light bulbs that hang on dangling cords from the ceiling; in the center are several quartet tables with chairs, for dining; at far left is the counter with six stools before it, running the depth of the setting; behind the counter are the usual restaurant equipment and paraphernalia (coffee percolator, dishes, glasses, electric refrigerator, etc.); on top of the counter are several large plates of doughnuts, sweet rolls, etc., under glass covers. At the far right, close to the outside entrance door, are a magazine stand and a rack of shelves piled with paperback novels and books. At back center is an old-fashioned Franklin stove. At the back right is a great window that provides a view of the local scenery. Against the wall, beneath the window, are two long benches meant for waiting passengers. At the back left is the rear door, close to the upper end of the counter. Above this door is a dim hand-painted sign, "Rest Rooms in the Rear."*

It is 1:00 A.M. on a night in early March and a near blizzard is raging outside. Through the windows we can see the sweeping wind and flying snow. Inside, by comparison, the scene is warm and cozy, the Franklin stove radiating all the heat of which it is capable. Two young women, in uniforms that have lost their starched freshness, are employed behind the counter. ELMA is a big-eyed girl still in high school. GRACE is a more seasoned character in her thirties or early forties. A bus is expected soon and they are checking, somewhat lackadaisically, the supplies. Outside, the powerful, reckless wind comes and goes, blasting against everything in its path, seeming to shake the very foundation of the little restaurant building; then subsiding, leaving a period of uncertain stillness.

When the curtain goes up, ELMA stands far right, looking out the large plate-glass window, awed by the fury of the elements. GRACE is at the telephone.

ELMA Listen to that wind. March is coming in like a lion. (GRACE *jiggles the receiver on the telephone with no results*) Grace, you should come over here and look out, to see the way the wind is blowing things all over town.

GRACE Now I wonder why I can't get th' operator.

ELMA I bet the bus'll be late.

GRACE (*Finally hanging up*) I bet it won't. The roads are O.K. as far as here. It's *ahead* they're havin' trouble. I can't even get the operator. She must have more calls than she can handle.

ELMA (*Still looking out the window*) I bet the bus doesn't *have* many passengers.

GRACE Prob'ly not. But we gotta stay open even if there's only *one*.

ELMA I shouldn't think anyone would take a trip tonight unless he absolutely *had* to.

GRACE Are your folks gonna worry, Elma?

ELMA No—Daddy said, before I left home, he bet this'd happen.

GRACE (*Going behind counter*) Well, you better come back here and help me. The bus'll be here any minute and we gotta have things ready.

ELMA (*Leaving the window, following* GRACE) Nights like this, I'm glad I have a home to go to.

GRACE Well, I got a home to go to, but there ain't anyone in it.

ELMA Where's your husband now, Grace?

GRACE How should I know?

ELMA Don't you miss him?

GRACE No!

ELMA If he came walking in now, wouldn't you be glad to see him?

GRACE You ask more questions.

ELMA I'm just curious about things, Grace.

GRACE Well, kids your age *are*. I don't know. I'd be happy to see him, I guess, if I knew he wasn't gonna stay very long.

ELMA Don't you get lonesome, Grace, when you're not working down here?

GRACE   Sure I do. If I didn't have this restaurant to keep me busy, I'd prob'ly go nuts. Sometimes, at night, after I empty the garbage and lock the doors and turn out the lights, I get kind of a sick feelin', 'cause I sure don't look forward to walkin' up those stairs and lettin' myself into an empty apartment.

ELMA   Gee, if you feel that way, why don't you write your husband and tell him to come back?

GRACE   *(Thinks a moment)*   'Cause I got just as lonesome when he was here. He wasn't much company, 'cept when we were makin' love. But makin' love is *one* thing, and bein' lonesome is another. The resta the time, me and Barton was usually fightin'.

ELMA   I guess my folks get along pretty well. I mean . . . they really seem to like each other.

GRACE   Oh, I know *all* married people aren't like Barton and I. Not all! *(Goes to telephone again)* Now, maybe I can get the operator. *(Jiggles receiver)* Quiet as a tomb.
(Hangs up)

ELMA   I *like* working here with you, Grace.

GRACE   Do you, honey? I'm glad, 'cause I sure don't know what I'd do without ya. Week ends especially.

ELMA   You know, I dreaded the job at first.

GRACE   *(Kidding her)*   Why? Thought you wouldn't have time for all your boy friends? (ELMA *looks a little sour)* Maybe you'd have more boy friends if you didn't make such good grades. Boys feel kind of embarrassed if they feel a girl is smarter than they are.

ELMA   What should I do? Flunk my courses?

GRACE   I should say not. You're a good kid and ya got good sense. I wish someone coulda reasoned with *me* when I was your age. But I was a headstrong brat, had to have my own way. I had my own way all right, and here I am now, a grass widow runnin' a restaurant, and I'll prob'ly die in this little town and they'll bury me out by the backhouse.
(WILL, the sheriff, comes in the front door, wind and snow flying through the door with him. He is a huge, saturnine man, well over six feet, who has a thick black beard and a scar on his forehead. He wears a battered black hat, clumsy overshoes, and a heavy mackinaw. He looks somewhat forbidding)

WILL *(On entering)* You girls been able to use your phone?

GRACE No, Will. The operator don't answer.

WILL That means *all* the lines are down. 'Bout time fer the Topeka bus, ain't it?

GRACE Due now.

WILL You're gonna have to hold 'em here, don't know how long. The highway's blocked 'tween here and Topeka. May be all night gettin' it cleared.

GRACE I was afraid a that.

WILL They got the highway gang workin' on it now and the telephone company's tryin' to get the lines back up. March is comin' in like a lion, all right.

GRACE Yah.

WILL *(Taking off his mackinaw, hanging it, going to the fire to warm his hands)* The station house's *cold.* Got any fresh coffee?

GRACE It just went through, Will. Fresh as ya could want it.

WILL *(Goes to counter)* A storm like this makes me mad. (GRACE *laughs at his remark and gives him a cup of coffee)* It *does.* It makes me mad. It's just like all the elements had lost their reason.

GRACE Nothin' you can do about a wind like *that.*

WILL Maybe it's just 'cause I'm a sheriff, but I like to see things in order.

GRACE Let the wind blow! I just pray to God to leave a roof over my head. That's about all a person *can* do.
(The sound of the bus is heard outside, its great motor coming to a stop)

WILL Here it is.

GRACE Better fill some water glasses, Elma. Remember, the doughnuts are left over from yesterday but it'll be all right to serve 'em. We got everything for sandwiches but *cheese.* We got no cheese.

WILL You *never* got cheese, Grace.

GRACE I guess I'm kinda self-centered, Will. I don't care for cheese m'self, so I never think t'order it for someone else.

ELMA Gee, I'm glad I'm not traveling on the bus tonight.

GRACE   I wonder who's drivin' tonight. This is Carl's night, isn't it?

ELMA   I think so.

GRACE   Yes it is. *(Obviously the idea of* CARL *pleases her. She nudges* ELMA *confidentially)* Remember, honey, *I* always serve Carl.

ELMA   Sure, Grace.

(The door swings open, some of the snow flying inside, and CHERIE, *a young blond girl of about twenty, enters as though driven. She wears no hat, and her hair, despite one brilliant bobby pin, blows wild about her face. She is pretty in a fragile, girlish way. She runs immediately to the counter to solicit the attention of* GRACE *and* ELMA. *She lugs along an enormous straw suitcase that is worn and battered. Her clothes, considering her situation, are absurd: a skimpy jacket of tarnished metal cloth edged with not luxuriant fur, a dress of sequins and net, and gilded sandals that expose brightly enameled toes. Also, her make-up has been applied under the influence of having seen too many movies. Her lipstick creates a voluptuous pair of lips that aren't her own, and her eyebrows also form a somewhat arbitrary line. But despite all these defects, her prettiness still is apparent, and she has the appeal of a tender little bird. Her origin is the Ozarks and her speech is Southern)*

CHERIE *(Anxious, direct)*   Is there some place I kin hide?

GRACE *(Taken aback)*   What?

CHERIE   There's a *man* on that bus . . . I wanta *hide.*

GRACE *(Stumped)*   Well, gee . . . I dunno.

CHERIE *(Seeing the sign above the rear door, starting for it)*   I'll hide in the powder room. If a tall, lanky cowboy comes in here, you kin just tell him I disappeared.

GRACE *(Her voice stopping* CHERIE *at the door)*   Hey, you can't hide out there. It's cold. You'll freeze your . . .

CHERIE *(Having opened the door, seeing it is an outside toilet)*   Oh! It's outside.

GRACE   This is just a country town.

CHERIE *(Starting again)*   I kin stand anything fer twenty minutes.

GRACE *(Stopping her again)*   I got news for ya. The bus may be here all night.

CHERIE *(turning)*   What?

GRACE   The highway's blocked. You're gonna have to stay here till it's cleared.

CHERIE *(Shutting the door, coming to counter, lugging her suitcase. She is about to cry)*   Criminey! What am I gonna do?

GRACE *(Coming from behind counter, going to front door)*   I better go out and tell Carl 'bout the delay.

CHERIE *(Dropping to a stool at the counter)*   What am I gonna do? What am I ever gonna do?

ELMA *(In a friendly way)*   There's a little hotel down the street.

CHERIE   What ya take me for? A millionaire?

WILL *(Coming to* CHERIE *with a professional interest)*   What's the trouble, miss?

CHERIE *(Looking at* WILL *suspiciously)*   You a p'liceman?

WILL   I'm the local sheriff.

ELMA *(Feeling some endorsement is called for)*   But everyone likes him. Really!

CHERIE   Well . . . I ain't askin' t'have no one arrested.

WILL   Who says I'm gonna arrest anyone? What's your trouble?

CHERIE   I . . . I need protection.

WILL   What from?

CHERIE   There's a man after me. He's a cowboy.

WILL *(Looking around)*   Where is he?

CHERIE   He's on the bus, asleep, him and his buddy. I jumped off the bus the very second it stopped, to make my getaway. But there ain't no place to *get* away to. And he'll be in here purty soon. You just *gotta* make him lemme alone.

WILL   Ya meet him on the bus?

CHERIE   No. I met him in Kansas City. I work at the Blue Dragon night club there, down by the stockyards. *He* come there with the annual rodeo, and him and the resta the cowboys was at the night club ev'ry night. Ev'ry night there was a big fight. The boss says he ain't gonna let the cowboys in when they come back next year.

WILL   Then he followed ya on the bus?

CHERIE   He *put* me on the bus. I'm bein' abducted.

WILL   Abducted! But you took time to pack a suitcase!

CHERIE   I was goin' somewhere else, tryin' to get away from him, but he picked me up and carried me to the bus and put me on it. I din have nothin' to say about it at all.

WILL   Where's he plan on takin' ya?

CHERIE   Says he's got a ranch up in Montana. He says we're gonna git married soon as we get there.

WILL   And yor against it?

CHERIE   I don't wanta go up to some God-forsaken ranch in Montana.

WILL   Well, if this cowboy's really takin' ya against yor will, I s'pose I'll have to stop him from it.

CHERIE   You just don't know this cowboy. He's mean.

WILL   I reckon I kin handle him. You relax now. I'll be around mosta the night. If there's any trouble, I'll put a stop to it.

ELMA   You're safe with Will here. Will is very respected around here. He's never lost a fight.

WILL   What're ya talkin' about, Elma? Of course I've lost a fight . . . once.

ELMA   Grace always said you were *invincible*.

WILL   There ain't no one that's . . . *invincible*. A man's gotta learn that, the sooner the better. A good fighter has gotta know what it is to *get* licked. Thass what makes the diff'rence 'tween a fighter and a *bully*.

CHERIE   (*Shuddering*)   There's gonna be trouble. I kin feel it in my bones. (*Enter* DR. GERALD LYMAN, *a man of medium height, about fifty, with a ruddy, boyish face that smilingly defies the facts of his rather scholarly glasses and iron-gray hair. He wears an old tweed suit of good quality underneath a worn Burberry. His clothes are mussed, and he wears no hat, probably having left it somewhere; for he has been drinking and is, at present, very jubilant. He looks over the restaurant approvingly*)

DR. LYMAN   Ah! "This castle hath a pleasant seat."

CHERIE *(To* ELMA*)*   Could I hide my suitcase behind the counter, so's he won't see it when he comes in? I ain't gonna say anything to him at all 'bout not goin' on to Montana with him. I'm just gonna let 'im think I'm goin' till the bus pulls out and he finds I ain't on it. Thass th' only thing I know t' do.

ELMA *(Taking the suitcase and putting it behind counter)*   Oh, you needn't worry with Will here.

CHERIE   Think so? *(She studies* WILL*)* Looks kinda like Moses, don't he?

ELMA   He *is* a very religious man. Would you believe it? He's a deacon in the Congregational Church.

CHERIE *(Just because she happens to think of it)*   My folks was Holy Rollers. Will ya gimme a cup of coffee, please? Lotsa cream.
(ELMA *draws a cup of coffee for her. Then* CARL, *the bus driver, comes in, followed by* GRACE. CARL *is a hefty man, loud and hearty, who looks very natty in his uniform)*

WILL *(Calling to him from across the room)*   Howdy, Carl! You bring this wind?

CARL *(Hollering back)*   No! It brought *me!*
(This greeting probably has passed between them a dozen times, but they still relish it as new)

GRACE   Aren't you the comedian?

CARL   The wind is doin' ninety miles an hour. The bus is doin' twenty. What's *your* guess about the roads, Will?

WILL   They got the highway gang out. It may take a few hours.

CARL   Telephone lines down, too?

WILL   Yah. But they're workin' on 'em.
(DR. LYMAN, having got his extremities warmed at the fire, seeks CARL *privately to make certain clarifications)*

DR. LYMAN   Driver, it seems to me we are still in the state of Kansas. Is that right?

CARL   What do ya mean, *still?* You been in the state of Kansas about a half-hour.

DR. LYMAN   But I don't understand. I was told, when I left Kansas City, that I would be across the state line immediately. And now I find . . .

CARL *(Eying* DR. LYMAN *suspiciously)*   You was kinda anxious to get across that state line, too, wasn't you, Jack?

DR. LYMAN *(Startled)*   Why . . . what ever do you mean?

CARL   Nothin'. Anyway, you're across the line now. In case you didn't know it, Kansas City is in *Missouri.*

DR. LYMAN   Are you joking?

CARL   There's a Kansas City, Kansas, too, but *you* got on in Kansas City, Missouri. That's the trouble with you easterners. You don't know anything about any of the country west of the Hudson River.

DR. LYMAN   Come, come now. Don't scold.

GRACE *(As* CARL *gets out of his heavy coat)*   Carl, let me hang up your coat fer ya, while you get warm at the stove.
(DR. LYMAN'S *eyes brighten when he sees* ELMA, *and he bows before her like a cavalier)*

DR. LYMAN   "Nymph, in thy orisons be all my sins remembered!"

ELMA *(Smiling)*   I'm sorry your bus is held up.

DR. LYMAN   Oohh! Is that a nice way to greet me?

ELMA *(Confused)*   I mean . . .

DR. LYMAN   After my loving greeting, all you can think of to say is, "I'm sorry your bus is held up." Well, I'm not. I would much rather sit here looking into the innocent blue of your eyes than continue riding on that monotonous bus.

ELMA   Don't you have to get somewhere?

DR. LYMAN   I have a ticket in my pocket to Denver, but I don't have to get there. I never have to get *any*where. I travel around from one town to another just to prove to myself that I'm *free.*

ELMA   The bus probably won't get into Denver for another day.

DR. LYMAN   Ah, well! What is our next stop?

ELMA   Topeka.

DR. LYMAN   Topeka? Oh, yes! that's where the famous hospital is, isn't it?

ELMA   The Menninger Clinic? Yes, it's a very famous place. Lots of movie stars go there for nervous breakdowns and things.

DR. LYMAN *(Wryly)* Does the town offer anything else in the way of diversion?

ELMA It's the capital of Kansas. It's almost as big as Kansas City. They have a university and a museum, and sometimes symphony concerts and plays. I go over there every Sunday to visit my married sister.

DR. LYMAN Aren't there any Indian tribes around here that have war dances?

ELMA *(laughing)* No, silly! We're very civilized.

DR. LYMAN I'll make my own judgment about that. Meanwhile, you may fix me a double shot of rye whiskey . . . on the rocks.

ELMA I'm sorry, sir. We don't sell drinks.

DR. LYMAN You don't sell drinks?

ELMA Not intoxicating drinks. No, sir.

DR. LYMAN Alas!

ELMA We have fresh coffee, homemade pies and cakes, all kinds of sandwiches . . .

DR. LYMAN No, my girl. You're not going to sober me up with your dainties. I am prepared for such emergencies. *(Draws a pint bottle of whiskey from his overcoat pocket)* You may give me a bottle of your finest lemon soda.

ELMA *(whispering)* You'd better not let Will see you do that. You're not supposed to.

DR. LYMAN Who is *he*, the sheriff?

ELMA Yes. Lots of people do spike their drinks here and we never say anything, but Will would have to make you stop if *he* saw you.

DR. LYMAN I shall be *most* cautious. I promise.
(She sets the bottle of soda before him as he smiles at her benignly. He pours some soda in a glass, then some whiskey, and ambles over to a table, far right, sitting down with his drink before him. WILL moves over to CARL, who's at the end of the counter, chiding GRACE, where the two of them have been standing, talking in very personal voices that can't be overheard)

WILL I sure don't envy ya, Carl, drivin' in weather like this.

CARL *(Making it sound like a personal observation)* Yah! March is comin' in like a *lion*.

WILL   This all the passengers ya got?

CARL   There's a coupla crazy cowboys rolled up in the back seat, asleep. I thought I woke 'em, but I guess I didn't.

WILL   Shouldn't you go out and do it now?

CARL   I'd jest as soon they stayed where they're at. One of 'em's a real troublemaker. You know the kind, first time off a ranch and wild as a bronco. He's been on the make fer this li'l blonde down here . . . (*Indicates* CHERIE)

WILL   She was tellin' me.

CARL   I've had a good mind to put him off the bus, the way he's been actin'. I say, there's a time and place for ev'rything.

WILL   That bus may get snowbound purty soon.

CARL   I'll go wake 'em in a minute, Will. Just lemme have a li'l *time* here. (WILL *sizes up the situation as* CARL *returns his attention to* GRACE, *then* WILL *picks up a copy of the Kansas City* Star, *sitting down close to the fire to read*) Ya know what, Grace? This is the first time you and I ever had more'n twenty minutes t'gether.

GRACE (*Coyly*)   So what?

CARL   Oh, I dunno. I'll prob'ly be here mosta the night. It'd sure be nice to have a nice li'l apartment to go to, some place to sit and listen to the radio, with a good-lookin' woman . . . somethin' like you . . . to talk with . . . maybe have a few beers.

GRACE   That wouldn't be a hint or anything, would it?

CARL (*Faking innocence*)   Why? Do you have an apartment like that, Grace?

GRACE   Yes, I do. But I never told *you* about it. Did that ornery Dobson fella tell you I had an apartment over the restaurant?

CARL (*In a query*)   Dobson? Dobson? I can't seem to remember anyone named Dobson.

GRACE   You know him better'n *I* do. He comes through twice a week with the Southwest Bus. He told me you and him meet in Topeka sometimes and paint the town.

CARL   Dobson? Oh, yah, I know Dobson. Vern Dobson. A prince of a fella.

GRACE   Well, if he's been gabbin' to you about my apartment, I can tell ya he's oney been up there *once*, when he come in here with his hand cut, and I took him up there to bandage it. Now that's the oney time he was ever up there. On my word of honor.

CARL   Oh, Vern Dobson speaks very highly of you, Grace. Very highly.

GRACE   Well . . . he better. Now, what ya gonna have?

CARL   Make it a ham and cheese on rye.

GRACE   I'm sorry, Carl. We got no cheese.

CARL   What happened? Did the mice get it?

GRACE   None of your wise remarks.

CARL   O.K. Make it a ham on rye, then.

GRACE   *(At breadbox)*   I'm sorry, Carl, but we got no rye, either.

DR. LYMAN   *(Chiming in, from his table)*   I can vouch for that, sir. I just asked for rye, myself, and was refused.

CARL   Look, mister, don't ya think ya oughta lay off that stuff till ya get home and meet the missus?

DR. LYMAN   The *missus*, did you say? *(He laughs)* I have no missus, sir. I'm *free*. I can travel the universe, with no one to await my arrival anywhere.

CARL   *(To* GRACE, *bidding for a little sympathy)*   That's all I ever get on my bus, drunks and hoodlums.

GRACE   How's fer whole wheat, Carl?

CARL   O.K. Make it whole wheat.

DR. LYMAN   *(To* ELMA, *as she brings him more soda)*   Yes, I am free. My third and last wife deserted me several years ago . . . for a ballplayer. *(He chuckles as though it were all a big absurdity)*

ELMA   *(A little astounded)*   Your *third*?

DR. LYMAN   Yes, my third! Getting married is a careless habit I've fallen into. Sometime, really, I *must* give it all up. Oh, but she was pretty! Blonde, like the young lady over there. *(He indicates* CHERIE) And Southern, too, or pretended to be. However, she was kinder than the others when we parted. She didn't care about money. All she wanted was to find new marital bliss with her ballplayer, so I never had to pay her alimony . . . as if I could. *(He chuckles, sighs and recalls another)* My

second wife was a different type entirely. But she was very pretty, too. I
have always exercised the most excellent taste, if not the best judgment.
She was a student of mine, when I was teaching at an eastern university.
Alas! she sued me for divorce on the grounds that I was incontinent and
always drunk. I didn't have a chance to resign from that position.
(Still he manages to chuckle about it)

CHERIE *(From the counter)*   Hey! how much are them doughnuts?
(She is counting the coins in her purse)

ELMA *(Leaving* DR. LYMAN, *hurrying back to counter)*   I'll make you a special
price, two for a nickel.

CHERIE   O.K.

DR. LYMAN *(Musingly, he begins to recite as though for his own enjoyment)*
              "That time of year thou may'st in me behold
              When yellow leaves, or none, or few, do hang
              Upon those boughs—"

CHERIE *(Shivering, she goes to the stove)*   I never was so cold in my life.

ELMA *(Setting the doughnuts before her)*   Do you honestly work in a night
club?

CHERIE *(Brightening with this recognition)*   Sure! I'm a *chanteuse*. I call
m'self *Cherie*.

ELMA   That's French, isn't it?

CHERIE   I dunno. I jest seen the name once and it kinda appealed t'me.

ELMA   It's French. It means "dear one." Is that all the name you use?

CHERIE   Sure. Thass all the name ya need. Like Hildegarde. She's a *chanteuse*, too.

ELMA   *Chanteuse* means singer.

CHERIE   How come *you* know so much?

ELMA   I'm taking French in high school.

CHERIE   Oh! *(A reflective pause)* I never got as far as high school. See, I was
the oldest girl left in the fam'ly after my sister Violet ran away. I had two
more sisters, both younger'n me, and five brothers, most of 'em older.
Was they mean! Anyway, I had to quit school when I was twelve, to stay
home and take care a the house and do the cookin'. I'm a real good cook.
Honest!

ELMA Did you *study* singing?

CHERIE *(Shaking her head)* Huh-uh. Jest picked it up listenin' to the radio, seein' movies, tryin' to put over my songs as good as them people did.

ELMA How did you get started in the night club?

CHERIE I won a amateur contest. Down in Joplin, Missouri. I won the second prize there . . . a coupla boys won *first* prize . . . they juggled milk bottles . . . I don't think that's fair, do you? To make an artistic performer compete with jugglers and knife-throwers and people like that?

ELMA No, I don't.

CHERIE Anyway, second prize was good enough to get me to Kanz City t'enter the contest there. It was a real *big* contest and I didn't win any prize at all, but it got me the job at the Blue Dragon.

ELMA Is that where you're from, Joplin?

CHERIE *(With an acceptance of nature's catastrophes)* No. Joplin's a *big* town. I lived 'bout a hundred miles from there, in River Gulch, a li'l town in the Ozarks. I lived there till the floods come, three years ago this spring, and washed us all away.

ELMA Gee, that's too bad.

CHERIE I dunno where any a my folks are now, 'cept my baby sister Nan. We all just separated when the floods come and I took Nan into Joplin with me. She got a job as a waitress and I went to work in Liggett's drug store, till the amateur contest opened.

ELMA It must be fun working in a night club.

CHERIE *(A fleeting look of disillusionment comes over her face)* Well . . . it ain't all roses.

CARL *(Leaving GRACE for the moment)* You gonna be here a while, Will?

WILL I reckon.

CARL I'm gonna send them cowboys in here now, and leave *you* to look after 'em.

WILL I'll do my best.

CARL Tell ya somethin' else, Will.
     (CARL *looks at* DR. LYMAN *cautiously, as though he didn't want to be over-*

heard by him, then moves very closely to WILL *and whispers something in his ear.* WILL *looks very surprised)*

WILL   I'll be jiggered.

CARL   So, ya better keep an eye on *him*, too.
   (Starts off)

WILL   Ain't you comin' back, Carl?

CARL   *(Obviously he is faking, and a look between him and* GRACE *tells us something is up between them. He winks at her and stretches)*   To tell the truth, Will, I git so darn *stiff*, sittin' at the wheel all day, I thought I'd go out fer a long walk.

WILL   In this blizzard? You gone crazy?

CARL   No. That's just the kinda fella I am, Will. I like to go fer long walks in the rain and snow. Freshens a fella up. Sometimes I walk fer hours.

WILL   Ya do?

CARL   Yah. Fer hours. That's just the kinda fella I am.
   (He saunters out now, whistling to show his nonchalance)

WILL   *(To* GRACE*)*   Imagine! Goin' out fer a walk, a night like this.

GRACE   Well, it's really very good for one, Will. It really is.

CHERIE   *(Leaning over counter to talk to* ELMA *privately)*   He said he was gonna wake him up. Then he'll be in here pretty soon. You won't let on I said anything 'bout him, will ya?

ELMA   No. Cross my heart.
   *(*DR. LYMAN *is suddenly reminded of another poem, which he begins to recite in full voice)*

DR. LYMAN

>   "Shall I compare thee to a summer's day?
>   Thou art more lovely and more temperate:
>   Rough winds do shake the darling buds of May,
>   And summer's lease hath all too short a date."

ELMA   *(Still behind counter, she hears* DR. LYMAN, *smiles fondly, and calls to him across room)*   Why, that's one of my favorite sonnets.

DR. LYMAN   It is? Do *you* read Shakespeare?

ELMA   I studied him at school, in English class. I loved the sonnets. I memorized some of them myself.

DR. LYMAN *(Leaving table, returning to counter)* I used to know them *all,* by heart. And many of the plays I could recite in their entirety. I often did, for the entertainment and the annoyance of my friends.
(He and ELMA *laugh together)*

ELMA Last fall I memorized the Balcony Scene from *Romeo and Juliet.* A boy in class played Romeo and we presented it for convocation one day.

DR. LYMAN Ah! I wish I had been there to see.
*(*CHERIE *feels called upon to explain her own position in regard to Shakespeare, as* ELMA *resumes work behind counter)*

CHERIE Where I went to school, we din read no Shakespeare till the ninth grade. In the ninth grade everyone read *Julius Caesar.* I oney got as far as the eighth. I seen Marlon Brando in the movie, though. I sure do like that Marlon Brando.

DR. LYMAN *(Now that* CHERIE *has called attention to herself)* Madam, where is thy Lochinvar?

CHERIE *(Giggling)* I don't understand anything you say, but I just love the way you say it.

DR. LYMAN And *I* . . . understand *every*thing I say . . . but privately despise the way I say it.

CHERIE *(Giggling)* That's so cute. *(A memory returns)* I had a very nice friend once that recited poetry.

DR. LYMAN *(With spoofing seriousness)* Whatever could have happened to him?

CHERIE I dunno. He left town. His name was Mr. Everett Brubaker. He sold second-hand cars at the corner of Eighth and Wyandotte. He had a lovely Pontiac car-with-the-top-down. He talked nice, but I guess he really wasn't any nicer'n any of the others.

DR. LYMAN The others?

CHERIE Well . . . ya meet quite a few men in the place I worked at, the Blue Dragon night club, out by the stockyards. Ever hear of it?

DR. LYMAN No, and I deeply regret the fact.

CHERIE You're just sayin' that. An educated man like you, you wouldn't have no use fer the Blue Dragon.

DR. LYMAN *(With a dubious look)* I wouldn't?
(The front door swings open again and the two cowboys, BO DECKER *and*

VIRGIL BLESSING, *enter. Their appearance now is rumpledly picturesque and they both could pass, at first glance, for outlaws.* BO *is in his early twenties, is tall and slim and good-looking in an outdoors way. Now he is very unkempt. He wears faded jeans that cling to his legs like shedding skin; his boots, worn under his jeans, are scuffed and dusty; and the Stetson on the back of his head is worn and tattered. Over a faded denim shirt he wears a shiny horsehide jacket, and around his neck is tied a bandanna.* VIRGIL *is a man in his forties who seems to regard* BO *in an almost parental way. A big man, corpulent and slow-moving, he seems almost an adjunct of* BO. *Dressed similarly to* BO, *perhaps a trifle more tidy, he carries a guitar in a case and keeps a bag of Bull Durham in his shirt pocket, out of which he rolls frequent cigarettes. Both men are still trying to wake up from their snooze, but* BO *is quick to recognize* CHERIE. *Neither cowboy has thought to shut the door behind them, and the others begin to shiver)*

BO *(In a full voice, accustomed to speaking in an open field)* Hey! Why din anyone wake us up? Virg'n I mighta froze out there.

GRACE Hey! Shut the door.

BO *(Calling across the room)* Cherry! how come you get off the bus, 'thout lettin' me know? That any way to treat the man you're gonna marry?

WILL *(Lifting his eyes from the paper)* Shut the door, cowboy!
(BO doesn't even hear WILL, but strides across the room to CHERIE, who is huddled over the counter as though hoping he might overlook her. VIRGIL, still rubbing sleep out of his eyes, lingers open-mouthed in the open doorway)

BO Thass no way to treat a fella, Cherry, to slip off the bus like ya wanted to get rid of him, maybe. And come in here and eat by yourself. I thought we'd have a li'l snack t'*gether*. Sometimes, I don't understand you, Cherry.

CHERIE Fer the hunderth time, my name ain't *Cherry*.

BO I cain't say it the way you do. What's wrong with Cherry?

CHERIE It's kinda embarrassin'.

WILL *(In a firmer, louder voice)* Cowboy, will you have the decency to shut that door!
(VIRGIL now responds immediately and quickly closes the door as BO turns to WILL)

BO *(There is nothing to call him for the moment but insolent)* Why, what's the matter with you, mister? You afraid of a little fresh air? (WILL *glowers but* BO *is not fazed)* Why, man, ya oughta breathe real deep and git yor lungs full of it. Thass the trouble with you city people. You git *soft.*

VIRGIL *(Whispering)*   He's the sheriff, Bo.

BO *(In full voice, for* WILL'S *benefit)*   S'posin' he *is* the sheriff! What's that matter t'*me?* That don't give him the right t'insult my manners, does it? No man ever had to tell *me* what t'do, did he, Virge? Did he?

VIRGIL   No. No. But there allus comes a time, Bo, when . . .

BO *(Ignoring* VIRGIL, *speaking out for the benefit of all)*   My name's Bo Decker. I'm twenty-one years old and own me m'own ranch up in Timber Hill, Montana, where I got a herd a fine Hereford cattle and a dozen horses, and the finest sheep and hogs and chickens anywhere in the country. And I jest come back from a rodeo where I won 'bout ev'ry prize there *was,* din I, Virge? *(Joshingly, he elbows* VIRGIL *in the ribs)* Yap, I'm the prize bronco-buster, 'n steer-roper, 'n bulldogger, anywhere 'round. I won 'em all. And what's more, had my picture taken by *Life* magazine. *(Confronting* WILL*)* So I'd appreciate your talkin' to me with a little respect in yor voice, mister, and not go hollerin' orders to me from across the room like I was some no-'count servant. (WILL *is flabbergasted)*

CHERIE *(Privately to* ELMA)   Did ya ever see anybody like him?

WILL *(Finally finds his voice and uses it, after a struggle with himself to sound just and impartial)*   You was the last one in, cowboy, and you left the door open. You shoulda closed it, I don't care *who* y'are. That's all I'm saying.

BO   Door's closed now. What ya arguin' 'bout? *(Leaving a hushed and somewhat awed audience,* BO *strides over to the counter and drops to a stool)* Seems like we're gonna be here a while, Virge. How's fer some grub?

VIRGIL *(Remaining by magazine counter)*   Not yet, Bo. I'm chewin' t'backy.

BO *(Slapping a thigh)*   Thass ole Virge for ya. Allus happy long's he's got a wad a t'backy in his mouth. Wall, I'm gonna have me a li'l snack. *(To* ELMA*)* Miss, gimme 'bout three hamburgers.

ELMA   Three? How do you want them?

BO   I want 'em *raw.*
   (CHERIE *makes a sick face.* DR. LYMAN *quietly withdraws, taking his drink over to the window)*

ELMA   Honest?

BO   It's the only way t'eat 'em, raw, with a thick slice a onion and some piccalilli.

ELMA *(Hesitant)*   Well . . . if you're sure you're not joking.

BO *(His voice holding* ELMA *on her way to refrigerator)*   Jest a minute, miss. That ain't all. I'd also like me some ham and eggs . . . and some potaty salad . . . and a piece a pie. I ain't so pertikler what *kinda* pie it is, so long as it's got that murang on top of it.

ELMA   We have lemon and choc'late. They both have meringue.

BO *(Thinking it over)*   Lemon'n choc'late. I like 'em both. I dunno which I'd ruther have. *(Ponders a moment)* I'll have 'em *both,* miss.
(CHERIE *makes another sick face)*

ELMA   Both?

BO   Yep! 'N set a quart of milk beside me. I'm still a growin' boy. (ELMA *starts preparations as* BO *turns to* CHERIE) Travelin' allus picks up my appetite. That all you havin', jest a measly doughnut?

CHERIE   I ain't hungry.

BO   Why not?

CHERIE   I jest ain't.

BO   Ya oughta be.

CHERIE   Well—I ain't!

BO   Wait till I get ya up to the Susie-Q. I'll fatten ya up. I bet in two weeks time, ya won't recognize yorself. *(Now he puts a bearlike arm around her, drawing her close to him for a snuggle, kissing her on the cheek)* But doggone, I *love* ya, Cherry, jest the way ya are. Yor about the cutest li'l piece I ever did see. And, man! when I walked into that night club place and hear you singin' my favorite song, standin' before that orkester lookin' like a angel, I told myself then and there, she's fer *me.* I ain't gonna leave this place without her. And now I got ya, ain't I, Cherry?

CHERIE *(Trying to avoid his embrace)*   Bo . . . there's people here . . . they're lookin' . . .
(And she's right. They are)

BO   What if they are? It's no crime to show a li'l affection, is it? 'Specially, when we're gonna git married. It's no crime I ever heard of.
(He squeezes her harder now and forces a loud, smacking kiss on the lips. CHERIE *twists loose of him and turns away)*

CHERIE　Bo! fer cryin' out loud, lemme *be!*

BO　Cherry, thass no way to talk to yor husband.

CHERIE　That's all ya done since we left Kanz City, is maul me.

BO　Oh, is zat so? *(This is a deep-cutting insult)* Wall, I certainly ain't one to *pester* any woman with my affections. I never had to *beg* no woman to make love to me. *(Calling over his shoulder to* VIRGIL*)* Did I, Virge? I never had to coax no woman to make love to me, *did* I?

VIRGIL　*(In a voice that sounds more and more restrained)*　No . . . no . . .

BO　*(Still in full voice)*　No! Ev'rywhere I go, I got all the wimmin I want, don't I, Virge? I gotta fight 'em to keep 'em off me, don't I, Virge? *(*VIRGIL *is saved from having to make a response as* ELMA *presents* BO *with his hamburgers)*

ELMA　Here are the hamburgers. The ham and eggs will take a little longer.

BO　O.K. These'll gimme a start.
*(*GRACE *rubs her forehead with a feigned expression of pain)*

GRACE　Elma, honey, I got the darndest headache.

ELMA　I'm sorry, Grace.

GRACE　Can you look after things awhile?

ELMA　Sure.

GRACE　'Cause the only thing for me to do is go upstairs and lie down awhile. That's the only thing gonna do me any good at all.

WILL　*(From his chair)*　What's the matter, Grace?

GRACE　*(At the rear door)*　I got a headache, Will, that's just drivin' me *wild.*

WILL　That so?
*(*GRACE *goes out)*

DR. LYMAN　*(To* ELMA*)*　You are now the Mistress of the Inn.

ELMA　You haven't told me anything about your first wife.

DR. LYMAN　Now, how could I have omitted her?

ELMA　What was *she* like?

DR. LYMAN　*(Still in the highest of spirits)*　Oh . . . she was the loveliest of them all. I do believe she was. We had such an idyllic honeymoon together, a golden month of sunshine and romance, in Bermuda. She sued

me for divorce later, on the grounds of mental cruelty, and persuaded the judge that she should have my house and my motorcar, and an alimony that I still find it difficult to pay, for she never chose to marry again. She found that for all she wanted out of marriage, she didn't have to marry. *(He chuckles)* Ah, but perhaps I am being unkind.
(ELMA is a little mystified by the humor with which he always tells of his difficulties. BO now leans over the counter and interrupts)

BO   Miss, was you waitin' fer me to lay them eggs?

ELMA *(Hurrying to stove)*   Oh, I'm sorry. They're ready now.
(BO jumps up, grabs a plate and glides over the counter for ELMA to serve him from the stove)

BO   Them hamburgers was just a *horse d'oovrey*. *(He grins with appreciation of this word.* ELMA *fills his plate)* Thank ya, miss. *(He starts back for the stool but trips over* CHERIE'S *suitcase on the way)* Daggone! *(He looks down to see what has stopped him.* CHERIE *holds a rigid silence.* BO *brings his face slowly up, looking at* CHERIE *suspiciously)* Cherry! *(She says nothing)* Cherry, what'd ya wanta bring yor suitcase in here fer? *(She still says nothing)* Cherry, I'm askin' ya a civil question. What'd ya bring yor suitcase in fer? *Tell* me?

CHERIE *(Frightened)*   I . . . I . . . now don't you come near me, Bo.

BO   *(Shaking* CHERIE *by the shoulders)*   Tell me! What's yor suitcase doin' there b'hind the counter? What were ya tryin' to do, *fool* me? Was you plannin' to git away from me? That what you been sittin' here plannin' t'do?

CHERIE *(Finding it hard to speak while he is shaking her)*   Bo . . . lemme be . . . take your hands off me, Bo Decker.

BO   Tell me, Cherry. Tell me.
(Now WILL *intercedes, coming up to* BO, *laying a hand on his shoulder)*

WILL Leave the little lady alone, cowboy.

BO   *(Turning on* WILL *fiercely)*   Mister, ya got no right interferin' 'tween me and my feeancy.

WILL Mebbe she's yor feeancy and maybe she ain't. Anyway, ya ain't gonna abuse her while *I'm* here. Unnerstand?

BO   *Abuse* her?

WILL *(To* CHERIE)   I think you better tell him now, miss, jest how you feel about things.

(BO *looks at* CHERIE *with puzzled wonder)*

CHERIE *(Finding it impossible to say)*   I . . . I . . .

BO   What's this critter tryin' to say, Cherry?

CHERIE   Well . . . I . . .

WILL   You better tell him, miss.

CHERIE   Now, Bo, don't git mad.

BO   I'll git mad if I feel like it. What you two got planned?

CHERIE   Bo, I don't wanta go up to Montana and marry ya.

BO   Ya do too.

CHERIE   I do not!

BO   Anyways, you'll come to like it in time. I *promised* ya would. Now we been through all that b'fore.

CHERIE   But, Bo . . . I ain't goin'.

BO *(A loud blast of protest)*   What?

CHERIE   I ain't goin'. The sheriff here said he'd help me. He ain't gonna let you take me any farther. I'm stayin' here and take the next bus back to Kanz City.

BO *(Grabbing her by the shoulders to reassure himself of her)*   You ain't gonna do nothin' of the kind.

CHERIE   Yes, I am, Bo. You gotta b'lieve me. I ain't goin' with ya. That's final.

BO *(In a most personal voice, baffled)*   But, Cherry . . . we was *familiar* with each other.

CHERIE   That don't mean ya gotta *marry* me.

BO *(Shocked at her)*   Why . . . I oughta take you across my knee and blister yer li'l bottom.

CHERIE *(More frightened)*   Don't you touch me.

BO *(To* WILL)   You cain't pay no tension to what she says, mister. Womenfolk don't know their own minds. Never did.

(Back to CHERIE)

CHERIE Don't you come near me!

BO Yor gonna follow me back to Timber Hill and marry up. You just think you wouldn't like it now 'cause ya never been there and the whole idea's kinda strange. But you'll get over them feelin's. In no time at all, yor gonna be happy as a mudhen. I ain't takin' *no* fer an answer. By God, yor comin' along.
(*He grabs her forcefully to him, as* WILL *interferes again, pulling the two apart*)

WILL You're not takin' her with ya if she don't wanta go. Can't you get that through your skull? Now leave her be. (BO *stands looking at* WILL *with sullen hatred.* CHERIE *trembles.* VIRGIL *stands far right, looking apprehensive*)

BO (*Confronts* WILL *threateningly*) This ain't no biznes of yors.

WILL It's *my* business when the little lady comes t'me wantin' protection.

BO Is that right, Cherry? Did you go to the sheriff askin' fer pertection?

CHERIE (*Meekly*) . . . yes, I guess I did.

BO (*Bellowing out again*) Why? What'd ya need pertection for . . . from a man that wants to *marry* ya?

CHERIE (*Shuddering*) . . . 'cause . . .

BO (*Bellowing angrily*) 'Cause *why?* I said I *loved* ya, din I?

CHERIE (*About to cry*) I know ya did.

BO (*Confronting* WILL *with a feeling of angry unjustness*) See there? I told her I loved her and I wanta marry her. And with a world fulla crazy people goin' 'round killin' each other, *you* ain't got nothin' better t'do than stand here tryin' to keep me from it.

WILL Yor overlookin' jest one thing, cowboy.

BO (*With gruff impatience*) Yor so smart. Tell me what I'm overlookin'.

WILL Yor overlookin' the simple but important fack that the little lady don't love you.
(BO *now is trapped into silence. He can say nothing, and one can tell that* WILL *has named a fact that* BO *did not intend to face.* VIRGIL *watches him alertly. He can tell that* BO *is angry enough to attack* WILL *and is about to.* VIRGIL *hurries to* BO's *side, holding his arms as though to restrain him*)

VIRGIL *(Pacifyingly)*   Now, Bo. Take it easy, Bo. Don't blow your lid. He's the sheriff, Bo. Hold yor temper.

BO *(To* VIRGIL*)*   That polecat bastard! He said she din love me.

VIRGIL *(Trying to draw him away from the scene)*   Pay no 'tention, Bo. Come on over here and sit down. Ya gotta think things over, Bo.

BO *(Twisting loose from* VIRGIL*'s hold)*   Lemme be, Virge.

WILL   Ask the li'l lady, if ya don't b'lieve *me*. Ask her if she loves ya.

BO   I won't ask her nothin' of the kind.

WILL   All right then, take my word for it.

BO   I wouldn't take yor word for a cloudy day. I'm tellin' ya, she loves me. And *I* oughta know.
(CHERIE *flees to the counter, sobbing)*

WILL   Wall . . . she ain't gettin' back on the bus with ya. We'll leave it at that. So you better take my advice and sit down with yor friend there, and have a quiet game a pinochle till the bus gets on its way and takes you with it.

VIRGIL   Do like he tells ya, Bo. I think mebbe ya got the li'l lady all wrong, anyway.

BO *(A defender of womanhood)*   Don't you say nothin' against her, Virge.

VIRGIL   I *ain't* sayin' nothin' *against* her. I jest see no reason why you should marry a gal that says she don't love ya. That's all. And I kinda doubt she's as good a gal as you think she is. Now come on over here and sit down.

BO *(Turns restlessly from* VIRGIL*)*   I don't feel like sittin'.
(Instead, he paces up to the big window, standing there looking out, his back to the audience)

ELMA *(From behind counter, to* VIRGIL*)*   What shall I do with the ham and eggs?

VIRGIL   Just put 'em on the stove and keep 'em warm, miss. He'll have 'em a li'l later.

WILL *(To* CHERIE*)*   I don't think you'll be bothered any more, miss. If y'are, my station's right across the road. You kin holler.

CHERIE *(Dabbing at her eyes)*   Thank you very much, I'm sure.

WILL   Are you gonna be all right, Elma?

ELMA   *(Surprised at the question)*   Why yes, Will!
(WILL *just looks at* DR. LYMAN, *who, we can tell, is made to feel a little uncomfortable*)

WILL   I'll look in a little later.

ELMA   O.K., Will.
(WILL *goes to the door, takes a final look at* BO, *then goes out*)

DR. LYMAN   I don't know why, but . . . I always seem to relax more easily . . . when a sheriff leaves the room.
(He chuckles bravely)

ELMA   I think it's awfully unfair that people dislike Will just because he's a sheriff.

DR. LYMAN   But you see, my dear, he stands as a symbol of authority, the most dreaded figure of our time. Policemen, teachers, lawyers, judges, doctors, and I suppose, even tax collectors . . . we take it for granted that they are going to punish us for something we didn't do . . . or did do.

ELMA   But you said you were a teacher once.

DR. LYMAN   But not a successful one. I could never stay in one place very long at a time. And I hated having anyone *over* me, like deans and presidents and department heads. I never was a man who could take *orders* . . . from *anyone* . . . without feeling resentment. Right or wrong, I have always insisted on having my own way.
(BO *walks slowly down from his corner retreat, seeking* VIRGIL, *who is taking his guitar out of its case.* BO *speaks hesitantly, in a low voice*)

BO   What am I gonna do, Virge?

VIRGIL   Bo, ya jest gotta quit dependin' on me so much. I don't know what to tell ya to do, except to sit down and be peaceful.

BO   I—I can't be peaceful.

VIRGIL   All right then, pace around like a panther and be miserable.

BO   *(To himself)*   I—I jest can't believe it!

VIRGIL   *What* can't ya believe?

BO *(Now he becomes embarrassed)*   Oh . . . nothin'.

VIRGIL   If ya got anything on your chest, Bo, it's best to get it off.

BO   Well, I . . . I just never realized . . . a gal might not . . . love me.

CURTAIN

ACT TWO

SCENE: *Only a few minutes have elapsed since the close of* ACT ONE. *Our characters now are patiently trying to pass the time as best they can.* VIRGIL *has taken out his guitar and, after tuning it, begun to play a soft, melancholy cowboy ballad. He keeps his music an almost unnoticeable part of the background.* BO *lingers in the corner up right, a picture of troubled dejection.* CHERIE *has found a movie magazine, which she sets on one of the tables and reads.* DR. LYMAN *continues sitting at the bar, sipping his drink and courting* ELMA, *although* ELMA *does not realize she is being courted. She is immensely entertained by him.*

ELMA   . . . And where else did you teach?

DR. LYMAN   My last position was at one of those revolting little progressive colleges in the East, where they offer a curriculum of what they call *functional* education. Educators, I am sure, have despaired of ever teaching students *anything*, so they have decided the second-best thing to do is to *understand* them. Every day there would be a meeting of everyone on the entire faculty, with whom the students ever came into any contact, from the President down to the chambermaids, and we would put our collective heads together to try to figure out why little Jane or little Mary was not getting out of her classes what she *should*. The suggestion that perhaps she wasn't studying was too simple, and if you implied that she simply did not have the brains for a college education, you were being undemocratic.

ELMA   You must have disapproved of that college.

DR. LYMAN   My dear girl, I have disapproved of my entire life.

ELMA   Really?

DR. LYMAN   Yes, but I suppose I couldn't resist living it over again.
(There is a touch of sadness about him now)

ELMA   Did you resign from that position?

DR. LYMAN   One day I decided I had had enough. I walked blithely into the Dean's office and said, "Sir! I graduated *magna cum laude* from the University of Chicago, I studied at Oxford on a Rhodes Scholarship, and returned to take my Ph.D. at Harvard, receiving it with highest honors. I think I have the right to expect my students to try to understand *me.*"

ELMA *(Very amused)*   What did he say?

DR. LYMAN   Oh, I didn't wait for a response. I walked out of the door and went to the railroad station, where I got a ticket for the farthest place I could think of, which happened to be Las Vegas. And I have been traveling ever since. It's a merry way to go to pot.
(He chuckles)

ELMA   I had thought *I* might teach one day, but you don't make it sound very attractive.

DR. LYMAN   Ah, suit yourself. Don't let me influence you one way or the other. (ELMA *smiles and* DR. LYMAN *gives in to the sudden compulsion of clasping her hand)* You're a lovely young girl.

ELMA *(Very surprised)*   Why . . . thank you, Dr. Lyman.

DR. LYMAN *(Clears his throat and makes a fresh approach)*   Did you tell me you plan to go to Topeka tomorrow?

ELMA *(Looking at clock)*   You mean *today.* Yes. I have a ticket to hear the Kansas City Symphony. They come to Topeka every year to give a concert.

DR. LYMAN *(Feeling his way)*   You say . . . you stay with your sister there?

ELMA   Yes, then I take an early morning bus back here, in time for school Monday. Then after school, I come here to work for Grace.

DR. LYMAN *(Obviously he is angling for something)*   Didn't you say there was a university in Topeka?

ELMA   Yes. Washburn University.

DR. LYMAN   Washburn University—of course! You know, it just occurs to me that I should stop there to check some references on a piece of research I'm engaged on.

ELMA   Oh, I've been to Washburn library lots of times.

DR. LYMAN   You have? *(He shows some cunning, but obviously* ELMA *does not see it)* Perhaps you would take me there!

ELMA *(Hesitant)* Well, I . . .

DR. LYMAN I'll arrive in Topeka before you do, then meet your bus . . .

ELMA If you really want me to.

DR. LYMAN You can take me to the library, then perhaps we could have dinner together, and perhaps you would permit me to take you to the symphony.

ELMA *(Overjoyed)* Are you serious?

DR. LYMAN Why, of course I'm serious. Why do you ask?

ELMA I don't know. Usually, older people are too busy to take notice of kids. I'd just love to.

DR. LYMAN Then I may depend on it that I have an engagement?

ELMA Yes. Oh, that'll be lots of fun. I can't wait.

DR. LYMAN But, my dear . . . let's not tell anyone of our plans, shall we?

ELMA Why not?

DR. LYMAN You see . . . I have been married, and I am somewhat older than you, though perhaps not quite as old as you might take me to be . . . anyway, people might not understand.

ELMA Oh!

DR. LYMAN So let's keep our plans to ourselves. Promise?

ELMA O.K. If you think best.

DR. LYMAN I think it best.
  (VIRGIL has finished playing a ballad and CHERIE applauds)

CHERIE That was real purty, Virgil.

VIRGIL Thank ya, miss.
  (From his corner, BO has seen the moment's intimacy between them. He winces. CHERIE goes over to the counter and speaks to ELMA)

CHERIE Isn't there some other way of me gettin' back to Kanz City?

ELMA I'm sorry. The bus comes through here from Topeka, and it can't get through, either, until the road's cleared.

CHERIE I was jest gettin' sorta restless.
  (She sits at center table and lights a cigarette. Suddenly, the front door swings open and WILL appears, carrying a thermos jug)

WILL *(Crossing to counter)*   Elma, fill this up for me, like a good girl.

ELMA   Sure, Will.
(Takes thermos from him and starts to fill it at urn)

WILL   I'm goin' down the highway a bit to see how the men are gettin' on. Thought they'd enjoy some hot coffee.

ELMA   Good idea, Will.

WILL *(With a look around)*   Everyone behavin'?

ELMA   Of course.

WILL *(Puzzled)*   Grace not down yet?

ELMA   No.

WILL   I didn't see Carl any place outside. Suppose somethin' coulda happened to him?

ELMA   I wouldn't worry about him, Will.

WILL   I s'pose he can take care of himself. (ELMA *hands him thermos)* Thank you, Elma. *(He pays her, then starts back out, saying for the benefit primarily of* BO *and* DR. LYMAN) Oh, Elma. If anyone should be wantin' me, I won't be gone very long.
(He looks around to make sure everyone has heard him, then goes out. BO *has heard and seen him, and suddenly turns from his corner and comes angrily down to* VIRGIL)

BO   That dang sheriff! If it wasn't fer *him,* I'd git Cherry now and . . . I . . .

VIRGIL   Where would ya take her, Bo?

BO   There's a justice a the peace down the street. You can see his sign from the window.

VIRGIL   Bo, ya cain't *force* a gal to marry ya. Ya jest cain't do it. That sheriff's a stern man and he'd shoot ya in a minute if he saw it was his duty. Now, why don't ya go over to the counter and have yourself a drink . . . like the perfessor?

BO   I never did drink and I ain't gonna let no woman drive me to it.

VIRGIL   Ya don't drink. Ya don't smoke or chew. Ya oughta have *some* bad habits to rely on when things with women go wrong.
(BO thinks for a moment then sits opposite VIRGE)

BO   Virge. I hate to sound like some pitiable weaklin' of a man, but there's been times the last few months, I been so lonesome, I . . . I jest didn't know what t'do with m'self.

VIRGIL   It's no disgrace to feel that way, Bo.

BO   How 'bout you, Virge? Don't you ever git lonesome, too?

VIRGIL   A long time ago, I gave up romancin' and decided I was just gonna take bein' lonesome for granted.

BO   I wish I could do that, but I cain't.
(They now sit in silence. CHERIE, at the counter, lifts her damp eyes to ELMA, seeking a confidante)

CHERIE   Mebbe I'm a sap.

ELMA   Why do you say that?

CHERIE   I dunno why I *don't* go off to Montana and marry him. I might be a lot better off'n I am now.

ELMA   He says he *loves* you.

CHERIE   He dunno what love is.

ELMA   What makes you say that?

CHERIE   All he wants is a girl to throw his arms around and hug and kiss, that's all. The resta the time, he don't even know I exist.

ELMA   What made you decide to marry him in the first place?

CHERIE   *(Giving ELMA a wise look)*   Ya ain't very experienced, are ya?

ELMA   I guess not.

CHERIE   I never *did* decide to marry him. Everything was goin' fine till he brought up *that* subjeck. Bo come in one night when I was singin' "That Ole Black Magic." It's one a my best numbers. And he liked it so much, he jumped up on a chair and yelled like a Indian, and put his fingers in his mouth and whistled like a steam engine. Natur'ly, it made me feel good. Most a the customers at the Blue Dragon was too drunk to pay any attention to my songs.

ELMA   And you liked him?

CHERIE   Well . . . I thought he was awful *cute*.
(She shows a mischievous smile)

ELMA   I think he looks a little like Burt Lancaster, don't you?

CHERIE Mebbe. Anyway . . . I'd never seen a cowboy before. Oh, I'd seen 'em in movies, a course, but never in the *flesh* . . . Anyway, he's so darn healthy-lookin', I don't mind admittin', I was attracted, right from the start.

ELMA You were?

CHERIE But it was only what ya might call a *sexual* attraction.

ELMA Oh!

CHERIE The very next mornin', he wakes up and hollers, "Yippee! We're gettin' married." I honestly thought he was crazy. But when I tried to reason with him, he wouldn't listen to a word. He stayed by my side all day long, like a shadow. At night, a course, he had to go back to the rodeo, but he was back to the Blue Dragon as soon as the rodeo was over, in time fer the midnight show. If any other fella claimed t'have a date with me, Bo'd beat him up.

ELMA And you never told him you'd marry him?

CHERIE No! He kep tellin' me all week, he and Virge'd be by the night the rodeo ended, and they'd pick me up and we'd all start back to Montana t'gether. I knew that if I was around the Blue Dragon that night, that's what'd happen. So I decided to beat it. One a the other girls at the Blue Dragon lived on a farm 'cross the river in Kansas. She said I could stay with her. So I went to the Blue Dragon last night and just sang fer the first show. Then I told 'em I was quittin' . . . I'd been wantin' to find another job anyway . . . and I picked up my share of the kitty . . . but darn it, I had to go and tell 'em I was takin' the midnight bus. They had to go and tell Bo, a course, when he come in a li'l after eleven. He paid 'em five dollars to find out. So I went down to the bus station and hadn't even got my ticket, when here come Bo and Virge. He just steps up to the ticket window and says, "Three tickets to Montana!" I din know what to say. Then he dragged me onto the bus and I been on it ever since. And somewhere deep down inside me, I gotta funny feelin' I'm gonna end up in Montana.
(She sits now in troubled contemplation as ELMA *resumes her work. On the other side of the stage,* BO, *after a period of gestation, begins to question* VIRGIL)

BO Tell me somethin', Virge. We been t'gether since my folks died, and I allus wondered if mebbe I din spoil yer chances a settlin' down.

VIRGIL *(Laughs)* No, you never, Bo. I used to tell myself ya did, but I just wanted an excuse.

BO   But you been lookin' after me since I was ten.

VIRGIL   I coulda married up, too.

BO   Was ya ever in love?

VIRGIL   Oncet. B'fore I went to work on your daddy's ranch.

BO   What happened?

VIRGIL   Nuthin'.

BO   Ya ask her to marry ya?

VIRGIL   Nope.

BO   Why not?

VIRGIL   Well . . . there comes a time in every fella's life, Bo, when he's gotta give up his own ways . . .

BO   How ya mean?

VIRGIL   Well, I was allus kinda uncomfortable around this gal, 'cause she was sweet and kinda refined. I was allus scared I'd say or do somethin' wrong.

BO   I know how ya mean.

VIRGIL   It was cowardly of me, I s'pose, but ev'ry time I'd get back from courtin' her, and come back to the bunkhouse where my buddies was sittin' around talkin', or playin' cards, or listenin' to music, I'd jest relax and feel m'self so much at home, I din wanta give it up.

BO   Yah! Gals can scare a fella.

VIRGIL   Now I'm kinda ashamed.

BO   Y'are?

VIRGIL   Yes I am, Bo. A fella can't live his whole life dependin' on buddies. (BO *takes another reflective pause, then asks directly*)

BO   Why don't she like me, Virge?

VIRGIL   *(Hesitant)* Well . . .

BO   Tell me the truth.

VIRGIL   Mebbe ya don't go about it right.

BO   What do I do wrong?

VIRGIL   Sometimes ya sound a li'l bullheaded and mean.

BO   I do?

VIRGIL   Yah.

BO   How's a fella s'posed to act?

VIRGIL   I'm no authority, Bo, but it seems t'me you should be a little more gallant.

BO   Gall—? Gallant? I'm as gallant as I know how to be. You hear the way Hank and Orville talk at the ranch, when they get back from sojournin' in town, 'bout their women.

VIRGIL   They like to brag, Bo. Ya caint b'lieve ev'rything Hank and Orville say.

BO   Is there any reason a gal wouldn't go fer *me*, soon as she would fer Hank or Orville?

VIRGIL   They're a li'l older'n you. They learned a li'l more. They can be *gallant* with gals . . . when they *wanta* be.

BO   I ain't gonna *pertend*.

VIRGIL   I caint blame ya.

BO   But a gal *oughta* like me. I kin read and write, I'm kinda tidy, and I got good manners, don't I?

VIRGIL   I'm no judge, Bo. I'm used to ya.

BO   And I'm tall and strong. Ain't that what girls like? And if I do say so, m'self, I'm purty good-lookin'.

VIRGIL   Yah.

BO   When I get spruced up, I'm just as good-lookin' a fella as a gal might hope to see.

VIRGIL   I know ya are, Bo.

BO   (*Suddenly seized with anger at the injustice of it all*)   Then hellfire and damnation! Why don't she go back to the ranch with me?
(*His hands in his hip pockets, he begins pacing, returning to his corner like a panther, where he stands with his back to the others, watching the snow fly outside the window*)

ELMA (*Having observed* BO's *disquiet*)   Gee, if you only loved him!

CHERIE That'd solve ev'rything, wouldn't it? But I don't. So I jest can't see
m'self goin' to some God-forsaken ranch in Montana where I'd never see
no one but him and a lotta cows.

ELMA No. If you don't love him, it'd be awfully lonely.

CHERIE I dunno why I keep expectin' m'self to fall in love with someone,
but I do.

ELMA I know *I* expect to, some day.

CHERIE I'm beginnin' to seriously wonder if there *is* the kinda love I have
in mind.

ELMA What's that?

CHERIE Well . . . I dunno. I'm oney nineteen, but I been goin' with guys
since I was fourteen.

ELMA *(Astounded)* Honest?

CHERIE Honey, I almost married a cousin a mine when I was fourteen, but
Pappy wouldn't have it.

ELMA I never heard of anyone marrying so young.

CHERIE Down in the Ozarks, we don't waste much time. Anyway, I'm
awful glad I never married my cousin Malcolm, 'cause he turned out real
bad, like Pappy predicted. But I sure was crazy 'bout him at the time.
And I been losin' my head 'bout some guy ever since. But Bo's the first
one wanted to marry me, since Cousin Malcolm. And natur'ly, I'd like to
get married and raise a fam'ly and all them things, but . . .

ELMA But you've *never* been in love?

CHERIE Mebbe I have and din know it. Thass what I mean. Mebbe I don't
know what love is. Mebbe I'm expectin' it t'be somethin' it ain't. I jest
feel that, regardless how crazy ya are 'bout some guy, ya gotta feel . . .
and it's hard to put into words, but . . . ya gotta feel he *respects* ya.
Yah, thass what I means.

ELMA *(Not impudent)* I should think so.

CHERIE I want a guy I can look up to and respect, but I don't want one
that'll browbeat me. And I want a guy who can be sweet to me but I
don't wanta be treated like a baby. I . . . I just gotta feel that . . .
whoever I marry . . . has some real regard for me, apart from all the
lovin' and sex. Know what I mean?

ELMA *(Busily digesting all this)*   I think so. What are you going to do when you get back to Kansas City?

CHERIE   I dunno—There's a hillbilly program on one a the radio stations there. I might git a job on it. If I don't, I'll prob'ly git me a job in Liggett's or Walgreen's. Then after a while, I'll prob'ly marry some guy, whether I think I love him or not. Who'm *I* to keep insistin' I should fall in love? You hear all about love when yor a kid and jest take it for granted that such a thing really exists. Maybe ya have to find out fer yorself it don't. Maybe everyone's afraid to tell ya.

ELMA *(Glum)*   Maybe you're right . . . but I hope not.

CHERIE *(After squirming a little on the stool)*   Gee, I hate to go out to that cold powder room, but I guess I better not put it off any longer.
   (CHERIE *hurries out the rear door as* DR. LYMAN *sits again at the counter, having returned from the book shelves in time to overhear the last of* CHERIE'S *conversation. He muses for a few moments, gloomily, then speaks to* ELMA *out of his unconscious reflections)*

DR. LYMAN   How defiantly we pursue love, like it was an inheritance due, that we had to wrangle about with angry relatives in order to get our share.

ELMA   You shouldn't complain. You've had three wives.

DR. LYMAN   Don't shame me. I loved them all . . . with passion. *(An afterthought)* At least I *thought* I did . . . for a while.
   (He still chuckles about it as though it were a great irony)

ELMA   I'm sorry if I sounded sarcastic, Dr. Lyman. I didn't mean to be.

DR. LYMAN   Don't apologize. I'm too egotistical ever to take offense at anything people *say*.

ELMA   You're not egotistical at all.

DR. LYMAN   Oh, believe me. The greatest egos are those which are too egotistical to show just how egotistical they are.

ELMA   I'm sort of idealistic about things. I like to think that people fall in love and stay that way, forever and ever.

DR. LYMAN   Maybe we have lost the ability. Maybe Man has passed the stage in his evolution wherein love is possible. Maybe life will continue to become so terrifyingly complex that man's anxiety about his mere survival will render him too miserly to give of himself in any true relation.

ELMA You're talking over my head. Anyone can fall in love, I always thought . . . and . . .

DR. LYMAN   But two people, *really* in love, must give up something of themselves.

ELMA *(Trying to follow)*   Yes.

DR. LYMAN   That is the gift that men are afraid to make. Sometimes they keep it in their bosoms forever, where it withers and dies. Then they never know love, only its facsimiles, which they seek over and over again in meaningless repetition.

ELMA *(A little depressed)*   Gee! How did we get onto this subject?

DR. LYMAN *(Laughs heartily with sudden release, grabbing* ELMA'S *hand)*   Ah, my dear! Pay no attention to me, for whether there is such a thing as love, we can always . . . *(Lifts his drink)* . . . pretend there is. Let us talk instead of our forthcoming trip to Topeka. Will you wear your prettiest dress?

ELMA Of course. If it turns out to be a nice day, I'll wear a new dress Mother got me for spring. It's a soft rose color with a little lace collar.

DR. LYMAN   Ah, you'll look lovely, *lovely*. I know you will. I hope it doesn't embarrass you for me to speak these endearments . . .

ELMA No . . . it doesn't embarrass me.

DR. LYMAN   I'm glad. Just think of me as a fatherly old fool, will you? And not be troubled if I take such rapturous delight in your sweetness, and youth, and innocence? For these are qualities I seek to warm my heart as I seek a fire to warm my hands.

ELMA Now I *am* kind of embarrassed. I don't know what to say.

DR. LYMAN   Then say nothing, or nudge *me* and I'll talk endlessly about the most trivial matters.
(They laugh together as CHERIE *comes back in, shivering)*

CHERIE Brre, it's cold. Virgil, I wish you'd play us another song. I think we all need somethin' to cheer us up.

VIRGIL I'll make a deal with ya. I'll play if you'll sing.

ELMA *(A bright idea comes to her)*   Let's have a floor show! *(Her suggestion comes as a surprise and there is silence while all consider it)* Everyone here can do *something!*

DR. LYMAN   A brilliant idea, straight from Chaucer. You must read Juliet for me.

ELMA *(Not hearing* DR. LYMAN, *running to* VIRGIL)   Will you play for us, Virgil?

VIRGIL   I don't play opery music or jitterbug.

ELMA   Just play anything you want to play. *(To* BO) Will you take part? *(Stubbornly,* BO *just turns the other way)* Please! It won't be fun unless we all do something.

VIRGIL   G'wan, Bo.

BO   I never was no play-actor, miss.

VIRGIL   Ya kin say the Gettysburg Address.

BO *(Gruffly)*   I ain't gonna say it now.

VIRGIL   Then why don't ya do your rope tricks? Yer rope's out on the bus. I could get it for ya easy enough.

ELMA   Oh, please! Rope tricks would be lots of fun.

BO *(Emphatically)*   No! I ain't gonna get up before a lotta strangers and make a fool a m'self.

VIRGIL *(To* ELMA)   I guess he means it, miss.

ELMA   Shucks!

VIRGIL *(Quietly to* BO)   I don't see why ya couldn't a cooperated a little, Bo.

BO   I got too much on my mind to worry about doin' stunts.

ELMA *(To* CHERIE)   You'll sing a song for us, won't you, Cherie?

CHERIE   I will fer a piece a pie and another cup a coffee.

ELMA   Sure.
(CHERIE *hurries to* VIRGIL)

CHERIE   Virgil, kin you play "That Ole Black Magic"?

VIRGIL   You start me out and I think I can pick out the chords.
(CHERIE *sits by his side as they work out their number together.* ELMA *hurries to* DR. LYMAN)

ELMA   And you'll read poetry for us, won't you?

DR. LYMAN *(Already assuming his character)* Why, I intend to play Romeo opposite your Juliet.

ELMA Gee, I don't know if I can remember the lines.

DR. LYMAN *(Handing her a volume he has taken off the shelves)* Sometimes one can find Shakespeare on these shelves among the many lurid novels of juvenile delinquents. Here it is, *Four Tragedies of Shakespeare,* with my compliments.
(They begin to go over the scene, together as BO, *resentful of the closeness between* CHERIE *and* VIRGIL, *goes to them belligerently)*

BO *(To* CHERIE*)* Thass *my* seat.

ELMA *(Taking book from* DR. LYMAN*)* If I read it over a few times, it'll come back. Do you know the Balcony Scene?

CHERIE *(Jumping to her feet)* You kin have it.
(Hurries to ELMA, *at counter)*

DR. LYMAN My dear, I know the entire play by heart. I can recite it backwards.

CHERIE *(To* ELMA*)* I got a costume with me. Where can I change?

ELMA Behind the counter. There's a mirror over the sink.
*(*CHERIE *darts behind the counter, digging into her suitcase)*

BO *(To* VIRGIL*)* She shines up to *you* like a kitten to milk.

ELMA Gee, costumes and everything.
(She resumes her study with DR. LYMAN*)*

VIRGIL *(Trying to make a joke of it)* Kin *I* help it if I'm so darn attractive to women? *(Unfortunately* BO *cannot take this as a joke, as* VIRGIL *intended.* VIRGIL *perceives he is deeply hurt)* Shucks, Bo, it don't mean nothin'.

BO Maybe it don't mean nothin' to *you.*

VIRGIL She was bein' nice to me cause I was playin' my guitar, Bo. Guitar music's kinda tender and girls seem to like it.

BO Tender?

VIRGIL Yah, Bo! Girls like things t'be *tender.*

BO They do!

VIRGIL Sure they do, Bo.

BO   A fella gets "tender," then someone comes along and makes a sap outa him.

VIRGIL   Sometimes, Bo, but not always. You just gotta take a chance.

BO   Well . . . I allus tried t'be a *decent* sorta fella, but I don't know if I'm *tender*.

VIRGIL   I think ya are, Bo. You know how ya feel about deer huntin'. Ya never could do it. Ya couldn't any more *shoot* one a them sweet li'l deers with the sad eyes than ya could jump into boilin' oil.

BO   Are you makin' fun of me?

VIRGIL   *(Impatient with him)*   No, I'm not makin' fun of ya, Bo. I'm just tryin' to show ya that *you* got a tender side to your nature, same as anyone else.

BO   I s'pose I do.

VIRGIL   A course ya do.

BO   *(With a sudden feeling of injustice)*   Then how come Cherry don't come over and talk sweet to *me*, like she does to *you*?

VIRGIL   Ya *got* a tender side, Bo, but ya don't know how to *show* it.

BO   *(Weighing the verdict)*   I don't!

VIRGIL   No, ya just don't know how.

BO   How does a person go about showin' his tender side, Virge?

VIRGIL   Well . . . I dunno as I can tell ya.
      (ELMA *comes over to them ready to start the show*)

ELMA   Will you go first, Virgil?

VIRGIL   It's all right by me.

ELMA   O.K. Then I'll act as Master of the Ceremonies. *(Centerstage, to her audience)* Ladies and Gentlemen! Grace's Diner tonight presents its gala floor show of celebrated artists from all over the world! (VIRGIL *plays an introductory chord*) The first number on our show tonight is that musical cowboy, Mr. Virgil—*(She pauses and* VIRGIL *supplies her with his last name)*—Virgil Blessing, who will entertain you with his guitar.
      (*Applause.* ELMA *retires to the back of the room with* DR. LYMAN. VIRGIL *begins to play. During his playing,* BO *is drawn over to the counter, where he tries to further himself with* CHERIE, *who is behind the counter, dressing*)

BO *(Innocently)*   I think you got me all wrong, Cherry.

CHERIE   Don't you come back here. I'm dressing.

BO   Cherry . . . I think you misjudged me.

CHERIE   Be quiet. The show's started.

BO   Cherry, I'm really a very *tender* person. You jest don't know. I'm so tender-hearted I don't go deer huntin'. 'Cause I jest couldn't kill them "sweet li'l deers with the sad eyes." Ask Virge.

CHERIE   I ain't int'rested.

BO   Ya ain't?

CHERIE   No. And furthermore I think you're a louse fer comin' over here and talkin' while yor friend is tryin' to play the guitar.

BO   Ya talk like ya thought more a Virge than ya do a me.

CHERIE   Would ya go away and lemme alone?

BO *(A final resort)*   Cherry, did I tell ya 'bout my color-television set with the twenty-four-inch screen?

CHERIE   One million times! Now go 'way.
   (ELMA *begins to make a shushing noise to quiet* BO. *Finally* BO *dejectedly returns to the other side of the room, where* VIRGIL *is just finishing his number.* BO *sits down in the midst of* VIRGIL'S *applause*)

CHERIE   That was wonderful, Virge!

DR. LYMAN   Brilliant!   *(Together)*

ELMA   Swell! Play us another!

VIRGIL   No more just now. I'm ready to see the rest of ya do somethin'.

BO *(To* VIRGIL)   A lot *she* cares how tender I am!

ELMA *(Coming forth again as Master of Ceremonies)*   That was swell, Virgil. *(Turns back to* DR. LYMAN)   Are you ready?

DR. LYMAN *(Preening himself)*   I consider myself so.

ELMA *(Taking the book to* VIRGIL)   Will you be our prompter?

VIRGIL   It's kinda funny writin', but I'll try.

ELMA *(Back to* DR. LYMAN)   Gee, what'll we use for a balcony?

DR. LYMAN   That offers a problem.

(Together they consider whether to use the counter for ELMA *to stand on or one of the tables)*

BO *(To* VIRGIL) What is it these folks are gonna do, Virge?

VIRGIL *Romeo and Juliet* . . . by Shakespeare!

BO Shakespeare!

VIRGIL This Romeo was a great lover, Bo. Watch him and pick up a few pointers.
*(*CHERIE *comes running out from behind the counter now, a dressing gown over her costume, and she sits at one of the tables)*

CHERIE I'm ready.

BO *(Reading some of the lines from* VIRGIL'S *book)* "But, soft . . . what light through . . . yonder window breaks? It is the east . . . and Juliet is the sun . . . Arise, fair . . ."
(He has got this far only with difficulty, stumbling over most of the words. VIRGIL *takes the book away from him now)*

VIRGIL Shh, Bo!
*(*ELMA *comes forth to introduce the act)*

ELMA Ladies and gentlemen! you are about to witness a playing of the Balcony Scene from *Romeo and Juliet*. Dr. Gerald Lyman will portray the part of Romeo, and I'll play Juliet. My name is Elma Duckworth. The scene is the orchard of the Capulets' house in Verona, Italy. This table is supposed to be a balcony. (DR. LYMAN *helps her onto the table, where she stands, waiting for him to begin)* O.K.? (DR. LYMAN *takes a quick reassuring drink from his bottle, then tucks it in his pocket, and comes forward in the great Romantic tradition. He is enjoying himself tremendously. The performance proves to be pure ham, but there is pathos in the fact that he does not seem to be aware of how bad he is. He is a thoroughly selfish performer, too, who reads all his speeches as though they were grand soliloquies, regarding his Juliet as a prop)*

DR. LYMAN
"He jests at scars, that never felt a wound.
But, soft! what light through yonder window breaks?
It is the east, and Juliet is the sun!
(He tries to continue, but ELMA, *unmindful of cues and eager to begin her performance, reads her lines with compulsion)*
Arise . . . fair sun, and . . . kill the envious. . . ."

ELMA *(At same time as* DR. LYMAN)

"O Romeo, Romeo! wherefore art thou, Romeo?
Deny thy father and refuse thy name:
Or if thou wilt not, be but sworn my love,
And I'll no longer be a Capulet."

DR. LYMAN

"She speaks, yet she says nothing: what of that?
Her eye discourses; I will answer it.
I am too bold—"

BO *(To* VIRGIL)   Bold? He's drunk.

VIRGIL   Ssssh!

DR. LYMAN

". . . 'tis not to me she speaks:
Two of the fairest stars in all the heaven,
Having some business, do entreat her eyes
To twinkle in their spheres till they return."

ELMA

"Ay me!"

DR. LYMAN

"O! speak again, bright angel; for thou art
As glorious to this night, being o'er my head,
As is a winged messenger of heaven
Unto the white-upturned . . ."

(DR. LYMAN *continues with this speech, even though* BO *talks over him.*)

BO   I don't understand all them words, Virge.

VIRGIL   It's *Romeo and Juliet,* for God's sake. Now will you shut up?

DR. LYMAN *(Continuing uninterrupted)*

". . . wondering eyes
Of mortals, that fall back to gaze on him
When he bestrides the lazy-pacing clouds,
And sails upon the bosom of the air."

(He is getting weary but he is not yet ready to give up)

ELMA

" 'Tis but thy name that is my enemy;
Thou art thyself though, not a Montague.
What's Montague? it is nor hand, nor foot,
Nor arm, nor face, nor any other part

Belonging to a man. O! be some other name:
What's—"

DR. LYMAN *(Interrupts. Beginning to falter now)*
"I take thee at thy word.
Call me but love, and . . . I'll be new baptiz'd;
Henceforth . . . I never . . . will be Romeo."
(It is as though he were finding suddenly a personal meaning in the lines)

ELMA
"What man art thou, that, thus bescreen'd in night,
So stumblest on my counsel?"

DR. LYMAN *(Beginning to feel that he cannot continue)*
"By a name
I know not how to tell thee . . . who I am:
My name, dear saint, is . . . is *hateful* to myself."
(He stops here. For several moments there is a wondering silence. ELMA
signals VIRGIL*)*

VIRGIL *(Prompting)*
"Because it is an enemy to thee."

DR. LYMAN *(Leaving the scene of action, repeating the line dumbly, making his
way stumblingly back to the counter)*
"My name . . . is hateful . . . to myself . . ."
*(*ELMA *hurries to* DR. LYMAN'S *side.* VIRGIL *grabs hold of* BO, *pulls him back to
the floor and shames him)*

ELMA   Dr. Lyman, what's the matter?

DR. LYMAN   My dear . . . let us not continue this meaningless little act!

ELMA   Did I do something wrong?

DR. LYMAN   You couldn't possibly do anything wrong . . . if you tried.

ELMA   I can try to say the lines differently.

DR. LYMAN   Don't. Don't. Just tell your audience that Romeo suddenly is
fraught with remorse.
(He drops to a stool, ELMA *remaining by him a few moments, uncertainly.*
BO *turns to* VIRGIL*)*

BO   Virge, if thass the way to make love . . . I'm gonna give up.

ELMA *(To* VIRGIL*)*   I'm afraid he isn't feeling well.

VIRGIL *(To* ELMA*)*   I tried to prompt him.

ELMA *(To herself)*   Well, we've only got one more number. *(To* CHERIE*)* Are you ready?

CHERIE   Sure.

ELMA   Ladies and gentlemen, our next number is Mademoisell Cherie, the international *chanteuse,* direct from the Blue Dragon night club in Kansas City, *Cherie!*
(All applaud as CHERIE *comes forth,* VIRGIL *playing an introduction for her.* BO *puts his fingers through his teeth and whistles for her)*

CHERIE *(Takes off her robe, whispering to* ELMA*)*   Remember, I don't allow no table service during my numbers.

ELMA   O.K.
(In the background now, we can observe that DR. LYMAN *is drinking heavily from the bottle in his overcoat pocket.* CHERIE *gets up on one of the tables and begins singing "That Old Black Magic" with a chord accompaniment from* VIRGIL. *Her rendition of the song is a most dramatic one, that would seem to have been created from* CHERIE'S *observations of numerous torch singers. But she has appeal, and if she is funny, she doesn't seem to know it. Anyway, she rekindles* BO'S *most fervent love, which he cannot help expressing during her performance)*

BO *(About the middle of the song)*   Ain't she beautiful, Virge?

VIRGIL *(Trying to keep his mind on his playing)*   Shh, Bo!

BO   I'm gonna git her, Virge.

VIRGIL   Ssshh!

BO *(Pause. He pays no attention to anyone)*   I made up my mind. I told myself I was gonna git me a gal. Thass the only reason I entered that rodeo, and I ain't takin' no fer an answer.

VIRGIL   Bo, will you hush up and lemme be!

BO   Anything I ever wanted in this life I went out and got, and I ain't gonna stop now. I'm gonna git her.
*(*CHERIE *is enraged. She jumps down from her table and slaps* BO *stingingly on the face)*

CHERIE   You ain't got the manners God gave a monkey.

BO *(Stunned)*   Cherry!

CHERIE . . . and if I was a man, I'd beat the livin' daylights out of ya, and thass what some man's gonna do some day, and when it happens, I hope I'm there to *see*.
(She flounces back to her dressing room, as BO *gapes. By this time* DR. LYMAN *has drunk himself almost to insensibility, and we see him weaving back and forth on his stool, mumbling almost incoherently)*

DR. LYMAN "Romeo . . . Romeo . . . wherefore art thou? Wherefore art thou . . . Romeo?"
(He laughs like a loon, falls off the stool and collapses on the floor. ELMA *and* VIRGIL *rush to him.* BO *remains rooted, glaring at* CHERIE *with puzzled hurt)*

ELMA *(Deeply concerned)* Dr. Lyman! Dr. Lyman!

VIRGIL The man's in a purty bad way. Let's get him on the bench.
*(*ELMA *and* VIRGIL *manage to get* DR. LYMAN *to his feet as* BO *glides across the room, scales the counter in a leap and takes* CHERIE *in his arms)*

BO I was tellin' Virge I love ya. Ya got no right to come over and slap me.

CHERIE *(Twisting)* Lemme be.

BO *(Picking her up)* We're goin' down and wake up the justice of the peace and you're gonna marry me t'night.

CHERIE *(As he takes her in his arms and transports her to the door, just as* ELMA *and* VIRGIL *are helping* DR. LYMAN *onto the bench)* Help! Virgil, help!

BO Shut up! I'll make ya a good husband. Ya won't never have nothin' to be sorry about.

CHERIE *(As she is carried to the door)* Help! Sheriff! Help me, someone! Help me!
(The action is now like that of a two-ringed circus for ELMA *and* VIRGIL, *whose attention suddenly is diverted from the plight of* DR. LYMAN *to the much noisier plight of* CHERIE. BO *gets her, kicking and protesting, as far as the front door when it suddenly opens and* BO *finds himself confronted by* WILL)

WILL Put her down, cowboy!

BO *(Trying to forge ahead)* Git outta my way.

WILL *(Shoving* BO *back as* CHERIE *manages to jump loose from his arms)* Yor gonna do as I say.

BO I ain't gonna have no one interferin' in my ways.

(He makes an immediate lunge at WILL, *which* WILL *is prepared for, coming up with a fist that sends* BO *back reeling)*

VIRGIL *(Hurrying to* BO's *side)* Bo, ya cain't do this, Bo. Ya cain't pick a fight with the sheriff.

BO *(Slowly getting back to his feet)* By God, mister, there ain't no man ever got the best a me, and there ain't no man ever gonna.

WILL I'm ready and willin' to try, cowboy. Come on.
*(*BO *lunges at him again.* WILL *steps aside and lets* BO *send his blow into the empty doorway as he propels himself through it, outside. Then* WILL *follows him out, where the fight continues.* VIRGIL *immediately follows them, as* ELMA *and* CHERIE *hurry to the window to watch)*

CHERIE I knowed this was gonna happen. I knowed it all along.

ELMA Gee! I'd better call Grace.
(Starts for the rear door but GRACE *comes through it before she gets there.* GRACE *happens to be wearing a dressing gown)*

GRACE Hey, what the hell's goin' on?

ELMA Oh, Grace, they're fighting. Honest! It all happened so suddenly, I . . .

GRACE *(Hurrying to window)* Let's see.

CHERIE *(Leaving the window, not wanting to see any more, going to a chair by one of the tables)* Gee, I never wanted to cause so much trouble t'anyone.

GRACE Wow! Looks like Will's gettin' the best of him.

ELMA *(At the window, frightened by what she sees)* Oh!

GRACE Yap, I'll put my money on Will Masters *any* time. Will's got it up here. *(Points to her head)* Lookit that cowboy. He's green. He just swings out wild.

ELMA *(Leaving the window)* I . . . I don't want to watch any more.

GRACE *(A real fight fan, she reports from the window)* God, I love a good fight. C'mon Will—c'mon, Will—give him the old uppercut. That'll do it every time. Oh, oh, what'd I tell you, the cowboy's down. Will's puttin' handcuffs on him now.
*(*CHERIE *sobs softly.* ELMA *goes to her)*

ELMA Will'll give him first aid. He always does.

CHERIE Well . . . you gotta admit. He had it comin'.

GRACE (*Leaving the window now*) I'm glad they got it settled outside. (*Looks around to see if anything needs to be straightened up*) Remember the last time there was a fight in here, I had to put in a new window. (*She goes back up to her apartment, and we become aware once more of* DR. LYMAN, *who gets up from the bench and weaves his way center*)

DR. LYMAN It takes strong men and women to *love* . . . (*About to fall, he grabs the back of a chair for support*) People strong enough inside themselves to love . . . without humiliation. (*He sighs heavily and looks about him with blurred eyes*) People big enough to *grow* with their love and live inside a whole, wide new dimension. People brave enough to bear the responsibility of *being* loved and not fear it as a burden. (*He sighs again and looks about him wearily*) I . . . I never had the generosity to love, to give my own most private self to another, for I was *weak*. I thought the gift would somehow lessen *me*. Me! (*He laughs wildly and starts for the rear door*) Romeo! Romeo! I am disgusting! (ELMA *hurries after him, stopping him at the door*)

ELMA Dr. Lyman! Dr. Lyman!

DR. LYMAN Don't bother, dear girl. Don't ever bother with a foolish old man like me.

ELMA You're not a foolish old man. I like you more than anyone I've ever known.

DR. LYMAN I'm flattered, my dear, and pleased, but you're young. In a few years, you will turn . . . from a girl into a woman; a kind, thoughtful, loving, intelligent woman . . . who could only pity me. For I'm a child, a drunken, unruly child, and I've nothing in my heart for a true woman. (GRACE *returns in time to observe the rest of the scene. She is dressed now*)

ELMA Let me get you something to make you feel better.

DR. LYMAN No . . . no . . . I shall seek the icy comfort of the rest room. (*He rushes out the rear door*)

GRACE (*Feeling concern for* ELMA) Elma, honey, what's the matter? What was he sayin' to you, Elma? (*Goes to her and they have a quiet talk between themselves as the action continues.* GRACE *is quite motherly at these times. Now* VIRGIL *comes hurrying through the front door, going to* CHERIE.)

VIRGIL Miss, would ya help us? The sheriff says if you don't hold charges against Bo, he'll let him out to get back on the bus, if it ever goes.

CHERIE   So he can come back here and start maulin' me again?

VIRGIL   He won't do that no more, miss. I promise.

CHERIE   *You promise!* How 'bout him?

VIRGIL   I think you can trust him now.

CHERIE   Thass what I thought before. Nothin' doin'. He grabs ahold of a woman and kisses her . . . like he was Napoleon.

VIRGIL   *(Coming very close, to speak as intimately as possible)*   Miss . . . if he was to know I told ya this, he'd never forgive me, but . . . yor the first woman he ever made love to at all.

CHERIE   Hah! I sure don't b'lieve that.

VIRGIL   It's true, miss. He's allus been as shy as a rabbit.

CHERIE   *(In simple amazement)*   My God!

GRACE   *(To ELMA)*   Just take my advice and don't meet him in Topeka or anywhere else.

ELMA   I won't, Grace, but honest! I don't think he meant any harm. He just drinks a little too much. (DR. LYMAN *returns now through the rear door.* ELMA *hurries to him)* Dr. Lyman, are you all right?

DR. LYMAN   *(On his way to the bench)*   I'm an old man, my dear. I feel very weary.
(He stretches out on the bench, lying on his stomach. He goes almost immediately to sleep. ELMA *finds an old jacket and spreads it over his shoulders like a blanket. There is a long silence.* ELMA *sits by* DR. LYMAN *attentively.* CHERIE *is very preoccupied)*

GRACE   Let him sleep it off. It's all you can do.
(Now CARL *comes in the rear door. There is a look of impatient disgust on his face, as though he had just witnessed some revolting insult. He casts a suspicious look at* DR. LYMAN, *now oblivious to everything, and turns to* GRACE)

CARL   Grace, fer Christ sake! who puked all over the backhouse?

GRACE   Oh, God!
*(DR. LYMAN *snores serenely)*

CHERIE   *(Jumps up suddenly and grabs* VIRGIL'S *jacket off hook)*   Come on, Virge. Let's go.

VIRGIL   *(Enthused)*   I'm awful glad you're gonna help him, miss.

CHERIE   But if you're tellin' me a fib just to get him out of jail, I'll never forgive ya.

VIRGIL   It's no fib, miss. You're the first gal he ever made love to at all.

CHERIE   Well, I sure ain't never had that honor before.
(They hurry out together)

CURTAIN

SCENE: *By this time, it is early morning, about five o'clock. The storm has cleared, and outside the window we see the slow dawning, creeping above the distant hills, revealing a landscape all in peaceful white.*

BO, CHERIE and VIRGIL are back now from the sheriff's office. BO has returned to his corner, where he sits as before, with his back to the others, his head low. We can detect, if we study him, that one eye is blackened and one of his hands is bandaged. VIRGIL sits close to him like an attendant. DR. LYMAN is still asleep on one of the benches, snoring loudly. CHERIE tries to sleep at one of the tables. ELMA is clearing the tables and sweeping. The only animated people right now are CARL and GRACE. CARL is at the telephone, trying to get the operator, and GRACE is behind the counter.

CARL (*After jiggling the receiver*) Still dead.

(*He hangs up*)

GRACE (*Yawns*) I'll be glad when you all get out and I can go to bed. I'm tired.

CARL (*Returning to counter, he sounds a trifle insinuating*) Had enough a me, baby? (GRACE *gives him a look, warning him not to let* ELMA *overhear*) I'm kinda glad the highway was blocked tonight.

GRACE (*Coquettishly*) Y'are?

CARL Gave us a chance to become kinda acquainted, din it?

GRACE Kinda!

CARL Just pullin' in here three times a week, then pullin' out again in twenty minutes, I . . . I allus left . . . just wonderin' what you was like, Grace.

GRACE I always wondered about *you*, too, Carl!

CARL Ya did?

GRACE Yah. But ya needn't go blabbing anything to the other drivers.

CARL *(His honor offended)*   Why, what makes ya think I'd . . . ?

GRACE   Shoot! I know how you men talk when ya get t'gether. Worse'n women.

CARL   Well, not *me*, Grace.

GRACE   I certainly don't want the other drivers on this route, some of 'em especially, gettin' the idea I'm gonna serve 'em any more'n what they order over the counter.

CARL   Sure. I get ya. *(It occurs to him to feel flattered)* But ya . . . ya kinda *liked* me . . . din ya, Grace?

GRACE *(Coquettish again)*   Maybe I did.

CARL *(Trying to get more of a commitment out of her)*   Yah? Yah?

GRACE   Know what I first liked about ya, Carl? It was your hands. *(She takes one of his hands and plays with it)* I like a man with big hands.

CARL   You got *everything*, baby.
(For just a moment, one senses the animal heat in their fleeting attraction. Now WILL *comes stalking in through the front door, a man who is completely relaxed with the authority he possesses. He speaks to* GRACE*)*

WILL   One of the highway trucks just stopped by. They say it won't be very long now.

GRACE   I hope so.

WILL *(With a look around)*   Everything peaceful?

GRACE   Yes, Will.

WILL *(He studies* BO *for a moment, then goes to him)*   Cowboy, if yor holdin' any grudges against *me*, I think ya oughta ask yourself what you'd'a done in my *place*. I couldn't let ya carry off the li'l lady when she din wanta go, could I? *(*BO *has no answer. He just avoids* WILL'S *eyes. But* WILL *is determined to get an answer) Could* I?

BO   I don't feel like talkin', mister.

WILL   Well, I couldn't. And I think you might also remember that this li'l lady . . . *(*CHERIE *begins to stir)* if she wanted to . . . could press charges and get you sent to the penitentiary for violation of the Mann Act.

BO   The *what* act?

WILL   The Mann Act. You took a woman over the state line against her will.

VIRGIL   That'd be a serious charge, Bo.

BO   (*Stands facing* WILL)   I loved her.

WILL   That don't make any difference.

BO   A man's gotta right to the things he loves.

WILL   Not unless he deserves 'em, cowboy.

BO   I'm a hard-workin' man, I own me my own ranch, I got six thousand dollars in the bank.

WILL   A man don't deserve the things he loves, unless he kin be a little humble about gettin' em.

BO   I ain't gonna get down on my knees and *beg*.

WILL   Bein' humble ain't the same as bein' *wretched*. (BO *doesn't understand*) I had to learn that once, too, cowboy. I wasn't quite as old as you. I stole horses instead of women because you could *sell* horses. One day, I stole a horse off the wrong man, the Rev. Hezekiah Pearson. I never thought I'd get mine from any preacher, but he was very fair. Gave me every chance to put myself clear. But I wouldn't admit the horse was his. Finally, he did what he had to do. He thrashed me to within a inch of my life. I never forgot. 'Cause it was the first time in my life, I had to admit I was wrong. I was miserable. Finally, after a few days, I decided the only thing to do was to admit to the man how I felt. Then I felt different about the whole thing. I joined his church, and we was bosom pals till he died a few years ago. (*He turns to* VIRGIL) Has he done what I asked him to?

VIRGIL   Not yet, sheriff.

WILL   (*To* BO)   Why should ya be so scared?

BO   Who says I'm scared?

WILL   Ya gimme yor word, didn't ya?

BO   (*Somewhat resentful*)   I'm gonna do it, if ya'll jest gimme time.

WILL   But I warn ya, it ain't gonna do no good unless you really mean it.

BO   I'll mean it.

WILL   All right then. Go ahead.

(Slowly, reluctantly, BO *gets to his feet and awkwardly, like a guilty boy, makes his way over to the counter to* GRACE)

BO   Miss, I . . . I wanna apologize.

GRACE   What for?

BO   Fer causin' such a commotion.

GRACE   Ya needn't apologize to *me*, cowboy. I like a good fight. You're welcome at Grace's Diner *any* time. I mean *any* time.

BO *(With an appreciative grin)*   Thanks. *(Now he goes to* ELMA) I musta acted like a hoodlum. I apologize.

ELMA   Oh, that's all right.

BO   Thank ya, miss.

ELMA   I'm awfully sorry we never got to see your rope tricks.

BO   They ain't much. *(Pointing to the sleeping* DR. LYMAN) Have I gotta wake up the perfessor t'apologize t'him?

WILL   You can overlook the perfessor.
(He nods toward CHERIE, *whom* BO *dreads to confront, most of all. He starts toward her but doesn't get very far)*

BO   I cain't do it.

VIRGIL *(Disappointed)*   Aw, Bo!

BO   I jest cain't do it.

WILL   Why not?

BO   She'd have no respeck for me now. She saw me beat.

WILL   You gave me your promise. You owe that girl an apology, whether you got beat or not, and you're going to say it to her or I'm not lettin' you back on the bus.
(BO is in a dilemma. He wipes his brow)*

VIRGIL   G'wan, Bo. G'wan.

BO   Well . . . I . . . I'll try. *(He makes his way to her tortuously and finally gets out her name)* Cherry!

CHERIE   Yah?

BO Cherry . . . it wasn't right a me to treat ya the way I did, draggin' ya onto the bus, tryin' to make ya marry me whether ya wanted to or not. Ya think ya could ever forgive me?

CHERIE *(After some consideration)* I guess I been treated worse in my life.

BO *(Taking out his wallet)* Cherry . . . I *got* ya here and I think I oughta get ya back in good style. So . . . take this.
(He hands her a bill)

CHERIE Did the sheriff make you do this?

BO *(Angrily)* No, by God! He din say nothin' bout my givin' ya money.

WILL That's *his* idea, miss. But I think it's a good one.

CHERIE Ya don't have to gimme this much, Bo.

BO I want ya to have it.

CHERIE Thanks. I can sure use it.

BO And I . . . I wish ya good luck, Cherry . . . Honest I do.

CHERIE I wish you the same, Bo.

BO Well . . . I guess I said ev'rything that's to be said, so . . . so long.

CHERIE *(In a tiny voice)* So long.
(Awkward and embarrassed now, BO returns to his corner, and CHERIE sits back down at the table, full of wistful wonder)

WILL Now, that wasn't so bad, was it, son?

BO I'd ruther break in wild horses than have to do it again.
(WILL laughs heartily, then strolls over to the counter in a seemingly casual way)

WILL How's your headache, Grace?

GRACE Huh?

WILL A while back, you said you had a headache.

GRACE Oh, I feel fine now, Will.

WILL *(He looks at CARL)* You have a nice walk, Carl?

CARL Yah. Sure.

WILL Well, I think ya better go upstairs 'cause someone took your over-shoes and left 'em outside the door to Grace's apartment.

(WILL *laughs long and heartily, and* ELMA *cannot suppress a grin.* CARL *looks at his feet and realizes his oversight.* GRACE *is indignant*)

GRACE   Nosy old snoop!

WILL   I'll have me a cup of coffee, Grace, and one a these sweet rolls. (*He selects a roll from the glass dish on counter.*)

VIRGIL   Come on over to the counter now, Bo, and have a bite a breakfast.

BO   I ain't hungry, Virge.

VIRGIL   Maybe a cup a coffee?

BO   I couldn't get it down.

VIRGIL   Now what's the matter, Bo? Ya oughta feel purty good. The sheriff let ya go and . . .

BO   I might as well a stayed in the jail.

VIRGIL   Now, what kinda talk is that? The bus'll be leavin' purty soon and we'll be back at the ranch in a coupla days.

BO   I don't care if I never see that dang ranch again.

VIRGIL   Why, Bo, you worked half yor life earnin' the money to build it up.

BO   It's the lonesomest damn place I ever did see.

VIRGIL   Well . . . I never thought so.

BO   It'll be like goin' back to a graveyard.

VIRGIL   Bo . . . I heard Hank and Orville talkin' 'bout the new school-marm, lives over to the Stebbins'. They say she's a looker.

BO   I ain't int'rested in no schoolmarm.

VIRGIL   Give yourself time, Bo. Yor young. You'll find lotsa gals, gals that'll love *you,* too.

BO   I want Cherry. (*And for the first time we observe he is capable of tears*)

VIRGIL (*With a futile shrug of his shoulders*)   Aw—Bo—

BO (*Dismissing him*)   Go git yorself somethin' t'eat, Virge. (BO *remains in isolated gloom as* VIRGIL *makes his slow way to the counter. Suddenly the telephone rings.* GRACE *jumps to answer it*)

GRACE My God! the lines are up. *(Into the telephone)* Grace's Diner! *(Pause)* It is? *(Pause)* O.K. I'll tell him. *(Hangs up and turns to* CARL*)* Road's cleared now but you're gonna have to put on your chains 'cause the road's awful slick.

CARL God damn! *(Gets up and hustles into his overcoat, going center to make his announcement)* Road's clear, folks! Bus'll be ready to leave as soon as I get the chains on. That'll take about twenty minutes . . . *(Stops and looks back at them)* . . . unless someone wants to help me. *(Exits.* WILL *gets up from the counter)*

WILL I'll help ya, Carl.
(Exits. CHERIE *makes her way over to* BO*)*

CHERIE Bo?

BO Yah?

CHERIE I just wanted to tell ya somethin', Bo. It's kinda personal and kinda embarrassin', too, but . . . I ain't the kinda gal you thought I was.

BO What ya mean, Cherry?

CHERIE Well, I guess some people'd say I led a real wicked life. I guess I have.

BO What you tryin' to tell me?

CHERIE Well . . . I figgered since ya found me at the Blue Dragon, ya just took it fer granted I'd had other boy friends 'fore you.

BO Ya had?

CHERIE Yes, Bo. Quite a few.

BO Virge'd told me that, but I wouldn't b'lieve him.

CHERIE Well, it's true. So ya see . . . I ain't the kinda gal ya want at all. *(*BO *is noncommittal.* CHERIE *slips back to her table.* ELMA *makes her way to the bench to rouse* DR. LYMAN*)*

ELMA Dr. Lyman! Dr. Lyman!
(He comes to with a jump, staring out wildly about him)

DR. LYMAN Where am I? *(Recognizing* ELMA*)* Oh, it's *you.* *(A great smile appears)* Dear girl. What a sweet awakening!

ELMA How do you feel?

DR. LYMAN That's not a polite question. How long have I been asleep here?

ELMA Oh—a couple of hours.

DR. LYMAN Sometimes Nature blesses me with a total blackout. I seem to remember absolutely nothing after we started our performance. How were we?

ELMA Marvelous.

DR. LYMAN Oh, I'm glad. Now I'll have a cup of that coffee you were trying to force on me last night.

ELMA All right. Can I fix you something to eat?

DR. LYMAN No. Nothing to eat.
(He makes a face of repugnance)

ELMA Oh, Dr. Lyman, you *must* eat something. Really.

DR. LYMAN *Must* I?

ELMA Oh, yes! Please!

DR. LYMAN Very well, for your sweet sake, I'll have a couple of three-minute eggs, and some toast and orange juice. But I'm doing this for *you*, mind you. Just for you.
(ELMA slips behind the counter to begin his breakfast, as VIRGIL gets up from the counter and goes to BO)

VIRGIL I'll go help the driver with his chains, Bo. You stay here and take care a that hand.
(He goes out. BO finds his way again to CHERIE)

BO Cherry . . . would I be molestin' ya if I said somethin'?

CHERIE No . . .

BO Well . . . since you brought the subject up, you *are* the first gal I ever had anything to do with. *(There is a silence)* By God! I never thought I'd hear m'self sayin' that, but I said it.

CHERIE I never woulda guessed it, Bo.

BO Ya see . . . I'd lived all my life on a ranch . . . and I guess I din know much about women . . . 'cause they're *diff'rent* from men.

CHERIE Well, natur'ly.

BO Every time I got around one . . . I began to feel kinda scared . . . and I din know how t'act. It was aggravatin'.

CHERIE   Ya wasn't scared with *me*, Bo.

BO   When I come into that night club place, you was singin' . . . and you smiled at me while you was singin', and winked at me a coupla times. Remember?

CHERIE   Yah. I remember.

BO   Well, I guess I'm kinda green, but . . . no gal ever done that to me before, so I thought you was singin' yor songs just fer *me*.

CHERIE   Ya did kinda attrack me, Bo . . .

BO   Anyway, you was so purty, and ya seemed so kinda warm-hearted and sweet. I . . . I felt like I *could* love ya . . . and I did.

CHERIE   Bo—ya think you really did love me?

BO   Why, Cherry! I couldn't be *familiar* . . . with a gal I din love.
(CHERIE *is brought almost to tears. Neither she nor* BO *can find any more words for the moment, and drift away from each other back to their respective places.* CARL *comes back in, followed by* VIRGIL *and* WILL. CARL *has got his overshoes on now. He comes center again to make an announcement*)

CARL   Bus headed west! All aboard! Next stop, Topeka!
(*He rejoins* GRACE *at the counter and, taking a pencil from his pocket, begins making out his report.* WILL *speaks to* BO)

WILL   How ya feelin' now, cowboy?

BO   I ain't the happiest critter that was ever born.

WILL   Just 'cause ya ain't happy now don't mean ya ain't gonna be happy t'morrow. Feel like shakin' hands now, cowboy?

BO *(Hesitant)*   Well . . .

VIRGIL   Go on, Bo. He's only trying to be friends.

BO *(Offering his hand, still somewhat reluctantly)*   I don't mind.
(*They shake*)

WILL   I just want you to remember there's no hard feelin's. So long.

BO   S'long.

WILL   I'm goin' home now, Grace. See you Monday.

GRACE   S'long, Will.

CARL   Thanks for helpin' me, Will. I'll be pullin' out, soon as I make out the reports.

WILL   (*Stops at the door and gives a final word to* CHERIE)   Montana's not a bad place, miss.
(*He goes out*)

VIRGIL   Nice fella, Bo.

BO   (*Concentrating on* CHERIE)   Maybe I'll think so some day.

VIRGIL   Well, maybe we better be boardin' the bus, Bo.
(*Without even hearing* VIRGIL, BO *makes his way suddenly over to* CHERIE)

BO   Cherry!

CHERIE   Hi, Bo!

BO   Cherry, I promised not to molest ya, but if you was to give yor permission, it'd be all right. I . . . I'd like to kiss ya g'bye.

CHERIE   Ya would? (BO *nods*) I'd like ya to kiss me, Bo. I really would. (*A wide grin cracks open his face and he becomes all hoodlum boy again, about to take her in his arms roughly as he did before, but she stops him*) Bo! I think this time when ya kiss me, it oughta be diff'rent.

BO   (*Not sure what she means*)   Oh!
(*He looks around at* VIRGIL, *who turns quickly away, as though admitting his inability to advise his buddy.* BO *then takes her in his arms cautiously, as though holding a precious object that was still a little strange to him*)

BO   Golly! When ya kiss someone fer serious, it's kinda scary, ain't it?

CHERIE   Yah! It is.
(*Anyway, he kisses her, long and tenderly*)

GRACE   (*At the counter*)   It don't look like he was molestin' her now.
(BO, *after the kiss is ended, is dazed. Uncertain of his feelings, he stampedes across the room to* VIRGIL, *drawing him to a bench where the two men can confer. The action continues with* DR. LYMAN, *at the counter, having his breakfast*)

DR. LYMAN   I could tell you with all honesty that this was the most delicious breakfast I've ever eaten, but it wouldn't be much of a compliment because I have eaten very few breakfasts.
(*They laugh together*)

ELMA   It's my favorite meal.

(Turns to the refrigerator as he brings bottle out secretly and spikes his coffee)

DR. LYMAN *(When* ELMA *returns)* Dear girl, let us give up our little spree, shall we? You don't want to go traipsing over the streets of the state's capital with an old reprobate like me.

ELMA Whatever you say.

DR. LYMAN I shall continue my way to Denver. I'm sure it's best.

ELMA Anyway, I've certainly enjoyed knowing you.

DR. LYMAN Thank you. Ah! sometimes it is so gratifying to feel that one is doing the "right" thing, I wonder that I don't choose to always.

ELMA What do you mean?

DR. LYMAN Oh, I was just rambling. You know, perhaps while I am in the vicinity of Topeka, I should drop in at that hospital and seek some advice.

ELMA Sometimes their patients come in here. They look perfectly all right to me.

DR. LYMAN *(To himself)* Friends have been hinting for quite a while that I should get psychoanalyzed. *(He chuckles)* I don't know if they had my best interests at heart or their own.

ELMA Golly. I don't see anything the matter with you.

DR. LYMAN *(A little sadly)* No. Young people never do. *(Now with a return of high spirits)* However, I don't think I care to be psychoanalyzed. I rather cherish myself as I am. *(The cavalier again, he takes her hand)* Good-bye, my dear! You were the loveliest Juliet since Miss Jane Cowl. *(Kisses her hand gallantly, then goes for his coat.* ELMA *comes from behind counter and follows him)*

ELMA Thank you, Dr. Lyman. I feel it's been an honor to know you. You're the smartest man I've ever met.

DR. LYMAN The smartest?

ELMA Really you are.

DR. LYMAN Oh, yes. I'm terribly smart. Wouldn't it have been nice . . . to be intelligent?
(He chuckles, blows a kiss to her, then hurries out the door. ELMA *lingers behind, watching him get on the bus)*

CARL (*To* GRACE)   Hey, know what I heard about the perfessor? The detective at the bus terminal in Kanz City is a buddy of mine. He pointed out the perfessor to me before he got on the bus. Know what he said? He said the p'lice in Kanz City picked the perfessor up for *loiterin'* round the schools.

GRACE (*Appalled*)   Honest?

CARL   Then they checked his record and found he'd been in trouble several times, for gettin' involved with young girls.

GRACE   My God! Did you tell Will?

CARL   Sure, I told him. They ain't *got* anything on the perfessor now, so there's nothin' Will could do. (ELMA *makes her way back to the counter now and hears the rest of what* CARL *has to say*) What gets *me* is why does he call hisself a doctor? Is he some kinda phony?

ELMA   No, Carl. He's a Doctor of Philosophy.

CARL   What's that?

ELMA   It's the very highest degree there is, for scholarship.

GRACE   Ya'd think he'd have philosophy enough to keep outa trouble.
(ELMA *resumes her work behind the counter now*)

CARL (*To* GRACE)   Sorry to see me go, baby?

GRACE   No . . . I told ya, I'm tired.

CARL (*Good-naturedly*)   Ya know, sometimes I get to thinkin', what the hell good is marriage, where ya have to put up with the same broad every day, and lookit her in the morning, and try to get along with her when she's got a bad disposition. This way suits me fine.

GRACE   I got no complaints, either. Incidentally, are you married, Carl?

CARL   Now, who said I was married, Grace? Who said it? You just tell me and I'll fix him.

GRACE   Relax! Relax! See ya day after tomorrow.
(*She winks at him*)

CARL (*Winks back*)   You might get surprised . . . what can happen in twenty minutes. (*Slaps* GRACE *on the buttocks as a gesture of farewell*) All aboard!
(*He hustles out the front door as* BO *hurries to* CHERIE)

GRACE (*To herself*)   He still never said whether he was married.

BO   Cherry?

CHERIE   (A *little expectantly*)   Yah?

BO   I been talkin' with my buddy, and he thinks I'm virgin enough fer the two of us.

CHERIE   (*Snickers, very amused*)   Honest? Did Virgil say that?

BO   Yah . . . and I like ya like ya are, Cherry. So I don't care how ya got that way.

CHERIE   (*Deeply touched*)   Oh God, thass the sweetest, tenderest thing that was ever said to me.

BO   (*Feeling awkward*)   Cherry . . . it's awful hard for a fella, after he's been turned down once, to git up enough guts to try again . . .

CHERIE   Ya don't need guts, Bo.

BO   (*Not quite sure what she means*)   I don't?

CHERIE   It's the last thing in the world ya need.

BO   Well . . . anyway, I jest don't have none now, so I'll . . . just have to say what I feel in my heart.

CHERIE   Yah?

BO   I still wish you was goin' back to the ranch with me, more'n anything I know.

CHERIE   Ya do?

BO   Yah. I do.

CHERIE   Why, I'd go anywhere in the world with ya now, Bo. Anywhere at all.

BO   Ya would? Ya would?
(*They have a fast embrace. All look*)

GRACE   (*Nudging* ELMA)   I knew this was gonna happen all the time.

ELMA   Gee, I didn't.
(*Now* BO *and* CHERIE *break apart, both running to opposite sides of the room,* BO *to tell* VIRGIL; CHERIE, ELMA)

BO   Hear that, Virge? Yahoo! We're gettin' married after all. Cherry's goin' back with me.

CHERIE *(At counter)*   Ain't it wonderful when someone so awful turns out t'be so nice? We're gettin' married. I'm goin' to Montana.
(CARL sticks his head through the door and calls impatiently)

CARL   Hey! All aboard, fer Christ's sake!
(Exits. BO grabs VIRGIL now by the arm)

BO   C'mon, Virge, y'old raccoon!

VIRGIL *(Demurring)*   Now look, Bo . . . listen t'me for a second.

BO *(Who can't listen to anything in his high revelry. One arm is around CHERIE, the other tugs at VIRGIL)*   C'mon! Doggone it, we wasted enough time. Let's git goin'.

VIRGIL   Listen, Bo. Now be quiet jest a minute. You gotta hear me, Bo. You don't need me no more. I ain't goin'.

BO *(Not believing his ears)*   You ain't *what?*

VIRGIL   I . . . I ain't goin' with ya, Bo.

BO *(Flabbergasted)*   Well, what ya know about that?

VIRGIL   It's best I don't, Bo.

BO   Jest one blame catastrophe after another.

VIRGIL   I . . . I got another job in mind, Bo. Where the feed's mighty good, and I'll be lookin' after the cattle. I meant to tell ya 'bout it 'fore this.

BO   Virge, I can't b'lieve you'd leave yor old sidekick. Yor jokin', man.

VIRGIL   No . . . I ain't jokin', Bo. I ain't.

BO   Well, I'll be a . . .

CHERIE   Virgil—I wish you'd come. I liked *you* . . . 'fore I ever liked Bo.

BO   Ya *know* Cherry likes ya, Virge. It jest don't make sense, yor not comin'.

VIRGIL   Well . . . I'm doin' the right thing. I know I am.

BO   Who's gonna look after the cattle?

VIRGIL   Hank. Every bit as good as *I* ever was.

BO *(Very disheartened)*   Aw, Virge, I dunno why ya have to pull a stunt like this.

VIRGIL   You better hurry, Bo. That driver's not gonna wait all day.

BO   *(Starting to pull* VIRGIL, *to drag him away just as he tried once with* CHERIE)   Daggone it, yor my buddy, and I ain't gonna let ya go. Yor goin' *with* Cherry and me cause we want ya . . .

VIRGIL   *(It's getting very hard for him to control his feelings)*   No . . . No . . . lemme be, Bo . . .

CHERIE   *(Holding* BO *back)*   Bo . . . ya can't do it that way . . . ya jest can't . . . if he don't wanta go, ya can't make him . . .

BO   But, Cherry, there ain't a reason in the world he shouldn't go. It's plum crazy.

CHERIE   Well, sometimes people have their *own* reasons, Bo.

BO   Oh? *(He reconsiders)* Well, I just hate to think of gettin' along without old Virge.

VIRGIL   *(Laughing)*   In a couple weeks . . . ya'll never miss me.

BO   *(Disheartened)*   Aw, Virge!

VIRGIL   Get along with ya now.

CHERIE   Virgil—*(Brightly)* Will ya come and visit us, Virgil?

VIRGIL   I'll be up in the summer.

BO   Where ya gonna be, Virge?

VIRGIL   I'll write ya th' address. Don't have time to give it to ya now. Nice place. Mighty nice. Now hurry and get on your bus.
   *(*CARL *honks the horn)*

BO   *(Managing a quick embrace)*   So long, old boy. So long!

VIRGIL   'Bye, Bo! G'bye!
   (Now, to stave off any tears, BO *grabs* CHERIE's *hand)*

BO   C'mon, Cherry. Let's make it fast.
   (Before they are out the door, a thought occurs to BO. *He stops, takes off his leather jacket and helps* CHERIE *into it. He has been gallant. Then he picks up her suitcase and they go out, calling their farewells behind them)*

CHERIE   'Bye—'bye—'bye, everyone! 'Bye!
   *(*VIRGIL *stands at the door, waving good-bye. His eyes look a little moist. In a moment, the bus's motor is heard to start up. Then the bus leaves)*

GRACE *(From behind counter)*   Mister, we gotta close this place up now, if Elma and me're gonna get any rest. We won't be open again till eight o'clock, when the day girl comes on. The next bus through is Albuquerque, at eight forty-five.

VIRGIL   Albuquerque? I guess that's as good a place as any.
(He remains by the front entrance, looking out on the frosty morning. ELMA *and* GRACE *continue their work behind the counter)*

ELMA   Poor Dr. Lyman!

GRACE   Say, did you hear what Carl told me about that guy?

ELMA   No. What was it, Grace?

GRACE   Well, according to Carl, they run him outa Kanz City.

ELMA   I don't believe it.

GRACE   Honey, Carl got it straight from the detective at the bus terminal.

ELMA *(Afraid to ask)*   What . . . did Dr. Lyman do?

GRACE   Well, lots of old fogies like him just can't let young girls alone. *(A wondering look comes over* ELMA'S *face)* So, it's a good thing you didn't meet him in Topeka.

ELMA   Do you think . . . he wanted to make *love*, to *me*?

GRACE   I don't think he meant to play hopscotch.

ELMA *(Very moved)*   Gee!

GRACE   Next time any guy comes in here and starts gettin' fresh, you come tell your Aunt Grace.

ELMA   I guess I'm kinda stupid.

GRACE   Everyone has gotta learn. *(Looking into refrigerator)* Now Monday, for sure, I gotta order some cheese.

ELMA   I'll remind you.

GRACE *(Coming to* ELMA, *apologetically)*   Elma, honey?

ELMA   Yes?

GRACE   I could kill Will Masters for sayin' anything about me and Carl. I didn't want you to know.

ELMA   I don't see why I shouldn't know, Grace. I don't wanta be a baby forever.

GRACE   Of course you don't. But still, you're a kid, and I don't wanta set no examples or anything. Do you think you can overlook it and not think bad of me?

ELMA   Sure, Grace.

GRACE   'Cause I'm a restless sort of woman, and every once in a while, I gotta have me a man, just to keep m'self from gettin' grouchy.

ELMA   It's not my business, Grace. *(She stops a moment to consider herself in the mirror, rather pleased)* Just think, he wanted to make love to *me*.

GRACE   Now don't start gettin' *stuck* on yourself.

ELMA   I'm not, Grace. But it's nice to know that someone *can* feel that way.

GRACE   You're not gonna have any trouble. Just wait'll you get to college and start meeting all those cute *boys*.
(GRACE *seems to savor this*)

ELMA   All right. I'll wait.

GRACE   You can run along now, honey. All I gotta do is empty the garbage.

ELMA   *(Getting her coat from closet behind counter)*   O.K.

GRACE   G'night!

ELMA   *(Coming from behind counter, slipping into her coat)*   Good night, Grace. See you Monday. *(Passing* VIRGIL*)* It was very nice knowing you, Virgil, and I just loved your music.

VIRGIL   Thank you, miss. G'night.
(ELMA *goes out*)

GRACE   We're closing now, mister.

VIRGIL   *(Coming center)*   Any place warm I could stay till eight o'clock?

GRACE   Now that the p'lice station's closed, I don't know where you could go, unless ya wanted to take a chance of wakin' up the man that runs the hotel.

VIRGIL   No—I wouldn't wanta be any trouble.

GRACE   There'll be a bus to Kanz City in a few minutes. I'll put the sign out and they'll stop.

VIRGIL   No, thanks. No point a goin' back there.

GRACE   Then I'm sorry, mister, but you're just left out in the cold. *(She carries a can of garbage out the rear door, leaving* VIRGIL *for the moment alone)*

VIRGIL *(To himself)*   Well . . . that's what happens to some people. *(Quietly, he picks up his guitar and goes out.* GRACE *comes back in, locks the back door, snaps the wall switch, then yawns and stretches, then sees that the front door is locked. The sun outside is just high enough now to bring a dim light into the restaurant.* GRACE *stops at the rear door and casts her eyes tiredly over the establishment. One senses her aloneness. She sighs, then goes out the door. The curtain comes down on an empty stage)*

The Dark at the Top
of the Stairs

THE DARK AT THE TOP OF THE STAIRS *was first presented by Saint Subber and Elia Kazan at The Music Box, New York City, on December 5, 1957, with the following cast:*

(IN ORDER OF APPEARANCE)

CORA FLOOD, *a young housewife*	*Theresa Wright*
RUBIN FLOOD, *her husband*	*Pat Hingle*
SONNY FLOOD, *the ten-year-old son*	*Charles Saari*
BOY OUTSIDE	*Jonathan Shawn*
REENIE FLOOD, *the sixteen-year-old daughter*	*Judith Robinson*
FLIRT CONROY, *a flapper friend of Reenie's*	*Evans Evans*
MORRIS LACEY, *Cora's brother-in-law*	*Frank Overton*
LOTTIE LACEY, *Cora's older sister*	*Eileen Heckart*
PUNKY GIVENS, *Flirt's boy friend*	*Carl Reindel*
SAMMY GOLDENBAUM, *Punky's friend*	*Timmy Everett*
CHAUFFEUR	*Anthony Ray*

DIRECTED BY Elia Kazan
SETTING BY Ben Edwards
COSTUMES BY Lucinda Ballard
LIGHTING BY Jean Rosenthal

Scenes

The home of Rubin Flood, his wife and two children, in a small Oklahoma town close to Oklahoma City. The time is the early 1920's.

ACT ONE	A Monday afternoon in early spring.

ACT TWO	After dinner, the following Friday.

ACT THREE	The next day, late afternoon.

ACT ONE

SCENE: *The setting for the entire play is the home of* RUBIN FLOOD *and his wife and two children, in a small Oklahoma town close to Oklahoma City. The time is the early 1920's, during an oil boom in the area. The house is comfortable and commodious, with probably eight or nine rooms. It is one of those square, frame houses built earlier in the century, that stand secure as blocks, symbols of respectability and material comfort.*

All we see of the FLOODS' *house is the living room, where the action of the play takes place. There is a flight of stairs at the far left. At the top of them is the upstairs hallway, which is not accessible to windows and sunlight. During the daytime scenes, this small area is in semidarkness, and at night it is black. When the hallway is lighted, we can see the feet of the characters who happen to be there. We are conscious of this area throughout the play, as though it holds some possible threat to the characters.*

On the far right, downstairs, is the outside entrance, with a small hallway one must go through before coming into the living room.

In the middle of the living room is a wicker table and two comfortable wicker chairs, placed one on each side. Upstage center are sliding doors leading into the parlor, where we see a player piano. To the left of these doors and under the stairway, is a swinging door leading into the dining room. Extreme downstage left is a fireplace and a large comfortable leather chair. This area is considered RUBIN'S. *In the rest of the room are book shelves, a desk, a few small tables and portraits of* CORA FLOOD'S *mother and father. Through a large window at the back, we see part of the front porch to the house, and can see characters coming and going.*

As for the atmosphere of the room, despite the moodiness of shadowy corners and Victorian (more or less) furnishings, there is an implied comfort and hospitality.

When the curtain goes up, it is a late Monday afternoon in the early spring, about five o'clock. Outside, the sun is setting, but the room is still filled with soft, warm light.

The stage is empty when the curtain rises. CORA *and* RUBIN *are both upstairs, he preparing to leave on a business trip.*

CORA *(Off)*   Rubin!

RUBIN *(Off)*   Yah!

CORA *(Off)*   How many times do I have to tell you to rinse your hands before you dry them on a towel? You leave the bathroom looking like a wild horse had been using it. (RUBIN *laughs*) I can smell the bay rum clear over here. My! You're certainly getting spruced up!

RUBIN *(Starting downstairs, carrying a suitcase. He is quite a good-looking man of thirty-six, still robust, dressed in Western clothes—a big Stetson, boots, narrow trousers, colorful shirt and string tie)*   I gotta look good for my customers.

CORA *(Calling down to him)*   How long will you be gone this time?

RUBIN   I oughta be home end of the week. Saturday.

CORA *(Calling down)*   That's better than you usually do. Where will you be?

RUBIN *(Goes to his corner, where he keeps his business paraphernalia)*   I've made out my route for ya. I've left it on the mantel.

NEWSBOY *(Calling into house from outside)*   Hey, Mr. Flood. Jonsey says your tire's ready at the garage.

RUBIN   O.K., Ed, I'll be down to get it.

CORA *(Coming downstairs)*   Rubin, you've waited this long to go, why don't you wait now until morning? Here it is almost suppertime. You won't be able to see any customers tonight, no matter where you go. Wait until morning. I'll get up early and fix you breakfast. I'll fix you biscuits, Rubin.

RUBIN   I shoulda been out first thing this mornin'. Monday, and I'm just gettin' away. I can make it to Muskogee tonight and be there first thing in the mornin'. I can finish up by noon and then get on to Chickasha.

CORA   I wish you were home more, Rubin.

RUBIN   I gotta make a livin'.

CORA   Other men make a living without traveling all over the country selling harness.

RUBIN   The way other men make a livin' is *their* business. I gotta make mine the best way I know how. I can't be no schoolmaster like your old man was when he brung you all out here from Pennsylvania. I can't be no dentist like your brother-in-law Morris. I was raised on a ranch and thought I'd spend my life on it. Sellin' harness is about all I'm prepared for . . . as long as there's any harness to sell.

CORA *(With a trace of self-pity)*   I envy women who have their husbands with them all the time. I never have anyone to take me any place. I live like a widow.

RUBIN   What do you want me to do? Give up my job and stay home here to pleasure you every day?

CORA *(She is often disturbed by his language)*   Rubin! Don't say that.

RUBIN   Jesus Christ, ya talk like a man had nothin' else to do but stay home and entertain you.

CORA   Rubin! It's not just myself I'm thinking of. It's the children. We have a daughter sixteen years old now. Do you realize that? Yes. Reenie's sixteen. And Sonny's ten. Sometimes they act like they didn't have a father.

RUBIN *(Sits at table to sharpen his knife)*   You're always tellin' me how good they do at school. The girl plays the piano, don't she? And the boy does somethin', too. Gets up and speaks pieces, or somethin' like that?
(In CORA's *sewing basket he finds a sock on which to wipe his knife)*

CORA *(Again she is shocked)*   Rubin! Not on a clean sock!

RUBIN   Seems to me you all get along all right without me.

CORA   Rubin, I worry about them. Reenie's so shy of people her own age, I don't know what to make of her. She's got no confidence at all. And I don't know how to give her any, but you could. Her eyes light up like candles every time you go near her.

RUBIN *(A little embarrassed)*   Come on now, Cora.

CORA   It's true . . . and the boy. Other boys tease him and call him names, Rubin. He doesn't know how to get along with them.

RUBIN   He oughta beat the tar outa the other boys.

CORA   He's not like you, Rubin. He's not like anyone I ever knew. He needs a father, Rubin. So does Reenie. Kids need a father when they're growing up, same as they need a mother.

RUBIN   You din allus talk like that. God almighty, when those kids was born, you hugged 'em so close to ya, ya made me think they was your own personal property, and I din have nothin' to do with 'em at all.

CORA　Rubin, that's not so.

RUBIN　The hell it ain't. Ya pampered 'em so much and coddled 'em, they thought I was just bein' mean if I tried to drill some sense into their heads.

CORA　Rubin. Don't say that.

RUBIN　You're always kissin' and makin' over the boy until I sometimes wonder who's top man around here.

CORA　Rubin!

RUBIN　I just said I wonder.

CORA　If I kept the kids too close to me, it's only because you weren't there, and I had to have *someone* close to me. I had to have *some*one.

RUBIN　You're like an old mare Pa used to have on the ranch. Never wanted to give up her colts. By God, she'd keep 'em locked inside her and make all us men dig inside her with our hands to get 'em out. She never wanted to let 'em go.

CORA　(A *little repelled by the comparison*)　Rubin, I don't like what you just said.

RUBIN　Well, she was a good mare in every other way.

CORA　You talk shamefully at times.

RUBIN　Well . . . I got my own way of sayin' things and it's pretty hard to change.

CORA　(*Watching him primp before the mirror*)　You like being out on the road, don't you? You like to pretend you're still a young cowboy.

RUBIN　It wasn't a bad life.

CORA　Rubin, there are ever so many things you could do in town. Mr. Binny down here on the corner makes a very good living just selling groceries to the neighborhood people. We could find a store like that, Rubin, and the kids and I could help you, too. You'd be happier doing something like that, Rubin. I know you would.

RUBIN　Don't tell me how t'be happy. I told you over and over, I ain't gonna spend my life cooped up in no store.

CORA　Or a filling station, Rubin. You could run a filling station or a garage . . . .

RUBIN   God damn it, Cora. I don't mean to have that kinda life. I just wasn't cut out for it. Now, quit pickin' at me. We been married seventeen years now. It seems t'me, you'd be ready t'accept me the way I am, or start lookin' for a new man.

CORA   I don't want a new man. You know that.

RUBIN   Then start tryin' to put up with the one you got.

CORA   I do try.

RUBIN   'Cause he ain't gonna change. Kiss me g'bye. *(Playfully rough with her)* You come here and kiss me.
(He grabs her in a fast embrace, and they kiss)

CORA   *(Cautiously)*   Rubin, you've got to leave me some money.

RUBIN   How much you gonna need?

CORA   Uh . . . could you let me have maybe twenty-five dollars?

RUBIN   *(Hitting the ceiling)*   Twenty-five dollars? I'm only gonna be gone till Saturday.

CORA   I have a lot of expenses this week, and . . .

RUBIN   *I* pay the bills.

CORA   I take care of the utilities, Rubin. And we have a big gas bill this month, last month was so cold. And Reenie's invited to a big birthday party out at the country club. The Ralston girl, and Reenie has to take her a present.

RUBIN   Me? Buy presents for Harry Ralston's girl when he owns half this town?

CORA   I don't often ask for this much.

RUBIN   *(Taking a bill from his wallet)*   Twenty's the best I can do.

CORA   Thank you, Rubin. The Ralstons are giving Mary Jane a big dance. *(Finding a button loose on his coat)* Here, let me fix that.

RUBIN   Cora, that'll be all right.

CORA   It'll only take a minute, sit down. *(They sit, and CORA takes needle and thread from her sewing basket)* They're having a dance orchestra from Oklahoma City.

RUBIN   Harry and Peg Ralston puttin' on the dog now, are they?

CORA   Oh, yes. I hardly ever see Peg any more.

RUBIN   I guess they don't have time for any of their old friends, now that they've got so much money.

CORA   Anyway, they've asked Reenie to the party, I'm thankful for that.

RUBIN   The country club, huh? By God, I'd die in the poorhouse 'fore I'd ever do what Harry Ralston done.

CORA   Now, Rubin . . .

RUBIN   I mean it. He shot hisself in the foot to collect enough insurance money to make his first investment in oil.

CORA   Do you believe all those stories?

RUBIN   Hell, yes, I believe it. I know it for a fact. He shot hisself in the foot. He oughta be in jail now. Instead, he's a social leader, givin' parties out at the country club. And I'm supposed to feel real proud he invited my daughter. Hurry up.

CORA   I ran into Peg downtown during the winter. My, she was wearing a beautiful fur coat. Gray squirrel. And she was wearing a lot of lovely jewelry, too.

RUBIN   She's spendin' his money as fast as old Harry makes it.

CORA   Why shouldn't she have a few nice things?

RUBIN   They tell me they both started drinkin' now. They go out to those country club parties and get drunk as lords.

CORA   Peg didn't used to be like that.

RUBIN   They're all like that now. The town's gone oil-boom crazy. Chamber of Commerce says we're the wealthiest town per capita in all the Southwest. I guess they're not exaggeratin' much, either, with all this oil money, those damned Indians ridin' around in their limousines, gettin' all that money from the government, millions of dollars. Millions of dollars, and nobody knows what to do with it. Come on, hurry up now . . .

CORA   (Finishing with the button)   Rubin, if you want to make an investment, if you should hear of something absolutely sure, you can take that money Mama left me when she died. Two thousand dollars, Rubin. You can make an investment with that.

RUBIN   There ain't no such thing as a *sure thing* in the oil business.

CORA   Isn't there?

RUBIN   No. Ya can make a million dollars or lose your ass overnight.

CORA   Rubin, you don't have to use words like that.

RUBIN   I do a good job supportin' ya, don't I?

CORA   Of course.

RUBIN   Then let's let well enough alone.

CORA   I was only thinking, it makes you feel kind of left out to be poor these days.
    (*Suddenly, from outside, we hear the sounds of young boys' jeering voices*)

BOYS' VOICES
    Sonny Flood! His name is mud!
    Sonny runs home to Mama!
    Sonny plays with paper dolls!
    Sonny Flood, his name is mud!

CORA   See, there! (*She jumps up nervously and runs outside to face her son's accosters*) You boys run along. My Sonny hasn't done anything to hurt you. You go home now or I'll call your mothers, every last one of you. You should be ashamed of yourselves, picking on a boy who's smaller than you are.
    (SONNY *comes running into the house now. It is hard to discern his feelings*)

RUBIN   (*Follows* CORA *out to the porch*)   Cora, cut it out.

CORA   I can't stand quietly by while they're picking on my boy!

RUBIN   It's *his* battle. He's gotta fight it out for hisself.

CORA   If they touch one hair of that boy's head I'll destroy them.

VOICE   (*One last heckler*)   Sonny Flood, his name is mud!

CORA   I'll destroy them.
    (CORA *re-enters the house*)

VOICE   Sonny Flood, his name is mud.

RUBIN   (*Still on the porch*)   Hey, come here, you fat butterball.

BOY   Hi, Mr. Flood.

RUBIN   How you doin', Jonathan? Let me see how you're growin'. (*He lifts the boy up*) Gettin' fat as a pig. Say hello to your pa for me.
    (*The boy runs off and* RUBIN *comes back inside*)

CORA   Sonny, did they hurt you?

SONNY   No.

CORA   What started it this time?

SONNY   I don't know.

CORA   Did you say anything to make them mad?

SONNY   No.

CORA   They're just jealous because you make better grades than they do. They're just jealous, the little beasts.

RUBIN   Son!

SONNY   Huh?

RUBIN   Want me to teach you how to put up a good fight?

SONNY   *(Turning away from his father)*   I don't think so.

RUBIN   *(To* CORA)   What else can I do? Buy him a shotgun?

CORA   There should be *something* we can do. *Something.*

RUBIN   Everybody's gotta figure out his own way of handlin' things, Cora. Whether he fights or whether he runs.

CORA   I hate for anything to make me feel so helpless.

RUBIN   I gotta be goin'.

CORA   Say good-bye to your father, Sonny.

RUBIN   *(Making a point of being friendly)*   Good-bye, son.

SONNY   *(Diffidently)*   G'bye.

RUBIN   *(Giving up)*   Oh, hell.

CORA   Isn't there anything you can say to him?

RUBIN   Cora, if that boy wants me to help him, he's gotta come to me and tell me how. I never know what's on his mind.

CORA   You're just not interested.

RUBIN   Oh, hell, I give up. I plain give up.
    (Exasperated, RUBIN *bolts outside,* CORA *anxiously following him to the door)*

CORA Rubin . . . Rubin . . . *(We hear* RUBIN'S *car drive off.* CORA *comes back inside)* Why don't you listen to your father, Sonny? Why don't you let him help you?

SONNY Where's Reenie?

CORA She's downtown. Your father isn't here very often. Why don't you try and get along with him when he is?

SONNY *(Wanting to evade the issue)* I don't know.

CORA Most boys your age *worship* their fathers.

SONNY I like him, all right. Where are my movie stars?

CORA Forget your movie stars for a minute. You have a father to be proud of, Sonny. He and his family were pioneers. They fought Indians and buffalo, and they settled this country when it was just a wilderness. Why, if there was a movie about them, you couldn't wait to see it.

SONNY Mom, it just makes it worse when you come out and tell those boys you're going to call their mothers.

CORA You just won't listen to me, will you? You just won't listen to anyone. You're so set in your ways.

SONNY I want my movie stars.

CORA I put them in the book shelves when I was straightening up this morning. The only pastime you have is coming home here and playing with those pictures of movie stars. (SONNY *gets out his scrapbook and spreads it on the floor)*

SONNY I like them.

CORA That's all the friends you have. Not real friends at all. Just *pictures* of all the lovely friends you'd *like* to have. There's a mighty big difference between pictures of people and the way people really are.

SONNY I like pictures.

CORA Maybe you should get out and play with the other boys more often, Sonny.

SONNY They play stupid games.

CORA People distrust you if you don't play the same games they do, Sonny. It's the same after you grow up.

SONNY I'm not going to play games just to make them like me.

CORA (*Suddenly warm and affectionate*)   Come to me, Sonny. I wish I understood you better, boy.

SONNY   I don't see why.

CORA (*Caressing him*)   No, I don't suppose you do. You're a speckled egg, and the old hen that laid you can't help wondering how you got in the nest. But I love you, Sonny. More than anything else in the world.

SONNY   Mom, can I go to a movie tonight?

CORA   You know the rules. One movie a week, on Friday night.

SONNY   Please, Mom. It's a real special movie tonight. Honest, I just *got* to see it.

CORA   Oh, I bet. It's always something special and you've just got to see it like your very life depended on it. No. You're supposed to study on week nights. Now, stay home and study.

SONNY   I've already got all my lessons.

CORA   You have to speak at Mrs. Stanford's tea party next Saturday. Why don't you memorize a new recitation?

SONNY   I can't find anything I like.

CORA   Oh! I found a cute little poem in the Oklahoma City paper this morning. It's about a little boy who hates to take castor oil. It starts off:
"Of all the nasty things, gee whiz!
I think the very worst there is . . ."

SONNY (*Obviously bored*)   I want to do something serious.

CORA   Serious! Like what?

SONNY   I dunno.

CORA   Goodness, it seems to me we've got enough serious things in the world without you getting up to recite sad pieces.
(*Outside the window, we see* FLIRT *and* REENIE *come onto the porch, giggling*)

SONNY   I'm tired of all those stupid pieces you cut out of the papers.

CORA   My goodness! Aren't we getting superior! Oh, here's your sister, Sonny. Be a little gentleman and open the door for her.

REENIE (*Sticking her head in through the door, asking cautiously*)   Is Daddy gone, Mom?

CORA Yes, he's gone. The coast is clear.

REENIE (*Runs to* CORA *excitedly. She is a plain girl with no conscious desire to be anything else*) Oh, Mom, it's the prettiest dress I ever had.

CORA Bring it in.

REENIE Come on in, Flirt.

FLIRT (*Enters carrying a large dress box. She is a vivacious young flapper of the era*) Hello, Mrs. Flood.

CORA Hello, Flirt.
(FLIRT *opens the box*)

REENIE And they took up the hem and took in the waist so that it fits me just perfectly now.

FLIRT I think it's simply scrumptious, Mrs. Flood.

CORA Thank you, Flirt. Hold it up, Reenie.

FLIRT Yes, hold it up.

REENIE (*Holding the dress before her*) Is Dad going to be awfully mad, Mom?

CORA I told you, he's not going to know anything about it for a while, Reenie. He gave me some money before he left, enough for me to make a small down payment. My, I bet Flirt thinks we're terrible, plotting this way.

FLIRT Shucks, no. Mama and I do the same thing.

REENIE Oh, Mom. You should see the dress Flirt got.

FLIRT It's all red, with spangles on it, and a real short skirt. It's just darling. Daddy says he feels like disowning me in it.

CORA Did you buy your dress at Delman's, too, Flirt?

FLIRT (*She can't help boasting an advantage*) No. Mama takes me into Oklahoma City to buy all my clothes.

CORA Oh!

SONNY (*Feeling the dress*) Look, it's got stars.

REENIE (*Snapping angrily*) Sonny, take your dirty hands off my new dress.

SONNY (*Ready to start a fight any time* REENIE *is*) My hands are *not* dirty! So there.

REENIE   You make me mad. Why don't you go outdoors and play ball instead of staying in the house all the time, spying on everything I do. Mother, why don't you make him go out and play?

SONNY   It's my house as much as it's yours, and I've got as much right to be here as you do. So there!

CORA *(Always distressed by their fighting)*   Reenie. He only wanted to touch the dress. He likes pretty things, too.

FLIRT   Gee whiz, he hasn't done anything, Reenie.

CORA   Of course he hasn't. You kids are just antagonistic to each other. You scrap all the time.

SONNY   I hate you.

REENIE   I hate you, too.

CORA   Now stop that. Is that any way for a brother and sister to talk? I'm not going to have any more of it. Flirt, are you taking the Ralston girl a birthday present?

FLIRT   Mama got me a compact to give her. It's the only thing we could think of. She already has everything under the sun.

CORA   Yes, I suppose so. Her parents are so wealthy now. Well, I'll have to shop for something for Reenie to take her.

FLIRT   You know, my folks knew the Ralstons before he made all his money. Mama says Mrs. Ralston used to clerk in a millinery store downtown.

CORA   Yes, I knew her then.

FLIRT   And my daddy says that Mr. Ralston was so crazy to make money in oil that he shot himself in the foot. Isn't that awful?

SONNY   Why did he do that?
    (REENIE *goes into the parlor to try on her dress.* SONNY *sits at the table.* FLIRT *fascinates him)*

FLIRT   So he could collect enough insurance money to make his first investment in oil. Did you hear that story, too, Mrs. Flood?

CORA   Oh, yes . . . you hear all kinds of stories about the Ralstons now.

FLIRT   And you know, some of the women out at the country club didn't want to give Mr. Ralston a membership because they disapproved of *her.*

CORA Is that so?

FLIRT But when you've got as much money as the Ralstons do, I guess you can be a member of *anything*. I just hate Mary Jane Ralston. Some of the boys at school think she's pretty but I think she's a *cow*. I'm not being jealous, either. I guess if I had as much money to spend on clothes as she does, I'd have been voted the prettiest girl in school, too. Anyway, I'm absolutely positive she peroxides her hair.

CORA Really?

REENIE *(Poking her head out between the sliding doors)* Are you sure?

FLIRT Yes. Because she and I play on the same volley ball team in gym class, and her locker is right next to mine, and . . .

CORA *(Reminding her of* SONNY'S *presence)* Flirt!

FLIRT Isn't it terrible for me to say all these things, when I'm going to her birthday party? But I don't care. She just invited me because she had to. Because my daddy's her daddy's lawyer.

SONNY *(As* REENIE *comes out of parlor wearing her new dress, he makes a grotesque face and props his feet on the table)* Ugh . . .

CORA Oh, Reenie! it's lovely. Sonny, take your feet down. Let me see! Oh, Reenie. He did a fine job. Flirt! tell me more about the young man who's taking Reenie to the party.

FLIRT He's a Jew, Mrs. Flood.

CORA Oh, he is?

REENIE Do you think it's all right for me to go out with a Jew, Mom?

CORA Why, of course, dear, if he's a nice boy.

FLIRT His name is Sammy Goldenbaum, and he comes from Hollywood, California, and his mother's a moving-picture actress.

CORA Really?

REENIE Flirt just found that out, Mom. I didn't know it before.

SONNY *(All ears)* A moving-picture actress!

FLIRT Yes, but she just plays itsy-bitsy parts in pictures. I saw her once. She played a real stuck-up society woman, and she was Gloria Swanson's rival. You see, they were in love with the same man, Thomas Meighan, and she told all these lies about Gloria Swanson to make people think

Gloria Swanson wasn't nice, so she could marry Thomas Meighan her-self. But Thomas Meighan found out all about it, finally, and . . .

REENIE Mom, what's a Jewish person like?

CORA Well, I never knew many Jewish people, Reenie, but . . .

FLIRT I've heard that some of them can be awful fast with girls.

CORA I'm sure they're just like any other people.

FLIRT (*Dancing coquettishly about room*) They don't believe in Christian-ity.

CORA Most of them don't.

REENIE But do they act different?

CORA (*Not really knowing*) Well . . .

FLIRT My daddy says they always try to get the best of you in business.

CORA There are lots of very nice Jewish people, Reenie.

FLIRT Oh, sure! Gee whiz, of course.

REENIE I don't know what to expect.

FLIRT Kid, he's a *boy*. That's all you have to know.

CORA There are Jewish families over in Oklahoma City, but I guess there aren't any here in town.

FLIRT Oh, yes there are, Mrs. Flood. The Lewises are Jewish, only they changed their name from Levin so no one would know.

CORA I guess I did hear that some place.

REENIE Mom, I feel sort of scared to go out with someone so different.

FLIRT (*She never seems aware of her casual offensiveness*) Oh, you're crazy, Reenie. Gee whiz, I'd never go steady with a Jewish boy, but I'd sure take a date with one—if I didn't have any other way of going.

CORA Now, Reenie, I'm sure that any friend of the Givens boy is nice, whether he's Jewish or not. And besides, his mother's a movie actress. Think of that.

FLIRT Yes, but not a famous one.

CORA (*To* REENIE) Now, you have a nice date to the party, and a lovely new dress to wear. You can be sure you'll have a good time.

FLIRT Gosh, yes! After all, a party's a party. And it's out at the country club, and they're having a swell dance orchestra from Oklahoma City, and they're giving favors. I can't wait. Fix your hair real cute and you'll look all right. *(Looks at her wrist watch)* Oh, heck! I've got to go home.

CORA Do you want to stay here for supper, Flirt?

FLIRT No. It's my night to fix supper for the folks. My mother makes me fix supper once a week, cook's night out. She says it's good for me to learn something about homemaking. Isn't that crazy? They only think I know how to cook is salmon loaf. I learned how to make it in domestic science class. I've made salmon loaf every Monday night now for the whole year. Kid, can you help me study for that stupid old civics test we're having next week?

REENIE I guess so.

FLIRT Civics! Why can't they teach us something in that old school that'd do us some good?

CORA Good-bye, Flirt.

FLIRT Good-bye, Mrs. Flood, good-bye, Reenie. Oh, Sonny, you come over to *my* house and play sometime. I know how to be nice to little boys.

CORA Good-bye! (FLIRT *exits*) Sonny, you've got to go to the store now if we're going to have anything for supper tonight.

SONNY Mom! Can I get a candy bar?

CORA Wouldn't you rather have the nickel to put in your piggy bank?

SONNY No—I want a candy bar.

CORA All right. If you promise not to eat it before supper.

REENIE I want one, too. I want a nut Hershey.

CORA Bring one for Reenie, too.

SONNY She can get her own candy bar.

REENIE He's mean, Mom.

SONNY I don't care. She makes me mad, and I don't like her.

CORA Sonny, she's your sister.

SONNY I don't care. I don't like her.
(He exits)

CORA   Oh, God, some day you kids are going to be sorry. When you can't even get along with people in your own family, how can you expect to get along with people out in the world? *(Goes to the window and looks out, protectively)* Poor Sonny, every time he leaves the house, those neighborhood bullies pick on him. I guess they've all gone home now. (REENIE *takes off her new dress and throws it on a chair*)

REENIE   I don't know if I like Flirt or not.

CORA *(Comes away from the window)*   Why, what's the matter?

REENIE   The only reason she likes me is because I help her with her studies. (REENIE *goes into the parlor, gets her daytime clothes, and comes back into the living room to put them on*)

CORA   Why do you say that?

REENIE   I just do.

CORA   You don't think *anyone* likes you, do you?

REENIE   Mom, maybe we shouldn't have bought the dress.

CORA   What?

REENIE   I mean it, Mom. Dad'd be awful mad if he knew.

CORA   I told you, he's not going to know.

REENIE   Won't he be here the night of the party?

CORA   No. And even if he were, he wouldn't notice the dress was new unless you told him about it.

REENIE   Just the same, Mom, I don't feel right about it.

CORA   Why don't you feel right?

REENIE   Because . . . the dress cost so much, and what good is it going to do me? I never have a good time at those dances, anyway. No one ever dances with me.

CORA   This time it's going to be different. You've got a new dress, and you've got a nice young man coming here all the way from California to be your escort. Think of it. Why, most young girls would be too excited to breathe.

REENIE   It's just a *blind* date.

CORA   What are you talking about?

REENIE They give blind dates to all the girls in town that nobody else wants to take.

CORA Daughter, I'm sure that's not so.

REENIE Oh, Mom, you just don't know.

CORA I do too.

REENIE Besides, he's Jewish. I never knew a Jewish boy before. I'm scared.

CORA Daughter, you're just looking for excuses. You just don't want to go, do you? Reenie, don't you want to have friends?

REENIE Yes, but . . .

CORA You're not going to make friends just staying home playing the piano, or going to the library studying your lessons. I'm glad you're studious and talented, but those things aren't enough just in themselves.

REENIE I don't want to talk about it any more.

CORA You're going to have to talk about these things someday. Where are you going?

REENIE To practice the piano.
(She goes into the parlor and starts playing scales)

CORA *(Angrily impatient)* That's where you spend half your life, *practicing* at the piano. (REENIE *bangs on piano exasperatedly and exits to dining room)* But will you get up and play for people so they'll know how talented you are? No. You hide your light under a bushel. You stay home and play behind closed doors, where no one can hear you except your own family. All you do is *pity* yourself at the piano. That's all. You go in there and pity yourself, playing all those sad pieces.
(REENIE comes out of dining room, and calms herself by watering her plants)

REENIE Mom, I just couldn't get up before an audience and play. I just couldn't.

CORA Why couldn't you? What good is it for your father to have bought the piano? What use is it? (REENIE *begins to sob)* Now, don't cry, Reenie. I'm sorry. (REENIE *goes into parlor and resumes her monotonous scales.* CORA *goes to telephone)* Long distance? Give me three-six-oh-seven-J in Oklahoma City, please. *(There is a wait of several moments)* Hello, Lottie. . . . Lottie, can you and Morris come over to dinner Friday night? I haven't seen you for so long, I want to talk with you, Lottie. I've just got to see some of my own flesh and blood. *(We hear* RUBIN's *car slam to a stop outside; the car door slams and then he comes stomping up to the front porch)* Reenie's going to a big party out at the country club, and I thought I'd have a nice dinner first. . . . Rubin won't be here and I'll want company. Please come. Oh, I'm so glad. I'll be looking forward to seeing you.

RUBIN *(Bursting into the house)*   What the hell's been goin' on behind my back? *(Sees the innocent dress lying on a chair)* There it is!

CORA *(Her phone call over)*   Rubin!

RUBIN *(Displaying the dress as evidence)*   So this is what ya wanted the extra money for. Fine feathers! Fine feathers! And ya buy 'em when my back is turned.

CORA   Rubin, we were going to tell you. . . .

RUBIN   A man has t'go downtown and talk with some of his pals before he knows what's goin' on in his own family.

CORA   Who told you?

RUBIN   That's all right who told me. I got my own ways a findin' out what goes on when my back is turned.

CORA   You didn't leave town at all. You've been down to that dirty old pool hall.

RUBIN   I got a right to go to the pool hall whenever I damn please.

CORA   I thought you were in such a hurry to get out of town. Oh, yes, you had to get to Muskogee tonight.

RUBIN   I can still make it to Muskogee. *(Finds the price tag on the dress)* Nineteen seventy-five! Lord have mercy! Nineteen seventy-five.

CORA   Did Loren Delman come into the pool hall while you were there? Did he? Did he tell you? If he did I'll never buy anything in that store again.

RUBIN   That'd suit me just fine.

CORA   Oh, why couldn't he have kept his mouth shut? I was going to pay for the dress a little at a time, and . . .

RUBIN   "The finest dress I had in the store," he says, walkin' into the Arcade with a big cigar stuck in his mouth, wearin' a suit of fine tailored clothes. "I just sold your wife the finest dress I had in the store."

CORA Oh, that makes me furious.

RUBIN Jesus Christ, woman, whatta you take me for, one a those million-aire oil men? Is that what you think you're married to?

REENIE (*Pokes her head in through parlor door, speaking with tears and anxiety*) I told you he'd be mad, Mom. Let's take the dress back, Mom. I don't want to go to the party anyhow.

CORA (*Angrily impatient*) Get back in that parlor, Reenie, and don't come in here until I tell you to.
(CORA *slams the parlor doors shut*)

RUBIN See there! That girl don't even want the dress. It's *you*, puttin' all these high-fallutin' ideas in her head about parties, and dresses and nonsense.

CORA Rubin, of course Reenie doesn't want to go to the party. She never wants to go any place. All she wants to do is lock herself in the parlor and practice at the piano, or go to the library and hide her nose in a book. After all, she's going to want to get married one of these days, isn't she? And where's she going to look for a husband? In the public library?
(RUBIN *goes to his corner, sits in his big leather chair, and draws a pint of whiskey out of his desk drawer*)

RUBIN I bought her a fine dress . . . just a little while back.

CORA Oh, you did?

RUBIN Yes, I did.

CORA That's news to me. When?

RUBIN Just a few months ago. Sure I did.

CORA I certainly never saw it. What'd it look like?

RUBIN It was white.

CORA Rubin Flood, that was the dress you bought her three years ago when she graduated from the eighth grade. And she hasn't had a new dress since then, except for a few school clothes.

RUBIN Why couldn't she wear the white dress to the party?

CORA Because she's grown three inches since you got her that dress, and besides I cut it up two years ago and dyed it black and made her a skirt out of it to wear with a middy.

RUBIN   Just the same, I ain't got money to throw away on no party togs. I just ain't got it.

CORA   Oh, no. You don't have money when we need something here at home, do you?

RUBIN   I'm tellin' ya, right now I don't.

CORA   But you always have money for a bottle of bootleg whiskey when you want it, don't you? And I daresay you've got money for a few other things, too, that I needn't mention just at present.

RUBIN   What're ya talkin' about?

CORA   *You* know what I'm talking about.

RUBIN   The hell I do.

CORA   I know what goes on when you go out on the road. You may tell me you spruce up for your customers, but I happen to know better. Do you think I'm a fool?

RUBIN   I don't know what you're talkin' about.

CORA   I happen to have friends, decent, self-respecting people, who tell me a few things that happen when you visit Ponca City.

RUBIN   You mean the Werpel sisters!

CORA   It's all right, who I mean. I have friends over there. That's all I need to say.

RUBIN   Those nosy old maids, the Werpel sisters! God damn! Have they been runnin' to you with stories?

CORA   Maybe you don't have money to buy your daughter a new dress, but it seems you have money to take Mavis Pruitt to dinner whenever you're over there, and to a movie afterwards, and give her presents.

RUBIN   I've known Mavis . . . Pruitt ever since I was a boy! What harm is there if I take her to a movie?

CORA   You're always too tired to take *me* to a movie when you come home.

RUBIN   Life's different out on the road.

CORA   I bet it is.

RUBIN   Besides, I din ask her. She come into the Gibson House one night when I was havin' my dinner. What could I do but let her join me?

CORA She went to the Gibson House because she knew *you* were there. I know what kind of woman she is.

RUBIN She's not as bad as she's painted. That poor woman's had a hard time of it, too.

CORA Oh, she has!

RUBIN Yes, she has. I feel sorry for her.

CORA Oh, you do!

RUBIN Yes, I do. Is there any law that says I can't feel sorry for Mavis Pruitt?

CORA She's had her eye on you ever since I can remember.

RUBIN Oh, shoot!

CORA What happened to the man she left town with after we were married?

RUBIN He run off and left her.

CORA For good reason, too, I bet. I also heard that she was seen sporting a pair of black-bottom hose shortly after you left town, and that you were seen buying such a pair of hose at the Globe Dry Goods Store.

RUBIN By God, you got yourself a real detective service goin', haven't you?

CORA I don't ask people to tell me these things. I wish to God they didn't.

RUBIN All right. I bought her a pair of hose. I admit it. It was her birthday. The hose cost me sixty-eight cents. They made that poor woman happy. After all, I've known her ever since I was a boy. Besides, I was a li'l more flush then.

CORA How do you think it makes me feel when people tell me things like that?

RUBIN Ya oughtn'ta listen.

CORA How can I help it?

RUBIN *(He has to stop to remember to call Mavis Pruitt by her full name, to keep* CORA *from suspecting too much familiarity between them)* There's nothin' 'tween me and Mavis . . . Pruitt . . . Mavis Pruitt, nothin' for you to worry about.

CORA There's probably a woman like her in every town you visit. That's why you want to get out of town, to go frisking over the country like a young stallion.

RUBIN You just hush your mouth. The daughter'll hear you.

CORA *(Indulging in a little self-pity)* A lot you care about your daughter. A lot you care about any of us.

RUBIN You don't think I care for ya unless I set ya on my knee and nuzzle ya.

CORA What you need for a wife is a squaw. Why didn't you marry one of those Indian women out on the reservation? Yes. She'd make you rich now, too, wouldn't she? And you wouldn't have to pay any attention to her at all.
(SONNY *is seen coming onto porch*)

RUBIN All right. Maybe that's what I *shoulda* done.

CORA Oh. So you want to throw it up to me!

RUBIN Throw what?
(SONNY *quietly enters the room, carrying a sack of groceries.* CORA *and* RUBIN *are too far into battle to notice him*)

CORA You know what, Rubin Flood.

RUBIN I don't know nothin'.

CORA You never *wanted* to marry me.

RUBIN I never said that.

CORA It's true, isn't it?

RUBIN I'm tellin' ya, it ain't.

CORA It is. I've felt it all these years.
(SONNY *crosses and goes through the parlor into the dining room, still unobserved by* RUBIN *and* CORA)

RUBIN All right. If you're so determined to think it, then go ahead. I admit, in some ways I din wanna marry nobody. Can't ya understand how a man feels, givin' up his freedom?

CORA And how does a woman feel, knowing her husband married her only because . . . because he . . . (CORA *now spots* REENIE *spying between the parlor doors. She screams at her*) Reenie, get away from there!

RUBIN   None of this is what we was arguin' about in the first place. We was arguin' about the dress. Ya gotta take it back.

CORA   *I won't.*

RUBIN   *Ya will.*

CORA   Reenie's going to wear her new dress to the party, or you'll have to bury me.

RUBIN   You'll take that dress back to Loren Delman, or I'm leavin' this house for good and never comin' back.

CORA   Go on. You're only home half the time as it is. We can get along without you the rest of the time.

RUBIN   Then that's what you're gonna do. There'll be ice-cream parlors in hell before I come back to this place and listen to your jaw.
(He bolts into the hallway)

CORA   Get out! Get out and go to Ponca City. Mavis Pruitt is waiting. She's probably getting lonesome without you.
(SONNY quietly enters from the dining room, and watches)

RUBIN   By God, Cora, it's all I can do to keep from hittin' you when you talk like that.

CORA   *(Following him into hallway, taunting him. Here they are both unseen by audience)*   Go on and hit me! You wouldn't dare! *(But he does dare. We hear the sound of his blow, which sends CORA reeling back into parlor)* Rubin!
(REENIE watches from the parlor. SONNY is still in the living room)

RUBIN   I'll go to Ponca City, and drink booze and take Mavis to the movies, and raise every kind of hell I can think of. T'hell with you!
(He bolts outside)

CORA   *(Running to the door)*   Don't you ever set foot in this house again, Rubin Flood. I'll never forget what you've said. Never! Don't you ever come back inside this house again!
(We hear RUBIN'S car drive off now. CORA returns to the living room, still too dazed to be sure what has happened)

SONNY   Gee, Mom. That was the worst fight you ever had, wasn't it?

CORA   How long have you been standing there, Sonny?

SONNY   Since he hit you.

REENIE *(Coming forth)*   Did he mean it about not coming back? Oh, Mom, why did you have to say all those things? I love Daddy. Why do you say those things to him?

CORA   Oh, God, I hate for you kids to see us fight this way.

SONNY   What did he mean, he didn't want to marry you?

CORA   You're not old enough to understand these things, Sonny.

SONNY   Did he hurt you, Mom. Did he?

CORA   I'm still too mad to know whether he did or not.

REENIE   I don't think he'll ever come back. What'll we do, Mom?

CORA   Now, don't worry, Reenie.

REENIE   Will we have to go to the poorhouse?

CORA   No, of course not. Now, quit worrying.

REENIE   But if Daddy doesn't come back?

CORA   I still have the money my mother left me, haven't I? And if worst comes to worst we can always go to Oklahoma City and move in with your Aunt Lottie and Uncle Morris.

SONNY *(Jumping up and down in glee)*   Goody, goody, goody. I wanta move to Oklahoma City.

REENIE   Listen to him, Mom. He's *glad* Daddy's gone. He's *glad.*

SONNY   I don't care. I wanta move to Oklahoma City.

REENIE   I don't. *This* is home. *This* is. And I don't want to move.

CORA   Now, children!

REENIE   I hate you.

SONNY   I hate you, too. So there! Oklahoma City! Oklahoma City! I wanta move to Oklahoma City!

CORA   Stop it! There's been enough fighting in this house for one night. Reenie, take your dress upstairs and hang it in the closet.

REENIE   I hate the old dress now. It's the cause of all the trouble. I hate it.

CORA   You do what I tell you. You take that dress upstairs and hang it in the closet. You're going to go to that party if I have to take you there myself. (REENIE *starts upstairs*) The next time you're invited to a party, I'll let you go in a hand-me-down.

SONNY *(With the joy of discovering a new continent)* Oklahoma City.

CORA *(Wearily)* I'll go out and fix supper, although I don't imagine any of us will feel like eating.

SONNY I do. I'm hungry.

CORA *(A little amused)* Are you? Good. Come to me, Sonny! *(With a sudden need for affection)* Do you love me, boy? Do you love your old mom?

SONNY More than all the world with a fence around it.

CORA *(Clasping him to her)* Oh, God, what would I do without you kids? I hope you'll always love me, Sonny. I hope you always will. (REENIE *comes downstairs*) Where are you going, daughter?
(REENIE *looks disdainfully at them, and marches into the parlor, where, in a moment, we hear her playing a lovely Chopin nocturne*)

SONNY Mom, I'm going to sell my autographed photograph of Fatty Arbuckle. Millicent Dalrymple said she'd give me fifteen cents for it. And Fatty Arbuckle isn't one of my favorites any more. If I sold the photograph, I'd have enough to go to the movie tonight and buy a sack of popcorn, besides.

CORA *(Lying on the floor beside him)* If the world was falling to pieces all about you, you'd still want to go to the movies, wouldn't you?

SONNY I don't see why not.

CORA Your mother's unhappy, Sonny. Doesn't that mean anything to you?

SONNY Well . . . I'm sorry.

CORA I want you kids near me tonight. Can't you understand? Oh, God, wouldn't it be nice if life were as sweet as music! *(For a moment, mother and son lie together in each other's arms. Then* CORA *stands, as though fearing her own indulgence, and takes* SONNY *by the hand)* Come! Help me set the table, Sonny.

CURTAIN

ACT TWO

SCENE: *At rise of curtain, we hear a banging rendition of "Smiles" coming from the parlor, where* LOTTIE *is at the piano,* SONNY *by her side, both singing in hearty voices.* REENIE *stands listlessly watching, drying a dish.* MORRIS *sits in* RUBIN'S *chair, working one of those baffling little hand puzzles, which has got the best of him.* LOTTIE *proves to be a big, fleshy woman, a few years older than* CORA. *She wears a gaudy dress and lots of costume jewelry.* MORRIS *is a big defeated-looking man of wrecked virility.*

LOTTIE *and* SONNY *(Singing)*   "There are smiles that make us happy . . ."

CORA *(Coming into living room from kitchen)*   I won't need you to help me with the dishes, Reenie. I want you to go upstairs now and get ready for your party. *(Calls into parlor)* Sonny! Sonny!

MORRIS   Sure was a good dinner, Cora.

CORA   What, Morris?

MORRIS *(Trying to make himself heard above the piano)*   I said, it sure was a good dinner.

CORA   Thank you, Morris. Now go and get dressed, Reenie. (REENIE *reluctantly goes upstairs)* Sonny! Sonny! Lottie, will you please stop that racket. A body can't hear himself think.
(LOTTIE *and* SONNY *finish the chorus)*

CORA   Sonny, I said you've got to help me in the kitchen.

SONNY   Why can't Reenie?

CORA   She cleared the table for me, and now she has to bathe and get ready for her party.

SONNY   I have to do everything around here.

LOTTIE *(In the voice one uses to indulge a child)*   I think it's a shame. (SONNY *and* CORA *exit into the dining room.* LOTTIE *comes into the living room. To* MORRIS) Cora always was jealous because I could play the piano and she couldn't. *(Looks to see if* CORA *is out of hearing distance)* Do I have something to tell you! Do you know why she asked us over here? *(She hurries over to* MORRIS*)*

MORRIS   For dinner.

LOTTIE   No! She and Rubin have had another fight. She told me all about it while I was in the kitchen helping her get dinner on the table.

MORRIS   What about, this time?

LOTTIE   About a new dress she bought for Reenie. But what difference does that make? They could fight about anything. Only this time he hit her.

MORRIS   He did?

LOTTIE   Don't tell her I told you. Poor Cora. I guess maybe she has a hard time with Rubin.

MORRIS   Has Rubin walked out again?

LOTTIE   You guessed it. Do you know what she wants to do now, honey? She wants to bring the kids over to Oklahoma City to live *with us?* She says I suggested they do that some time ago. I guess maybe I did, but my God, I never thought they'd do it. We'd be perfectly miserable with her and the two kids living with us, wouldn't we, Morris? With only one extra bedroom, one of 'em would have to sleep on the davenport in the living room, and then what would happen when your patients started coming in the morning?

MORRIS   Yah. It wouldn't work out very well.

LOTTIE   No. Oh, my! The way she pampers those kids, Morris. If she had her way, she'd spoil 'em rotten.

MORRIS   What did you tell her, honey?

LOTTIE   Well, I haven't told her anything yet. I was so flabbergasted when she asked me, I just hemmed . . . (SONNY *enters the parlor to put away a big vase that* CORA *has just washed.* LOTTIE *sees him)* Hi! Honey.

SONNY   They got me working again.

LOTTIE   I think it's terrible.
*(*SONNY *exits into the dining room)*

LOTTIE   . . . and hawed until I could think of something to say. Oh, Morris, put away that puzzle and listen to me. She's going to come to you sometime this evening and ask you about it, and all you need to say is,

"I'm leaving all that in Lottie's hands, Cora." Can you remember that? Just say it real nice, like it was none of your business.

MORRIS   I'll remember.

LOTTIE   You say you will, but will you?

MORRIS   Yes, honey.

LOTTIE   I don't know. You're so afraid of hurting people's feelings.

MORRIS   That's not so.

LOTTIE   Oh, it is too. Don't I know! You had to go to see some psychologist over in Oklahoma City because you were so afraid of hurting your patients when you drilled their teeth. Now, confess it. It was actually making you sick, that you had to drill your patients' teeth and hurt them.

MORRIS   Honey, I wasn't really *sick* about it.

LOTTIE   You were too. Now remember what I say. Don't get *soft-hearted* at the last minute and tell Cora to bring the kids and come on over. My God, Morris, we'd be in the loony bin in less than two days with them in the house. Cora may be my own flesh and blood but I couldn't live with her to save my life. And I love those kids of hers. I do, Morris. But I couldn't live with them. They'd drive me crazy. You, too. You know they would.

CORA (*Enters the parlor to put napkins in the sideboard*)   Almost finished.

LOTTIE   You shoulda let me help you. (*But* CORA *has returned to the kitchen*) Cora said something to me about her getting a job at one of the big department stores over in Oklahoma City. Can you see her doin' a thing like that? I can't. "Cora," I said, "you wouldn't last two days at that kind of work, on your feet all day, taking people's sass." Well, I don't know if I convinced her or not, but I gave her something to think about. (*Sneaks back to parlor door to see if* CORA *is within earshot, then comes back to* MORRIS, *speaking in a very confidential voice*) Morris? Do you think Rubin still plays around with Mavis Pruitt over in Ponca City?

MORRIS (*Clamming up*)   I don't know, honey.

LOTTIE   You do too.

MORRIS   I'm telling you, I don't.

LOTTIE   You men, you tell each other everything, but you all want to protect each other. And wild horses and screaming ravens couldn't get you to talk.

MORRIS   Well, whatever Rubin does . . . like that . . . is *his* business.

LOTTIE   My! Don't we sound righteous all of a sudden! Well, I bet anything he still sees her.

MORRIS   Well, don't you let on to Cora.

LOTTIE   I won't. Did I ever tell you about the first time she met Rubin?

MORRIS   Yes, honey.

LOTTIE   I did not! Cora and I were coming out of the five-and-ten. She'd wanted to buy a little lace to put on a dress. And here comes Rubin, like a picture of Sin, riding down the street on a shiny black horse. My God, he was handsome. Neither of us knew who he was. But he looked at Cora and smiled, and Cora began to get all nervous and fluttery. And do you know what? He came by the house that very night and wanted to see her. Mama and Papa didn't know what to do. They stood around like they were afraid of Rubin. But Cora went out riding with him. He'd brought a buggy with him. And six weeks later they were married. Mama and Papa were worried sick. Rubin's people were all right, but they were ranchers. Kind of wild. And Cora only seventeen, not out of high school. I think that's the reason Papa had his stroke, don't you, Morris?

MORRIS   Maybe . . .

LOTTIE   I do. They just felt like Cora might as well be dead as married to a man like Rubin. But Cora was always a determined creature. Mama and Papa were no match for her when she wanted her own way.

MORRIS   Well, I like Rubin.

LOTTIE   I do, too, honey. I'm not saying anything against him. And he's made a lot better husband than I ever thought he would. But I'm glad *I'm* not married to him. I'd be worried to death all the time. I'm glad I'm married to a nice man I can trust.
(MORRIS *does not know how to respond to this endearment. He crosses the room troubledly*)

MORRIS   What'll Cora do if Rubin doesn't come back?

LOTTIE   Well, that's not our problem, honey.

MORRIS   Yes, but just the same, I . . .

LOTTIE   Listen, she's got a nice big house here, hasn't she? She can take in roomers if she has to. And Mama left her two thousand dollars when she died, didn't she? Yes, Cora was the baby, so Mama left the money to her. I'm not going to worry.

REENIE (*Upstairs*)   Aunt Lottie!

MORRIS   All right. I was just wondering.

LOTTIE   Now, remember. All you've got to say is, "I'm leaving all that to Lottie, Cora."

MORRIS   Yes, honey.
(REENIE *comes downstairs looking somewhat wan and frightened*)

LOTTIE   Shhhh! (*Now she turns to* REENIE *with a prepared smile*) Well, honey, aren't you getting ready for your party? Morris and I are dying to see your new dress.

REENIE   I don't feel well. I wish I didn't have to go.

LOTTIE (*Alarmed*)   You don't feel well? Did you tell your mother?

REENIE   Yes. But she won't believe me. I wish you'd tell her, Aunt Lottie.

LOTTIE (*Rushes excitedly into dining room, where we hear her speaking to* CORA)   Cora! Reenie says she isn't feeling well. Cora, I think maybe she shouldn't go to the party. She says she doesn't want to go. Cora, what do you think is wrong?

CORA (*Enters living room from dining room—followed by* LOTTIE)   There's nothing wrong with the child, Lottie.

LOTTIE   But she says she isn't feeling well, Cora. (*Turns to* REENIE) Come here, honey, let me see if you've got a temperature. No. Not a sign of temperature. Stick out your tongue. Are you sick at your stomach?

REENIE   Kind of.

LOTTIE   My God, Cora. Her little hands are like ice.

CORA (*Quite calm and wise*)   There's nothing wrong with the child, Lottie. She gets to feeling like this every time she goes to a party.

LOTTIE   She's not going to have a very good time if she doesn't feel well.

CORA   It's something she's got to get over, Lottie. Plans are already made now. I got her the dress and she's got a date with a boy who's come here all the way from California. Now, I'm not going to let her play sick and not go. The Ralston girl would never invite Reenie to another party as long as she lived if she backed out now.
(*Her strategy defeated,* REENIE *goes back up the stairs*)

LOTTIE   It's awful funny when a young girl doesn't want to go to a party, don't you think so, Morris? (*She watches* REENIE'S *departure, puzzledly*) I just thought of something. I've got a bottle of perfume I'm going to give her. It's Coty's L'Origan. Finest perfume made. One of the big drugstores in Oklahoma City was having an anniversary sale. With each box of Coty's face powder, they gave you a little bottle of perfume, stuck right on top of the box. Morris, run out to the car and get me that package. It's on the back seat. I'll take it upstairs to Reenie. It'll make her feel good, don't you think?

CORA   That's very thoughtful of you, Lottie.

MORRIS   (*On his way to door*)   You'll have her smelling like a fancy woman.

LOTTIE   (*With a sudden bite*)   How do *you* know what a fancy woman smells like?

MORRIS   I can make a joke, can't I?
(MORRIS *exits.* CORA *and* LOTTIE *sit on either side of the table*)

LOTTIE   It was a wonderful dinner, Cora.

CORA   I'm glad you thought so. It all tasted like ashes to me.

LOTTIE   Oh, now, Cora, quit taking on.

CORA   Seventeen years we've been married, Lottie, and we still can't get along.

LOTTIE   What are you talking about? Why, I've known times when you got along just fine . . . for months at a time.

CORA   When Rubin was gone.

LOTTIE   Cora, that's not so.

CORA   Lottie, it's not good for kids to see their parents fighting.

LOTTIE   Cora, you've got the two nicest kids in the whole world. Why, they're wonderful children, Cora.

CORA   I worry about them, Lottie . . . You saw Reenie just now. Here she is, sick because she's going to a party, when most girls her age would be tickled to death. And the other boys tease Sonny so.

LOTTIE   Oh, Reenie'll get over that. So will Sonny.

CORA   Kids don't just "get over" these things, in some magic way. These troubles stay with kids sometimes, and affect their lives when they grow up.

MORRIS *(Returns with a small package)*   This what you want?

LOTTIE   Yes. Reenie—I've got something for you, Reenie. I've got something here to make you smell good. Real French perfume. Morris says it'll make you smell like a fancy woman.
(She goes running upstairs, exuding her own brand of warmth and affection)

CORA   Lottie's awful good-hearted, Morris.

MORRIS   She thinks an awful lot of your kids, Cora.

CORA   I know she does. Morris, I've been thinking, wouldn't it be nice if Sonny and Reenie could go to those big schools you have in Oklahoma City? I mean . . .

LOTTIE *(Hurrying back downstairs)*   Cora, I wish you'd let me curl Reenie's hair for her. I could have her looking like a real baby doll. I'm an artist at it. Last week, Morris took me to a party at the Shrine, and everybody told me I had the prettiest head of hair at the whole party.

CORA   Go on and do it.

LOTTIE   I can't right now. She's in the bathtub. When are you going to get your hair bobbed, Cora?

CORA   Rubin doesn't like bobbed hair.

LOTTIE   Oh, he doesn't! You like my bobbed hair, don't you, Morris?

MORRIS   It's all right, honey.

LOTTIE   I'll be darned if I'd let any man tell me whether I could bob my hair or not. Why, I wouldn't go back to long hair now for anything. Morris says maybe I should take up smoking cigarettes now. Would you believe it, Cora? Women all over Oklahoma City are smoking cigarettes now. Isn't that disgraceful? What in God's name are we all coming to?

CORA *(There is too much on her mind for her to partake now of LOTTIE's small talk)*   I . . . I'd better finish up in the kitchen.
(She exits through the dining-room door)

LOTTIE   Morris, I don't know what to do. I just can't bear to see little Cora so unhappy.

MORRIS   After all, it's not your worry, honey.

LOTTIE   Oh, I know, but in a way it *is* my worry. I mean, I've always looked after Cora, ever since we were girls. I took her to her teacher the first day of school. I gave up the wishbone for her every time we had fried chicken. She was the baby of the family, and I guess we all felt we had to pamper her.

MORRIS   Honey, if you want to take in her and the kids, it's up to you. We'd manage somehow.

LOTTIE   Oh, God, Morris! Life'd be miserable.

SONNY *(Enters through parlor)*   Wanta see my movie stars, Aunt Lottie?

LOTTIE   I guess so, honey. (SONNY *goes into parlor to get scrapbooks as* LOTTIE *turns to* MORRIS *with a private voice*) Every time we come over here we've got to look at his movie stars.

MORRIS   Got any of Norma Talmadge?

SONNY *(Spreading the scrapbook on the floor before them)*   Sure.

LOTTIE   Norma Talmadge, Norma Talmadge! That's all you ever think about is Norma Talmadge. I don't know what you see in her. Besides, she's a Catholic.

MORRIS   Honey, you've just got a bug about the Catholics.

LOTTIE   Oh I do, do I! Maybe you'd like to marry Norma Talmadge someday and then let the Pope tell you what to do the rest of your life, making you swear to leave all your money to the church, and bring up all your children Catholic, and then join the Knights of Columbus and take an oath to go out and kill all the nice Protestant women when the day comes for the Catholics to take over the world.
(CORA *enters the parlor on her way to the sideboard, then wanders into the living room*)

MORRIS   Honey, where do you pick up these stories?

LOTTIE   Well, it's the truth. Marietta Flagmeyer told me. Cora, Marietta has this very close friend who used to be a Catholic but isn't any more. She even joined a convent, but she ran away because she found out all those things and wouldn't stand for them. This friend told Marietta that the Catholics keep the basements of their churches filled with guns and all kinds of ammunition . . .

CORA *(She has heard* LOTTIE's *rantings before)*   Lottie!
(*She shakes her head hopelessly and returns to the parlor, on her way to the kitchen*)

LOTTIE   . . . because some day they plan to rise and take over the world, and kill off all the rest of us who don't want to be Catholics. I believe every word of it, too.

MORRIS   Well . . . I still like Norma Talmadge. Got any of Bebe Daniels?

SONNY   Yes.
(He hands MORRIS *a picture, which* LOTTIE *snaps up first for an approving look)*

LOTTIE   I don't know what you see in her.
(She now passes the picture on to MORRIS*)*

MORRIS   You don't like any of the women stars, honey.

LOTTIE   I guess I don't. I hear they're all a bunch of trollops. *(To* SONNY*)* Honey, when is your daddy coming home?

SONNY   Oh, he's not coming back at all. He and Mom had a fight. Here's one of your favorites, Aunt Lottie.
(He hands her a picture)

LOTTIE   Who? Rudolph Valentino. He's not one of my favorites at all.

MORRIS   You saw *The Sheik* four times.

LOTTIE   That's just because Marietta Flagmeyer wanted me to keep her company.

MORRIS   Rudolph Valentino must be a Catholic, too. He's an Eyetalian.

LOTTIE   But he's not a Catholic. Marietta's friend has a book that lists all the people in Hollywood who are Catholics. *(She studies the picture very intently)* You know, it scares me a little to look at him. Those eyes, that seem to be laughing at you, and all those white teeth. I think it's a sin for a man to be as pretty as he is. Why, I'd be scared to death to let a man like him touch me. (CORA *returns now, without her apron; she is carrying a paper bag)* But you know, they say he's really a very nice man. Cora, do you know there's this woman over in Oklahoma City who worships Rudolph Valentino? That's the truth. Marietta knows her. She's made a little shrine to him down in her basement, and she keeps the room filled with candles and she goes down there every day and says a little prayer for him.

CORA   I thought you were going to fix Reenie's hair.

LOTTIE   Oh, yes. I guess she's out of the bathtub now.

CORA (*Puts the bag on the table*)   There's a lot of fried chicken left, Lottie. I brought you some to take home with you.

LOTTIE   Won't you and the kids want it?

CORA   They won't eat anything but the breast.

LOTTIE   Thanks, Cora.

CORA   Sonny, I don't want your pictures all over the floor when the young people come by for Reenie.

SONNY   All right.

MORRIS (*As* LOTTIE *takes a drumstick out of the bag*)   Honey, you just ate.

LOTTIE   Don't scold me, Daddy. (*She whispers boldly to him before starting upstairs*) Remember what I told you, Morris. (*Now she goes hurrying up the stairs*) Reenie! I'm coming up to fix your hair. I'm going to turn you into a real baby doll.

REENIE (*Upstairs*)   I'm in here, Aunt Lottie.
(MORRIS *draws over to the door, as though hoping to evade* CORA)

CORA   Morris . . . Morris! I suppose Lottie told you what's happened.

MORRIS   Well, uh . . . yes, Cora . . . she said something about it.

CORA   I guess now that maybe my folks were right, Morris. I shouldn't have married Rubin.

MORRIS   You're going to forget all this squabble after a while, Cora. So's Rubin.

CORA   I don't think we *should* forget it. I don't think we should *try* to come back together. I think I've failed.

MORRIS   Now, Cora, I think you're exaggerating things in your own mind.

CORA   Morris, I'm only thirty-four. That's still young. I thought I'd like to take the kids to Oklahoma City and put them in school there, and get myself a job in one of the department stores. I know I've never done work like that, but I think I'd like it, and . . . it seems to me that I've got to, Morris. I've got to.

MORRIS   Well, Cora . . . maybe . . .

LOTTIE (*Upstairs we see her feet treading the hallway*)   Let's go into the bathroom, Reenie, where the light's better.

MORRIS   It's awful hard, Cora, being on your feet all day.

CORA But I'd get used to it.

MORRIS Well . . . it's hard for me to advise you, Cora.

CORA Morris, I was wondering if maybe the kids and I could come and live with you and Lottie for a while. Just for a while. Until we got used to the city. Until I got myself a job and we felt more or less at home.

MORRIS Well, I . . . uh . . .

CORA I promise we wouldn't be any bother. I mean, I'd keep things straightened up after the kids, and do as much of the cooking as Lottie wanted me to do.

MORRIS Well, I . . . uh . . .

CORA I just don't know what else the kids and I can do, Morris.

MORRIS Yes. Well . . . Cora, I don't know just what to say.

CORA Would we be too much in the way, Morris?

MORRIS Oh, no. Of course not, Cora. *But . . .*

CORA *(Hopefully)* I think we could manage. And I'd pay our share of the bills. I'd insist on that.
(FLIRT, PUNKY and SAMMY are seen through the window, coming onto the porch)

MORRIS Well, Cora, I . . .

LOTTIE *(Comes hurtling halfway down the stairs, full of anxiety)* Cora, Reenie's sick. She's vomiting all over the bathroom.
(She bustles back upstairs as CORA starts to follow)

CORA Oh, my God! *(The doorbell rings, catching CORA for a moment)* Oh, dear! It's the young people after Reenie. Sonny, put on your manners and answer the door. (SONNY *runs to the door, stopping to turn on the porch light before opening it. We see the three young people on the porch outside—*FLIRT *in dazzling party dress, and the two boys in uniforms from a nearby military academy. One boy,* PUNKY GIVENS, *is seen drinking from a flask, preparing himself to meet people. Inside,* CORA *starts upstairs in worried concern)* Oh, dear! What could be wrong with the child? Morris, try to entertain the young people until I get back.
(CORA goes off. SONNY *swings open the door)*

SONNY Won't you come in?

FLIRT *(Comes dancing into the hallway, bringing the atmosphere of a chilly spring night with her)*   Hi, Sonny! Is your sister ready?

SONNY   Not yet.

FLIRT   Oh, shucks! *(Sticks her head out the door)* Come on in, fellows. We're going to have to wait. (PUNKY GIVENS *and* SAMMY GOLDENBAUM *make a colorful entrance. Both are dressed in uniforms of lustrous blue, which fit them like smooth upholstery.* FLIRT *begins the introductions)* Sammy, this is Sonny Flood, Reenie's little brother.
(SAMMY GOLDENBAUM *steps forth correctly, his plumed headgear in his hand. He is a darkly beautiful young man of seventeen, with lustrous black hair, black eyes and a captivating smile. Yet, something about him seems a little foreign, at least in comparison with the Midwestern company in which he now finds himself. He could be a Persian prince, strayed from his native kingdom. But he has become adept over the years in adapting himself, and he shows an eagerness to make friends and to be liked)*

SAMMY   Hi, Sonny!

SONNY *(Shaking hands)*   Hi!

FLIRT *(Bringing* PUNKY *up from the rear)*   And this is Punky Givens. *(She all but drags him from the dark corner of the hallway to face the lighted room full of people. For* PUNKY *is a disappointment as a human being. The military academy has done nothing as yet for his posture, and he wears his uniform as though embarrassed by its splendor. He offers a limp hand when being introduced, mumbles some incoherent greeting, and then retires in hopes that no one will notice him. These introductions made,* FLIRT *now notices* MORRIS)* Oh, hello! I'm Flirt Conroy. How're you?

MORRIS   How d'ya do? I'm Morris Lacey. Reenie's uncle. From Oklahoma City.

FLIRT   Oh, yes, I've heard her speak about you. Fellows, this is Dr. Lacey. He's Reenie's uncle. From Oklahoma City.

SAMMY *(Crossing the room to present himself to* MORRIS, *he is brisk and alert, even though his speech betrays a slight stammer)*   How do you do, sir? My name is G-Goldenbaum. Sammy, they call me.

MORRIS   Glad to know you, Sammy.

FLIRT   And this is Punky Givens. *(Nudging him)* Stand up straight, Punky.

MORRIS   Glad to know you, Punky. (PUNKY *mumbles.* MORRIS *now feels the*

burden of his responsibility as temporary host) Uh . . . anyone care for a
Life Saver?
(He offers a pack from his pocket, but no one is interested. LOTTIE *comes
bustling down the stairs, eager to take over the situation, exuberantly bab-
bling inconsequentials all the way down)*

LOTTIE Hello, everyone! I'm Lottie Lacey, Reenie's aunt. I'm Cora Flood's
sister. From Oklahoma City. Oklahoma City's a great big town now.
People say in another ten years it's going to be the biggest city in the
whole United States, bigger even than New York or Chicago. You're the
little Conroy girl, aren't you? I've heard my sister speak of you. My!
What a pretty red dress. Have you all met my husband? Dr. Lacey. He's
a dentist. Come over to Oklahoma City and he'll pull all your teeth. *(She
laughs heartily, and then her eyes slowly widen at the magnificent uniforms)* My goodness! Aren't those handsome getups?

SAMMY *(Stepping forth)* How do you do, ma'am? I'm Sammy
Goldenbaum. From California.

LOTTIE Oh, yes. Cora told me about the young man from California. He's
from Hollywood, Morris. His mother's in the movies. Has she played in
anything I might have seen?

SAMMY She was in T-Thomas Meighan's last picture. Her name is Gertrude Vanderhof. It was a very small part. She isn't a star or anything.

LOTTIE Gertrude Vanderhof! Did we see Thomas Meighan's last picture,
Morris? I don't believe so. I like Thomas Meighan, but we don't have
time to see *all* the movies. Do you think you ever saw Gertrude
Vanderhof in anything, Morris?
*(*LOTTIE *seems to refer to her husband on every topic without waiting for his
judgment. Nevertheless,* MORRIS *mulls over this last query as* FLIRT *interrupts)*

FLIRT Mrs. Lacey, have you met Punky Givens?

LOTTIE How do you do? I've heard my sister speak of you. Your people are
very prominent in town, aren't they? Yes, I've heard Cora speak of them.
*(*PUNKY *offers a hand and mumbles)* What did you say? *(He repeats his
mumble.* LOTTIE *is still at sea but makes the best of things)* Thank you very
much.
(At the top of the stairs, we see REENIE'S *feet trying to get up the courage to
bring her down, and we hear* CORA *coaxing her)*

CORA *(Off)* Go on, Reenie.
(But REENIE *can't make it yet. The feet go scurrying back to safety)*

LOTTIE (*Trying to avoid embarrassment*)   Well, I'm afraid you're all going to have to wait a few minutes. Reenie isn't quite ready.

CORA (*Upstairs*)   Reenie, not another word.

LOTTIE   Cora's upstairs now, helping her. I guess you'll have to entertain yourselves awhile. Do any of you play mah-jong?
(*She notices the bag of fried chicken, and hides it under the table*)

FLIRT   I want to play some music. Got any new piano rolls, Sonny?

SONNY   A few.
(*They run into the parlor, to the piano*)

FLIRT   Gee, I wish you had a Victrola like we do.

LOTTIE (*Sitting, turning her attention to* SAMMY)   My, you're a long way from home, aren't you?

SAMMY   Yes, ma'am.

LOTTIE   Morris and I went to California once. A Shriners' convention. Oh, we thought it was perfectly wonderful, all those oranges and things. Didn't we, Morris? I should think you'd want to go home on your spring vacation.

SAMMY   Well, I . . . I guess I don't really have a home . . . Mrs. Lacey.
(SONNY *wanders back from the parlor.* SAMMY *fills him with curiosity and fascination*)

LOTTIE   Did you tell me your mother lived out there?

SAMMY   Yes, but, you see, she's pretty busy in moving pictures, and . . . Oh, she feels awfully bad that she doesn't have more time for me. Really she does. But she doesn't have a place where I could stay right now . . . and . . . But, it's not *her* fault.

LOTTIE   Where's your father?

SAMMY   Oh, I never knew him.

LOTTIE   You never knew your father?

SAMMY   No. You see, he died before I was born. My mother has been married . . . a few times since then. But I never met any of her husbands . . . although they were all very fine gentlemen.

LOTTIE   Well—I just never knew anyone who didn't have a home. Do you spend your whole life in military academies?

SAMMY   Just about. I bet I've been in almost every military academy in the whole country. Well, I take that back. There's some I didn't go to. I mean . . . there's some that wouldn't take me.

SONNY *(Out of the innocent blue)* My mother says you're a Jew.

LOTTIE *(Aghast)* Sonny!

SAMMY   Well . . . yes, Sonny. I guess I am.

LOTTIE *(Consolingly)* That's perfectly all right. Why, we don't think a thing about a person's being Jewish, do we, Morris?

MORRIS   No. Of course not.

SAMMY   My father was Jewish. Mother told me. Mother isn't Jewish at all. Oh, my mother has the most beautiful blond hair. I guess I take after my father . . . in looks, anyhow. He was an actor, too, but he got killed in an automobile accident.

LOTTIE   That's too bad. Sonny, I think you should apologize.

SONNY   Did I say something bad?

SAMMY   Oh, that's all right. It doesn't bother me that I'm Jewish. Not any more. I guess it used to a little . . . Yes, it did used to a little.

LOTTIE *(Who must find a remedy for everything)* You know what you ought to do? You ought to join the Christian Science church. Now, I'm not a member myself, but I know this Jewish woman over in Oklahoma City, and she was very, very unhappy, wasn't she, Morris? But she joined the Christian Science church and has been perfectly happy ever since.

SONNY   I didn't mean to say anything wrong.

SAMMY   You didn't say anything wrong, Sonny.
(The piano begins playing "The Sheik of Araby" with precise, automatic rhythm. FLIRT *dances in from the parlor)*

FLIRT   Come on, Punky, let's dance. *(She sings)* The Sheik of Araby— boom—boom—boom—his heart belongs to me. Come *on*, Punky.

SAMMY *(Always courteous, to* LOTTIE*)* Would you care to dance, ma'am?

LOTTIE   Me? Good heavens, no. I haven't danced since I was a girl. But I certainly appreciate your asking. Isn't he respectful, Morris?
*(*LOTTIE *exits to dining room)*

SAMMY   Wanta wild West ride, Sonny?

(He kneels on the floor, permitting SONNY *to straddle his back. Then* SAMMY *kicks his feet in the air like a wild colt, as* SONNY *holds to him tight)*

FLIRT *(At the back of the room, instructs* PUNKY *in the intricacies of a new step)*   No, Punky. That's not it. You take one step to the left and then *dip.* See? Oh, it's a wonderful step, and all the kids are doing it.

LOTTIE *(Enters from kitchen with a plate of cookies, which she offers to* SAMMY *and* SONNY*)*   Would you like a cookie?

SAMMY *(Getting to his feet, the ride over)*   Gee, that gets to be pretty strenuous.
*(*FLIRT *and* PUNKY *now retire to the parlor where they indulge in a little private lovemaking)*

SONNY   Where did you get those clothes?

SAMMY   They gave them to me at the academy, Sonny.

FLIRT *(Protesting* PUNKY'S *advances)*   Punky, don't.
*(*LOTTIE *observes this little intimacy, having just started into the parlor with the plate of cookies. It rouses some of her righteousness)*

SAMMY   No. I take that back. They didn't *give* them to me. They never give you anything at that place. I paid for them. Plenty!

SONNY   Why do you wear a sword?

SAMMY *(Pulls the sword from its sheath, like a buccaneer, and goes charging about the room in search of imagined villains)*   I wear a sword to protect myself! See! To kill off all the villains in the world. *(He frightens* LOTTIE*)* Oh, don't worry, ma'am. It's not sharp. I couldn't hurt anyone with it, even if I wanted to. We just wear them for show.

SONNY *(Jumping up and down)*   Can I have a sword? I want a sword.

SAMMY   Do you, Sonny? Do you want a sword? Here, Sonny, I'll give you *my* sword, for all the good it'll do you.

LOTTIE *(To* MORRIS*)*   Cora will probably buy Sonny a sword now. *(Now* SONNY *takes the sword and imitates the actions of* SAMMY. LOTTIE *is apprehensive)* Now, you be careful, Sonny.

SAMMY   What do you want a sword for, Sonny?

SONNY *(With a lunge)*   To *show* people.

LOTTIE   Sonny! Be careful with that thing.

SAMMY   And what do you want to show people, Sonny?

SONNY   I just want to *show* 'em.
(*He places the sword between his arm and his chest, then drops to the floor, the sword rising far above his body, giving the appearance that he is impaled.* LOTTIE *is horrified*)

LOTTIE   Oh, darling—put it down. Sonny, please don't play with that nasty thing any more.
(SONNY *rises now and laughs with* SAMMY. LOTTIE *puts the sword away in the parlor, where she again comes upon* FLIRT *and* PUNKY, *now engaged in more serious necking. Morally outraged, she runs up the stairs to inform* CORA)

SAMMY   (*Kneeling beside* SONNY, *as though to make himself a physical equal*)   What'll we do now, Sonny? Are there any games you want to play? Do you want to fight Indians? or set bear traps? or go flying over volcanoes? or climb the Alps?

SONNY   (*Eagerly*)   Yes . . . yes.

SAMMY   Gee, so do I, Sonny. But we can't. Not tonight anyway. What else can we do?

SONNY   I can show you my movie stars.

SAMMY   I've had enough of movie stars. What else?

SONNY   I can speak a piece.

SAMMY   You can? (*Jumps to his feet*)   Hey, everyone! Stop the music. Sonny's going to speak a piece.
(SAMMY *stops the piano, which* FLIRT *finds quite annoying*)

LOTTIE   (*Hurrying downstairs*)   Did you hear that, Morris? Sonny's going to speak a piece.

FLIRT   (*To* SAMMY)   Hey, what are you doing?

SAMMY   (*To* SONNY)   Where do you want to stand, sir?

LOTTIE   He's got a little platform in the parlor where he practices.

SAMMY   (*Having taken over as impresario*)   Into the parlor, everyone. Into the parlor to hear Sonny speak his piece.

FLIRT   (*Pulling* PUNKY'S *arm*)   Come on, Punky. Come on. We *have* to listen, don't we?

SAMMY   Quiet, everyone. Quiet!
(*All enter the parlor, except* MORRIS, *who crosses toward the door, as though he hoped to escape, as* SONNY *begins the famous soliloquy with boyish*

fervor. MORRIS *looks as though he might share some of Hamlet's woes. After* SONNY *begins,* CORA *starts down the stairs with* REENIE.)

SONNY
"To be, or not to be: that is the question:
Whether 'tis nobler in the mind to suffer
The slings and arrows of outrageous fortune,
Or to take arms against a sea of troubles,
And by opposing end them? To die: to sleep;
No more; and, by a sleep to say we end
The heart-ache and the thousand natural shocks
That flesh is heir to, 'tis a consummation
Devoutly to be wish'd. To die, to sleep;
To sleep: perchance to dream: ay, there's the rub,
For in that sleep of death what dreams may come
When we have shuffled off this mortal coil,
Must give us pause. . . ."

CORA *(While* SONNY *is reciting)*   Oh, Sonny's reciting. Why, he's reciting Shakespeare. He must have gotten out that dusty volume of Shakespeare over in the bookcase, and memorized that speech all on his own. *(Points to* SAMMY *in the parlor)* Reenie, there's your young man. Isn't he handsome? Now you're going to have a good time. I can feel it in my bones. *(*SONNY *and* CORA *finish speaking at the same time. There is immediate loud acclaim for* SONNY*)*

SAMMY   That was *wonderful,* Sonny.
(All come into the living room now, SAMMY *carrying* SONNY *on his shoulders like a triumphant hero)*

LOTTIE   He's a second Jackie Coogan.

FLIRT   That was just wonderful, Sonny.

LOTTIE   Cora, you should have been here. Sonny recited Shakespeare. It was just wonderful.

CORA   Yes. I heard him.

SAMMY   Sonny's a genius. I'm going to take you to Hollywood, Sonny, and put you in the movies. You'll be the greatest actor out there, Sonny.

FLIRT   Oh, I think Shakespeare's just wonderful. I'm going to read him sometime, really I am.

CORA *(Going to* SAMMY*)*   Good evening, young man. I'm Mrs. Flood.

SAMMY *(Putting* SONNY *down)*   Beg your pardon, ma'am. I'm Sammy Goldenbaum.

CORA   Welcome. I see my son's been entertaining you.

SAMMY   He sure has, ma'am.

CORA   He started speaking pieces about a year ago. Just picked it up. Some people think he's talented.

SAMMY   I think so, too, ma'am. Very.

CORA *(Brings* REENIE *forth)*   Reenie! Sammy, this is my daughter Reenie.

SAMMY   Good evening, Reenie.

REENIE *(Reluctantly)*   Good evening.

SAMMY   You certainly look nice. That's a very beautiful dress.

FLIRT   Isn't it cute! I helped her pick it out. (CORA *quietly grabs* FLIRT'S *arm and prevents her from taking over)* Ouch!

SAMMY   Gee! I didn't expect you to be . . . like you are. I mean . . . well, Punky told me you were a friend of Flirt's, so I just naturally thought you'd be . . . well, kind of like Flirt is. Although Flirt is a very nice girl. I didn't mean to imply anything against her. But . . . *you're* very nice, too, in a different way.

REENIE *(Still a little distrustful)*   Thank you . . .

SAMMY   Would you call me *Sammy?*

REENIE   Sammy.

SAMMY   And may I call you Reenie?

REENIE   I guess so.

SAMMY   It's awfully nice of you to let me take you to the party. I know just how a girl feels, going out with some crazy guy she doesn't even know.

REENIE   Oh . . . that's all right. After all, you don't know anything about me, either.

SAMMY   You know, I've never been to many parties, have you?

REENIE   Not many.

SAMMY   I always worry that maybe people aren't going to like me, when I go to a party. Isn't that crazy? Do you ever get kind of a sick feeling in the pit of your stomach when you dread things? Gee, I wouldn't want to miss a party for anything. But every time I go to one, I have to reason with myself to keep from feeling that the whole world's against me. See, I've spent almost my whole life in military academies. My mother doesn't have a place for me, where she lives. She . . . she just doesn't know what else to do with me. But you mustn't misunderstand about my mother. She's really a very lovely person. I guess every boy thinks his mother is very beautiful, but my mother really is. She tells me in every letter she writes how sorry she is that we can't be together more, but she has to think of her work. One time we were together, though. She met me in San Francisco once, and we were together for two whole days. She let me take her to dinner and to a show and to dance. Just like we were sweethearts. It was the most wonderful time I ever had. And then I had to go back to the old military academy. Every time I walk into the barracks, I get kind of a depressed feeling. It's got hard stone walls. Pictures of generals hanging all over . . . oh, they're very fine gentlemen, but they all look so kind of hard-boiled and stern . . . you know what I mean. (CORA *and* LOTTIE *stand together, listening to* SAMMY's *speech with motherly expressions.* FLIRT *is bored.* PUNKY *is half asleep, and now he gives a sudden, audible yawn that startles everyone*) Well, gee! I guess I've bored you enough, telling you about myself.

CORA *and* LOTTIE   Oh, no. You haven't either.

FLIRT *(Impatient to get to the party)*   Come on, kids. Let's hurry.

SAMMY *(Tenderly, to* REENIE)   Are you ready?

CORA *(As though fearing* REENIE *might bolt and run)*   Reenie?

REENIE   Yes.

SAMMY   May I help you into your wrap?
   *(The word "*wrap*" is a false glorification of her Sunday coat, which he offers her, helping her into it)*

REENIE   Thank you.

CORA *(Whispering to* LOTTIE)   I wish I could have bought her one of those little fur jackets like Flirt is wearing.

FLIRT   Stand up straight, Punky, and say good night to everyone.
   *(*PUNKY *tries again, but remains inarticulate)*

CORA *(Assuming that* PUNKY *said good night)*   Good night, Punky. Tell your mother hello for me.

FLIRT Very pleased to have met you, Mr. and Mrs. Lacey. Good night, Mrs. Flood.

CORA Good night, Flirt.

LOTTIE *and* MORRIS Good night.

SONNY *(Pulling at* SAMMY's *coat tails)* Do you have to go?

SAMMY I'm afraid I do, Sonny.

SONNY Can I go, too? Please? Can I go, too?

SAMMY Gee, I don't know. *(He thinks a moment and then consults* FLIRT *and* PUNKY*)* Hey, is there any reason Sonny can't come along? I promise to look after him. Think what a great time he'd have.
(FLIRT *and* PUNKY *look dubious)*

SONNY *(Takes his welcome immediately for granted and dances about the room joyously)* Goody, goody! I'm going to the party. I'm going to the party.

REENIE *(Running to* CORA's *side)* Mother, I'm not going if Sonny goes too. Other girls don't have to be bothered by their little brothers.

CORA I agree with you, daughter.

FLIRT *(She loves to lash out when she has a victim)* No. It's not a kids' party, Sammy. That was a stupid idea. I think you should mind your own business.

CORA *(Trying to cool* FLIRT's *temper)* Now, Flirt.

FLIRT *(To* REENIE*)* He's always trying to boss everyone.

CORA *(To* SAMMY*)* I guess Sonny'd better not go.

SONNY *(Crying, jumping in protest)* I want to go to the party. I want to go to the party.

SAMMY *(Trying to be consoling)* I guess it was a pretty dumb idea, Sonny.

SONNY I WANT TO GO TO THE PARTY! I WANT TO GO TO THE PARTY!
(SONNY *flies into a real tantrum now, throws himself on the floor, pounding the floor with his fists and kicking it with his toes, his face red with rage.* CORA *and* LOTTIE *flutter about him like nervous hens)*

CORA Sonny! Sonny! Stop it this instant. Sonny, I'll not let you go to another movie for a whole month if you don't stop.

LOTTIE   Oh, what'll I do? Oh, here, Sonny, do you want a little cookie, sweetheart?

FLIRT   Now we'll never get there.

CORA   I never can do a thing with him when he throws one of these tantrums.

SAMMY   *(Quietly goes to* SONNY'S *side and speaks in a voice that is firm with authority, yet still thoughtful and considerate)*   Sonny, that's no way to behave.

SONNY   *(Suddenly quiet)*   Isn't it?

SAMMY   No, Sonny. You mustn't ever act like that.

SONNY   *(More reasonable now)*   But I want to go to the party.

SAMMY   But if you act that way, no one's *ever* going to ask you to a party.

SONNY   Aren't they?

SAMMY   No, Sonny. You have to be a good boy before people ask you to parties. Even then, they don't always ask you.

SONNY   I love parties more than anything else in the world.

SAMMY   So do I, Sonny. I love parties, too. But there's lots of parties I can't go to.

SONNY   Honest?

SAMMY   Honest. It was wrong of me to suggest that you go to the party tonight. You're not old enough yet. You'll be old enough someday though, and then you can go to all the parties you like.

SONNY   Can I?

SAMMY   Sure. Now, I tell you what I'll do. I'll gather up all the favors I can find at the party. Want me to? And I'll give them to your sister to bring home to you. And then you can have a party here all by yourself. Would you like that? You can throw a big party in Sammy's honor, without any old grownups around to interfere. Will that make you happy?

SONNY   Yes, yes.

SAMMY   O.K. Are we still buddies?

SONNY   Yes.

SAMMY   Forever and ever?

SONNY   Forever and ever.
(SONNY *impulsively hugs him*)

SAMMY   Gee! I love kids.

CORA *(Awed as though by a miracle)*   You're the first person in the entire world who's ever been able to do a thing with the boy when he goes into one of his tantrums.

SAMMY   You know, it's funny, but . . . I always seem to know just how kids feel.

FLIRT *(Still impatient)*   Come on, Sammy.
(FLIRT *and* PUNKY *exit*)

CORA   Good night, Sammy. I hope you'll be able to come back sometime.

SAMMY   Thank you, ma'am. It's very nice to feel welcome.

LOTTIE *and* MORRIS   Good night. Come over to see us sometime in Oklahoma City. It's a big town. You can stay in the extra bedroom. I hope you like cats.

CORA *(While* LOTTIE *and* MORRIS *are speaking)*   Oh, Reenie, don't forget your present. You're feeling better now, aren't you?

REENIE   Yes, Mom.

SAMMY *(Breaking away from* LOTTIE *and* MORRIS*)*   Excuse me.
(SAMMY *offers* REENIE *his arm now, and together they walk proudly out*)

CORA *(After they exit)*   Why, that's the nicest young man I ever met.

LOTTIE   I thought so, too, Cora. And my goodness, he was handsome. Morris says he felt sorry for him, though.

CORA   Sorry? Oh, Morris.

LOTTIE   He seemed like a perfectly happy boy to me. But Morris says he looked like a very unhappy boy to him. What makes you think that, Morris?

MORRIS   Oh . . . I don't know.

CORA   Unhappy? Why, he made himself right at home, didn't he?

LOTTIE   I should say he did. He was laughing and enjoying himself. But Morris says sometimes the people who act the happiest are really the saddest.

CORA   Oh, Morris.

LOTTIE Morris, I think you make these things up. Ever since you went to that psychologist, you've gone around imagining everyone's unhappy. (MORRIS *quietly gets up and walks to the door, leaving* LOTTIE *to wonder if she has said anything wrong*) Where are you going, Morris?

MORRIS Thought I'd go out for a little walk, honey.
(MORRIS *exits*)

LOTTIE (*Following him to the door*) Oh. Well, don't be gone long. We've got to get started back soon.

CORA Oh, please don't talk about going.

LOTTIE My God, Cora, we can't stay here all night. (*She peers out the window now, wondering about* MORRIS) Morris is funny, Cora. Sometimes he just gets up like that and walks away. I never know why. Sometimes he's gone for hours at a time. He says the walk helps his digestion, but I think it's because he just wants to get away from me at times. Did you ever notice how he is with people? Like tonight. He sat there when all the young people were here, and he didn't say hardly a word. His mind was a thousand miles away. Like he was thinking about something. He seems to be always thinking about something.

CORA Morris is nice to you. You've got no right to complain.

LOTTIE He's nice to me . . . in *some* ways.

CORA Good heavens, Lottie! He gave you those red patent-leather slippers, and that fox neckpiece . . . you should be grateful.

LOTTIE I know, but . . . there's *some* things he hasn't given me.

CORA Lottie! That's not his fault. You've got no right to hold that against him!

LOTTIE Oh, it's just fine for you to talk. You've got two nice kids to keep you company. What have I got but a house full of cats?

CORA Lottie, you always claimed you never wanted children.

LOTTIE Well . . . what else can I say to people?

CORA (*This is something of a revelation to her*) I just never knew.

LOTTIE (*Having suddenly decided to say it*) Cora . . . I can't let you and the kids come over and live with us.

CORA (*This is a blow to her*) Oh . . . Lottie.

LOTTIE   I'm sorry, Cora. I just can't do it.

CORA   Lottie, I was depending on you . . .

LOTTIE   Maybe you've depended on me too much. Ever since you were a baby, you've run to me with your problems, and now I've got problems of my own.

CORA   What am I going to do, Lottie?

LOTTIE   Call up Rubin and ask him to come back. Beg him to come back, if you have to get down on your knees.

CORA   I mustn't do that, Lottie.

LOTTIE   Why not?

CORA   Because we just can't keep from fighting, Lottie. You know that. I just don't think it's right, our still going on that way.

LOTTIE   Do you still love him?

CORA   Oh . . . don't ask me, Lottie.

LOTTIE   Do you?

CORA   Oh . . . yes.

LOTTIE   Cora, I don't think you should listen to the stories those old Werpel sisters tell you.

CORA   He's as good as admitted it, Lottie.

LOTTIE   Well, Cora, I don't think it means he likes you any the less, because he's seen Mavis Pruitt a few times.

CORA   No . . . I know he loves me.

LOTTIE   (Asking very cautiously)   Does he still want to be intimate?

CORA   That's only animal, Lottie. I couldn't indulge myself that way if I didn't feel he was being honorable.

LOTTIE   (Breaks into a sudden raucous laugh)   My God, a big handsome buck like Rubin! Who cares if he's honorable?

CORA   (A little shocked)   Lottie!

LOTTIE   (We see now a sudden lewdness in LOTTIE that has not been discernible before)   Cora, did you hear what the old maid said to the burglar? You see, the burglar came walking into her bedroom with this big, long billy club and . . .

CORA   Lottie!

LOTTIE *(Laughing so hard she can hardly finish the story)*   And the old maid
. . . she was so green she didn't know what was happening to her, she
said . . .

CORA   Lottie! That's enough. That's enough.

LOTTIE *(Shamed now)*   Shucks, Cora. I don't see what's wrong in having a
little fun just telling stories.

CORA   Sometimes you talk shamefully, Lottie, and when I think of the way
Mama and Papa brought us up . . .

LOTTIE   Oh, Mama and Papa, Mama and Papa! Maybe they didn't know as
much as we gave them credit for.

CORA   You're changed since you were a girl, Lottie.

LOTTIE   What if I am!

CORA   I never heard such talk.

LOTTIE   Well, that's all it is. It's only talk. Talk, talk, talk.

CORA   Lottie, are you sure you can't take us in?

LOTTIE   It'd mean the end of my marriage too, Cora. You don't understand
Morris. He's always nice and quiet around people, so afraid of hurting
people's feelings. But he's the most nervous man around the house you
ever saw. He'd try to make the best of it if you and the kids came over,
but he'd go to pieces. I know he would.

CORA   Honest?

LOTTIE   I'm not joking, Cora. My God, you're not the only one who has
problems. Don't think that for a minute.

CORA   A few moments ago, you said *you* had problems, Lottie . . .

LOTTIE   Problems enough.

CORA   Tell me, Lottie.

LOTTIE   Oh, why should I?

CORA   Doesn't Morris ever make love to you any more?

LOTTIE *(It takes her several moments to admit it)*   . . . No. It's been over
three years since he even touched me . . . that way.

CORA *(Another revelation)*   Lottie!

LOTTIE It's the God's truth, Cora.

CORA Lottie! What's wrong?

LOTTIE How do I know what's wrong? How does anyone ever know what's wrong with anyone else?

CORA I mean . . . is there another woman?

LOTTIE Not unless she visits him from the spirit world. *(This releases her humor again and she is diverted by another story)* Oh, say, Cora, did I tell you about this woman over in Oklahoma City who's been holding séances? Well, Marietta went to her and . . . *(But suddenly, again, she loses her humor and makes another sad admission)* Oh, no, there isn't another woman. Sometimes I wish there was.

CORA Lottie, you don't mean that.

LOTTIE How the hell do *you* know what I mean? He's around the house all day long, now that he's got his dental office in the dining room. Day and night, day and night. Sometimes I get tired of looking at him.

CORA Oh, Lottie . . . I'd always felt you and Morris were so devoted to each other. I've always felt you had an almost perfect marriage.

LOTTIE Oh, we're still devoted, still call each other "honey," just like we did on our honeymoon.

CORA But what happened? Something must have happened to . . .

LOTTIE Did you notice the way Morris got up out of his chair suddenly and just walked away, with no explanation at all? Well, something inside Morris did the same thing several years ago. Something inside him just got up and went for a walk, and never came back.

CORA I . . . just don't understand.

LOTTIE Sometimes I wonder if maybe I've been too bossy. Could be. But then, I always supposed that Morris *liked* me because I was bossy.

CORA I always envied you, having a husband you could boss.

LOTTIE Yes, I can boss Morris because he just isn't there any more to fight back. He doesn't care any more if I boss him or not.

CORA Just the same, he never hit you.

LOTTIE I wish he would.

CORA Lottie!

LOTTIE   I do. I wish to God someone *loved* me enough to hit me. You and Rubin fight. Oh, God I'd like a good fight. Anything'd be better than this *nothing*. Morris and I go around always being so sweet to each other, but sometimes I wonder maybe he'd like to kill me.

CORA   Lottie, you don't mean it.

LOTTIE   Do you remember how Mama and Papa used to caution us about men, Cora?

CORA   Yes, I remember.

LOTTIE   My God, they had me so afraid of ever giving in to a man, I was petrified.

CORA   So was I.

LOTTIE   Yes, you were until Rubin came along and practically raped you.

CORA   Lottie! I don't want Sonny to hear talk like that.

LOTTIE   Why not? Let him hear!

CORA   *(Newly aghast at her sister's boldness)*   Lottie!

LOTTIE   Why do we feel we always have to protect kids?

CORA   Keep your voice down. Rubin never did anything like that.

LOTTIE   Didn't he?

CORA   Of course not!

LOTTIE   My God, Cora, he had you pregnant inside of two weeks after he started seeing you.

CORA   Sssh.

LOTTIE   I never told. I never even told Morris. My God, do you remember how Mama and Papa carried on when they found out?

CORA   I remember.

LOTTIE   And Papa had his stroke just a month after you were married. Oh, I just thought Rubin was the wickedest man alive.

CORA   I never blamed Rubin for that. I was crazy in love with him. He just swept me off my feet and made all my objections seem kinda silly. He even made Mama and Papa seem silly.

LOTTIE   Maybe I shoulda married a man like that. I don't know. Maybe it was as much my fault as Morris'. Maybe I didn't . . . respond right . . . from the very first.

CORA   What do you mean, Lottie?

LOTTIE   Cora, I'll tell you something. Something I've never told another living soul. I never did enjoy it the way some women . . . say they do.

CORA   Lottie! You?

LOTTIE   Why do you say *me* like that? Because I talk kinda dirty at times? But that's all it is, is talk. I talk all the time just to convince myself that I'm alive. And I stuff myself with victuals just to feel I've got something inside me. And I'm full of all kinds of crazy curiosity about . . . all the things in life I seem to have missed out on. Now I'm telling you the truth, Cora. Nothing ever really happened to me while it was going on.

CORA   Lottie . . .

LOTTIE   That first night Morris and I were together, right after we were married, when we were in bed together for the first time, after it was all over, and he had fallen asleep, I lay there in bed wondering what in the world all the cautioning had been about. Nothing had happened to me at all, and I thought Mama and Papa musta been makin' things up.

CORA   Oh, Lottie!

LOTTIE   So, don't come to me for sympathy, Cora. I'm not the person to give it to you.
(*Outside there is a low rumble of thunder.* SONNY *enters from the dining room with a cup of flour paste and his scrapbook.* MORRIS *returns from his walk, his face mysterious and grave*)

MORRIS   We'd better be starting back now, honey. It looks like rain.

CORA   Oh, don't talk about leaving. Can't you and Lottie stay all night? I'd get up early and fix you breakfast. I'll fix you biscuits.

MORRIS   I can't, Cora. I got patients coming first thing in the morning.

LOTTIE   And I have to go home to let out the cats.

MORRIS   It was a wonderful dinner, Cora.

CORA   Thank you, Morris.

LOTTIE (*On a sudden impulse, she springs to her feet, hoists her skirt to her waist, and begins wrestling with her corset*)   My God, I'm gonna take off this corset and ride back home in comfort.

CORA (*Runs protectively to* SONNY, *and stands between him and* LOTTIE, *to prevent his seeing this display*)   Sonny! Turn your head.

LOTTIE   My God! That feels good. (*She rolls the corset under her arm and rubs the flesh on her stomach in appreciation of its new freedom. Then she reaches for the bag of fried chicken*) Thanks for the fried chicken, Cora. Oh, good! A gizzard. (*She brings out a gizzard to gnaw on*) It was a wonderful dinner. You're a better cook than I am.

CORA   That's not so.

LOTTIE   Kiss me good-bye, Sonny.

SONNY   Good-bye, Aunt Lottie.

LOTTIE (*Hugging him close*)   Good night, darling.

MORRIS   That was a fine recitation, Edwin Booth.

SONNY   Thank you, Uncle Morris.

LOTTIE (*Facing her husband with a bright smile, as though nothing but happiness had ever passed between them*)   I'm ready, Daddy.

MORRIS   All right, Mama. Good of you to have us, Cora.

CORA   Glad you could come, Morris.

LOTTIE (*At the door, thinks of one last piece of news she must impart to her sister before leaving*)   Oh, Cora! I forgot to tell you. Mamie Keeler's in the hospital.

MORRIS (*Goes out on the porch now*)   Looks like it's gonna rain any minute now.

CORA   What's wrong?

LOTTIE   Some kind of female trouble.

CORA   Oh . . . that's too bad.
(*But* LOTTIE *can tell by the sound of* CORA's *voice that she is too preoccupied now with her own worries to care about Mamie Keeler*)

LOTTIE   Oh, God, Cora . . . I just can't go off and leave you this way.

CORA   I'll be all right, Lottie.

LOTTIE   Look, Cora . . . if you and the kids wanta come over and stay with us . . . we'll manage somehow . . .

CORA   Oh, thank you, Lottie. *(They embrace as though recognizing the bond of their blood)* But I'm going to work this out for myself, Lottie.

LOTTIE   Good-bye, Cora.

MORRIS *(From outside)*   It's beginning to rain, honey.

LOTTIE   *(Hurrying out the door)*   Hold your horses, Morris. I'm coming. Don't be impatient now. *(They exit. Now* CORA *returns to the center of the room, feeling somehow deserted)*

SONNY   It's always so quiet after company leaves, isn't it?

CORA   Hush, Sonny. I'm trying to think.
(From outside, we hear the sound of MORRIS' *car driving off, and then the sound of the rain and the wind)*

SONNY   Let's move to California, Mom. Please, let's move to California.
(But CORA *has made a sudden decision. She rushes to the telephone)*

CORA   Long distance. *(A moment's wait)* This is Mrs. Flood, three-two-one. I want to talk to Mr. Rubin Flood at the Hotel Boomerang in Blackwell . . . Yes, I'll wait.

SONNY *(In an innocent voice)*   I bet he isn't there. I bet anything.

CORA   Hello? He isn't? Would you ask them if he's been there this week? *(A moment's wait)* He hasn't! Oh . . . Well, please tell him, if he does come, to call his family immediately. It's very important.
(A fallen expression on her face, she sits for a moment, wondering what next move to make. Then she hears a car approaching from the distance. She jumps up and runs to the window)

SONNY   It isn't Dad. I can always tell the sound of his car. *(*CORA *comes back to the middle of the room)*

CORA   Run along to bed now, Sonny. It's late. I have to go out and empty the pan under the icebox.
*(*CORA *goes out through the dining-room door.* SONNY *walks slowly, hesitantly, to the foot of the stairs and stands there, looking up at the blackness at the top. He stands there several moments, unable to force himself to go further. From the kitchen we hear* CORA'S *muffled sobs.* SONNY *cries out in fear)*

SONNY Mom!
(CORA *returns now, not wanting* SONNY *to know she has been crying*)

CORA Sonny, I thought I told you to go upstairs. *(She looks at him now and sees his embarrassed fear)* Sonny, why are you so afraid of the dark?

SONNY 'Cause . . . you can't see what's in front of you. And it might be something awful.

CORA You're the man of the house now, Sonny. You mustn't be afraid.

SONNY I'm not afraid . . . if someone's with me.
(CORA *walks over to him and takes his hand*)

CORA Come, boy. We'll go up together.
(They start up the stairs to face the darkness hovering there like an omen)

CURTAIN

SCENE: *It is the next day, late afternoon. Outside, there is a drizzling rain that has continued through the day.* REENIE *has not dressed all day. She sits by the fire in her robe, rubbing her freshly shampooed hair with a towel.* CORA *enters from the dining room, wearing a comfortable old kimono. She looks at the tray by* REENIE'S *side.*

CORA   Reenie! Is that all you feel like eating?

REENIE   Yes.

CORA   But that's all you've had all day, Reenie. You don't eat enough to keep a bird alive.

REENIE   I . . . I'm not hungry, Mom.

CORA   Now quit feeling sorry for yourself, just because you didn't have a good time last night.

REENIE   Mom, is Dad coming back?

CORA   I don't know. I tried to call him last night but couldn't get him.

REENIE   Aren't you mad at him any more?

CORA   No . . . I'm not mad.

REENIE   Even though he hit you?

CORA   Even though he hit me. I was defying him to do it . . . and he did. I can't blame him now.

REENIE   Do you think he *will* be back, Mom?

CORA   This is the day he was supposed to come back. It's almost suppertime and he still isn't here.

REENIE   But it's been raining, Mom. I'll bet the roads are bad.

CORA   You love your father, don't you?

REENIE   Yes.

CORA   Well, I'm glad. The people we love aren't always perfect, are they? But if we love them, we have to take them as they are. After all, I guess I'm not perfect, either.

REENIE   You are too, Mom. You're absolutely perfect, in every way.

CORA   No, I'm not, Reenie. I . . . I have my own score to settle for. I've always accused your father of neglecting you kids, but maybe I've hurt you more with pampering. You . . . and Sonny, too.

REENIE   What do you mean, Mom?

CORA   Oh, nothing. I can't say anything more about it right now. Forget it. (For some reason we don't yet know, she tries to change the subject) Are you feeling a little better now?

REENIE   I guess so.

CORA   Well, the world isn't going to end just because your young man went off and left you.

REENIE   Oh, Mom. It was the most humiliating thing that ever happened to me.

CORA   Where do you think Sammy went?

REENIE   He went out to the cars at intermission time with some other girl.

CORA   To spoon?

REENIE   They call it necking.

CORA   Are you sure of this?

REENIE   Mom, that's what all the boys do at intermission time. They take girls and go out to the cars. Some of them don't even come back for the rest of the dance.

CORA   But are you sure Sammy did that? Did you see him?

REENIE   No, Mom. I just know that's what he did.

CORA   Wouldn't you have gone out to one of the cars with him?

REENIE   (With self-disparagement)   Oh, Mom.

CORA   What makes you say "Oh, Mom" that way?

REENIE   He wouldn't have liked me that way.

CORA   But why? Why not?

REENIE   I'm just not *hot stuff* like the other girls.

CORA   Reenie, what an expression! You're pretty. You're every bit as pretty as Flirt or Mary Jane. Half a woman's beauty is in her confidence.

REENIE   Oh, Mom.

CORA   Reenie, I've tried to raise you proper, but . . . you're sixteen now. It's perfectly natural if a boy wants to kiss you, and you let him. It's all right if you *like* the boy.

REENIE   *(A hesitant admission)*   Oh . . . Sammy kissed me.

CORA   *(Quite surprised)*   He did?

REENIE   On the way out to the party, in Punky's car. Flirt and Punky were in the front seat, Sammy and I in the back. Punky had a flask . . .

CORA   The little devil!

REENIE   Mom, most of those wealthy boys who go away to school are kind of wild.

CORA   Go on.

REENIE   Well, Punky and Flirt started necking, very first thing. Flirt, I don't mean to be tattling, but she *is* kind of fast.

CORA   I guessed as much. You aren't tattling.

REENIE   Well, Sammy and I felt kind of embarrassed, with no one else to talk to, and so he took my hand. Oh, he was very nice about it, Mom. And then he put an arm around me, and said . . . "May I kiss you, Reenie?" And I was so surprised, I said yes before I knew *what* I was saying. And he kissed me. Was it all right, Mom?

CORA   Did you like the young man? That's the important thing.

REENIE   Yes, I . . . I liked him . . . very much. *(She sobs helplessly)* Oh, Mom.

CORA   There, there, Reenie dear. If he's the kind of young man who goes around kissing all the girls, you don't want to worry about him any more. You did right to leave the party!

REENIE   Did I, Mom?

CORA   Of course you did. I'm very disappointed in Sammy. I thought he was such a nice boy. But I guess appearances can be deceiving.

REENIE   Oh, Mom!

CORA   There, there, dear. There are plenty of other young men in the world. You're young. You're not going to have to worry.

REENIE   *(Struggling to her feet)*   Mom, I don't think I ever want to get married.

CORA   Reenie!

REENIE   I mean it, Mom.

CORA   You're too young to make a decision like that.

REENIE   I'm serious.

CORA   What makes you say such a thing? Tell me.

REENIE   I don't want to fight with anyone, like you and Daddy.

CORA   Oh, God.

REENIE   Every time you and Daddy fight, I just feel that the whole house is going to cave in all around me.

CORA   Then I *am* to blame.

REENIE   And I think I'd be lots happier, just by myself, teaching school, or working in an office building.

CORA   No, daughter. You need someone after you grow up. You need someone.

REENIE   But I don't want to. I don't *want* to need anyone, ever in my life. It's a horrible feeling to need someone.

CORA   *(Disturbed)*   Daughter!

REENIE   Anyway, the only times I'm really happy are when I'm alone, practicing at the piano or studying in the library.

CORA   Weren't you happy last night when Sammy kissed you?

REENIE   I guess you can't count on happiness like that.

CORA   Daughter, when you start getting older, you'll find yourself getting lonely and you'll want someone; someone who'll hear you if you get sick and cry out in the night; and someone to give you love and let you give your love back to him in return. Oh, I'd hate to see any child of mine miss that in life. *(There is a moment of quiet realization between them. Then we hear the sound of a car drawing up to the house.* CORA, *running to the window, is as excited as a girl)* That must be your father! No, it's Sonny. In a big limousine. He's getting out of the car as if he owned it.

Mrs. Stanford must have sent him home with her chauffeur. *(She gives "chauffeur" its American pronunciation.* SONNY, *in his Sunday suit, bursts into the house waving a five-dollar bill in his mother's face)*

SONNY   Mom. Look, Mom! Mrs. Stanford gave me five dollars for speaking my piece. See? Five whole dollars. She said I was the most talented little boy she ever saw. See, Mom? Then she got out her pocketbook and gave me five whole dollars. See?

CORA   I declare. Why, Sonny, I'm proud of you, boy. That's the very first money you ever earned, and I'm very proud.

SONNY   And Mrs. Stanford sent me home with her chauffeur, too, Mom. *(He gives the word its French pronunciation)* That's the way you're supposed to pronounce it, chauf*feur*. It's French.

CORA   If you spend any more time at Mrs. Stanford's, you'll be getting too high-hat to come home. *(She notices* REENIE *starting upstairs)* We'll talk later, Reenie. (REENIE *exits.* CORA *again turns her attention to* SONNY) Did you have anything to eat?

SONNY   Oh, Mom, it was just delicious. She had all kinds of little sandwiches. Gee, they were good. And cocoa, too, Mom, with lots of whipped cream on top, in little white cups with gold edges. Gee, they were pretty. And lots of little cakes, too, with pink frosting and green. And ice cream, too. I just ate and ate and ate.

CORA   Good. That means I won't have to get you any supper.

SONNY   No. I don't want any supper. I'm going to the movies tonight. And to the Royal Candy Kitchen afterwards, to buy myself a great big sundae with chocolate and marshmallow and cherries and . . .

CORA   Now, wait a minute, Sonny. This is the first money you've ever earned in your life, and I think you should save it.

SONNY   Oh, Mom!

CORA   I mean it. Five dollars is a lot of money, and I'm not going to let you squander it on movies and sundaes. You'll thank me for this some day. *(She takes his piggy bank from the bookcase)*

SONNY   I will not. I will not thank you!

CORA   Sonny.
(She takes the bill from him and drops it into the bank. SONNY *is wild at the injustice)*

SONNY   Look what you've done. I hate you! I wanta see the movie. I've just gotta see the movie. If I can't see the movie, I'll kill myself.

CORA   Such foolish talk!

SONNY   I mean it. I'll kill myself.

CORA   Now, be quiet, Sonny. I want to have a little talk.

SONNY   Can I sell the milk bottles for money?

CORA   No! Now quit pestering me about the movies. You've already talked me into letting you see one movie this week. I have scarcely any money now, and I can't spare a cent. (SONNY *is badly frustrated. He finds the favors that* SAMMY *promised him, displayed on the settee. He throws a handful of confetti recklessly into the air, then dons a paper hat, and blows violently on a paper horn*) Sonny! Stop that racket! You're going to have to clean up that mess.

SONNY   You won't let me have any fun at all.

CORA   The young man was very thoughtful to have sent you the favors. I wish he had been as thoughtful in other ways.

SONNY   Didn't Reenie have a good time at the party last night?

CORA   No.

SONNY   Serves her right. Serves her right.

CORA   Sonny! I'm not going to have any more talk like that. If you and your sister can't get along, you can at least have a little respect for one another. Now, come here, Sonny, I want to talk serious for a little while. (SONNY *taunts her with the horn*) Will you go sit down?

SONNY   What's the matter?
(He sits opposite her at the table)

CORA   Nothing. I just want to talk awhile.

SONNY   *(Suddenly solemn and apprehensive)*   Have I done something bad?

CORA   Well, I don't know if you have or if I have. Anyway, we've got to talk about it. Sonny, you mustn't come crawling into my bed any more. I let you do it last night, but I shouldn't have. It was wrong.

SONNY   I was scared.

CORA   Just the same, that's not to happen again, Sonny. It's not the same when a boy your age comes crawling into bed with his mother. You can't expect me to mean as much to you as when you were a baby. Can you understand, Sonny? (*He looks away from her with unconscious guilt. She studies him*) I think you're older in your feelings than I ever realized. You're a funny mixture, Sonny. In some ways, shy as your sister. In other ways, bold as a pirate.

SONNY   I don't like you any more at all.

CORA   Sonny!

SONNY   I don't care. You make me mad.

CORA (*Going to him*)   Oh, God, I've kept you too close to me, Sonny. Too close. I'll take the blame, boy. But don't be mad. Your mother still loves you, Sonny. (*But she sees that they are at an impasse*) Well, we won't talk about it any more. Run along to the store now, before it closes. (*We see* FLIRT's *face in the door window. She is knocking on the door and calling for* REENIE. CORA *hurries to let her in*) Flirt!

FLIRT (*Rushing inside*)   Where's Reenie? Reenie . . . Reenie. Oh, Mrs. Flood, I have the most awful news.

CORA   What is it, Flirt?

FLIRT (FLIRT's *face, her whole body are contorted by shock and confused grief*)   Oh, it's so awful.

CORA   Tell me.

FLIRT   Is Reenie here? I've got to tell her, too.

CORA (*Calls upstairs*)   Reenie, can you come down? Flirt is here.

REENIE (*Off*)   I'm coming.

FLIRT   Oh, Mrs. Flood, it's the most awful thing that ever happened in this town. It's the most awful thing I ever heard of happening anywhere.

CORA   Did something happen to you, or your family? . . .

FLIRT   No, it's Sammy.

CORA   Sammy? . . .

REENIE (*Coming downstairs*)   What is it, Flirt?

FLIRT   Kid! Sammy Goldenbaum . . . killed himself.
    (*There is a long silence*)

CORA   Where did you hear this, Flirt?

FLIRT Mrs. Givens told me. The hotel people over in Oklahoma City called her about it just a little while ago. They found a letter in Sammy's suitcase Mrs. Givens had written him, inviting him to come home with Punky.

CORA Oklahoma City?

FLIRT He went over there last night after he left the party. He took the midnight train. That's what they figured out, because he registered at the hotel this morning at two o'clock.

CORA How . . . did he do it, Flirt?

FLIRT (*Hides her face in her hands as though hiding from the hideous reality of it*) He . . . Oh, I just can't.

CORA There, there, honey.

FLIRT Oh, I'm such a silly about things. He . . . he jumped out of the window . . . on the fourteenth floor . . . and landed on the pavement below.

CORA Oh, my God.

FLIRT Oh . . . it's really the most terrible thing that ever happened to me. I never did know anyone who killed himself before.

CORA Does anyone have any idea what made him do it?

FLIRT No! Punky says that he used to get kind of moody at times, but Punky never expected him to do anything like *this*.

CORA Why did he go to Oklahoma City in the middle of the night?

FLIRT No one knows that either . . . for sure. But one thing did happen at the party. He was dancing with Mary Jane Ralston . . . that cow . . . just before intermission . . . and Mrs. Ralston . . . she'd had too much to drink . . . comes out in the middle of the floor and stops them.

CORA What for?

FLIRT Well, you know how Mrs. Ralston is. No one takes her very serious even if she does have money. Anyway, she came right out in the middle of the floor and gave Sammy a bawling out . . .

CORA A bawling out? Why?

FLIRT She said she wasn't giving this party for Jews, and she didn't intend for her daughter to dance with a Jew, and besides, Jews weren't allowed in the country club anyway. And that's not so. They are too allowed in the country club. Maybe they're not permitted to be members, but they're certainly allowed as guests. Everyone knows that. *(She turns now to* REENIE, *who has sat numb in a chair since* FLIRT'S *shocking announcement)* Where were you when it all happened?

REENIE   I . . . I . . .
(But she is inarticulate)

CORA   Reenie wasn't feeling well. She left the party and came home.

FLIRT   The other kids told me Sammy was looking for you everywhere. He was going around asking everyone, Where's Reenie?

CORA   That . . . that's too bad.

FLIRT   *(Turning to* CORA*)*   . . . But a thing like that isn't serious enough to make a boy kill himself, is it?

CORA   Well . . . he did.

FLIRT   An old blabbermouth like Mrs. Ralston?

CORA   She was a stranger to Sammy. She probably sounded like the voice of the world.

FLIRT   Gee . . . I just don't understand things like that. Do you know something else, Mrs. Flood? They called Sammy's mother way out in California, and told her, and I guess she was terribly sorry and everything, but she told them to go on and have the funeral in Oklahoma City, that she'd pay all the expenses, but she wouldn't be able to come for it because she was working. And she cried over the telephone and asked them please to try and keep her name out of the papers, because she said it wasn't generally known that she had a son.

CORA   There won't be anyone Sammy knows at the funeral, will there?

FLIRT   Mrs. Givens said Punky and his daddy could drive us over for it. Will you come, Reenie? *(*REENIE *nods)* Do you wanta come, too, Sonny? *(*SONNY *nods)* Well . . . it'll be day after tomorrow, in the afternoon. We'll all have to get excused from school. Oh, gee, it all makes me feel so kind of *strange.* Doesn't it *you,* kid? I think I'll go to Sunday School tomorrow. Do you wanta go with me, Reenie? *(*REENIE *nods yes)* Oh, I feel just terrible.
*(*FLIRT *bolts out the front door, as though wanting to run away from all that is tragic or sorrowful in life.* CORA *keeps silent for several moments, her eyes on* REENIE*)*

CORA   Where were you when Sammy went off?

REENIE   *(Twisting with grief)*   Stop it, Mom!

CORA   Tell me. Where were you?

REENIE   Don't, Mom!

CORA   *(Commanding)*   *Tell* me.

REENIE   I . . . was up in . . . the girls' room.

CORA   Where did you leave Sammy?

REENIE   As soon as we got to the party, Sammy and I started dancing. He danced three straight dances with me, Mom. Nobody cut in. I didn't think anybody was ever going to cut in, Mom. I got to feeling so humiliated I didn't know what to do. I just couldn't bear for Sammy to think that no one liked me.

CORA   Dear God!

REENIE   So I told Sammy there was someone at the party I had to talk to. Then I took him over to Mary Jane Ralston and . . . introduced him to her . . . and told him to dance with her.

CORA   Reenie!

REENIE   I . . . I thought he'd like her.

CORA   But you said that *you* liked Sammy. You told me you did.

REENIE   But, Mom, I just couldn't *bear* for him to think I was such a wallflower.

CORA   You ran off and *hid*, when an ounce of thoughtfulness, one or two kind words, might have saved him.

REENIE   I didn't *know*. I didn't *know*.

CORA   A nice young man like that, bright and pleasant, handsome as a prince, caught out here in this sandy soil without a friend to his name and no one to turn to when some thoughtless fool attacks him and he takes it to heart. (REENIE *sobs uncontrollably*) Tears aren't going to do any good now, Reenie. Now, you listen to me. I've heard all I intend to listen to about being so shy and sensitive and afraid of people. I can't respect those feelings any more. They're nothing but selfishness. (REENIE *starts to bolt from the room, just as* FLIRT *did, but* CORA's *voice holds her*) Reenie! It's a fine thing when we have so little confidence in ourselves, we can't stop to think of the other person.

SONNY *(Who has been a silent listener until now)*   I *hate* people.

CORA   Sonny!

SONNY   I *do.*

CORA   Then you're just as bad as Peg Ralston.

SONNY   How can you keep from hating?

CORA   There are all kinds of people in the world. And you have to live with them all. God never promised us any different. The bad people, you don't hate. You're only sorry they have to be. Now, run along to the store before it closes.
(SONNY goes out, and finds himself again confronted by the jeers of the neighborhood boys, which sound like the voices that have plagued humanity from the beginning of time)

BOYS' VOICES
Sissy Sonny!
Sonny Flood! His name is mud!
Sonny plays with dolls!
Sonny loves his mama!
(Hearing the voices, CORA runs to the door, but stops herself from going further)

CORA   I guess I can't go through life protecting him from bullies. *(She goes to REENIE)* I'm sorry I spoke so harshly to you, Reenie.

REENIE   He asked for *me* . . . for *me.* The only time anyone ever *wanted* me, or *needed* me, in my entire life. And I wasn't there. I didn't stop once to think of . . . Sammy. I've always thought I was the only person in the world who had any feelings at all.

CORA   Well . . . you're not, if that's any comfort. Where are you going, dear?

REENIE   *(Resignedly)*   I haven't done anything to my room all day. I . . . I still have to make my bed.
(REENIE exits upstairs)

CORA   *(Calling after her)*   It's Saturday. Change the linens. I put them in the attic to dry. *(CORA goes into the parlor to pull down the shades. RUBIN enters from the dining room. He is in his stocking feet, and is carrying several bags, which he drops onto the floor with a clatter. CORA comes running from the parlor)* My God!

RUBIN   I scare ya?

CORA   Rubin! I hate to be frightened so.

RUBIN   I din *mean* to frighten ya.

CORA   I didn't hear you drive in.

RUBIN   I didn't.

CORA   Where's the car?

RUBIN   It ain't runnin' right. Left it downtown at the garage. I walked home.

CORA   Why did you come in the back way?

RUBIN   Cora, what difference does it make if I come in the back way or the front way, or down the chimney? My boots was covered with mud. So I left 'em out on the back porch. I din wanta track up your nice, clean house. Now, wasn't that thoughtful of me?

CORA   Did you get my message?

RUBIN   What message?

CORA *(A little haughty)* Oh . . . nothing.

RUBIN   What message you talkin' about?

CORA   The route you left me said you'd be in Blackwell last night. I called you there, but . . . Well, I suppose you had better places to be.

RUBIN   That's right. I did. What'd ya call me for?

CORA *(Hurt)* I don't know now. You'll be wanting a hot bath. I'll go turn on the water tank. (CORA *exits through dining-room door.* RUBIN *sits in his big chair and drops his face into his hands with a look of sad discouragement. Then he begins to unpack one of the bags, taking out small pieces of harness and tossing them on the floor. In a few moments,* CORA *returns)* What made you decide to come back?

RUBIN   I lost my job.

CORA   What?

RUBIN   I said I lost my job.

CORA   Rubin! You've always sold more harness for the company than any of the other salesmen.

RUBIN   Yah. The on'y trouble is, *no* one's selling much harness today because no one's buyin' it. People are buyin' automobiles. Harness salesmen are . . . things of the past.

CORA   Do you mean . . . your company's going out of business?

RUBIN   That's it! You won the kewpie doll.

CORA   Oh, Rubin!

RUBIN   So that's why ya couldn't get me in Blackwell last night. I went somewhere else, regardless of what you were thinkin', lookin' for a job.

CORA   (*A little embarrassed with regret*)   Oh . . . I apologize, Rubin.

RUBIN   Oh, that's all right. You have to get in your li'l digs ev'ry once in a while. I'm used to 'em.

CORA   I'm really awfully sorry. Believe me.

RUBIN   I was in Tulsa, talkin' to some men at the Southwest Supply Company. They're hirin' lotsa new men to go out in the fields and sell their equipment.

CORA   (*Seizing her opportunity*)   Rubin Flood, now that you've lost one traveling job, I'm not going to let you take another. You go downtown the first thing Monday morning and talk to John Fraser. He's bought out all the Curley Cue markets in town, and he needs men to manage them. He'd give you a job in a minute. Now, you do what I say, Rubin.

RUBIN   (*He looks at her for several moments before getting to his feet*)   God damn! I come home here t'apologize to you for hittin' ya. I been feelin' all week like the meanest critter alive, because I took a sock at a woman. My wife, at that. I walked in here ready to *beg* ya to forgive me. Now I feel like doin' it all over again. Don't you realize you can't talk to a man like that? Don't you realize that every time you talk that way, I just gotta go out and raise more hell, just to prove to myself I'm a free man? Don't you know that when you talk to a man like that, you're not givin' him credit for havin' any brains, or any guts, or a spine, or . . . or a few other body parts that are pretty important, too? All these years we been married, you never once really admitted to yourself what kinda man I am. No, ya keep talkin' to me like I was the kinda man you think I *oughta* be. (*He grabs her by the shoulders*) Look at me. Don't you know who I am? Don't you know who I am?

CORA   Rubin, you're hurting me.

RUBIN   I'm takin' the job if I can get it. It's a damn good job, pays good money.

CORA   I don't care about money.

RUBIN   No, you don't! Not until you see Peg Ralston come waltzin' down the street in a new fur coat, and then you start wonderin' why old Rubin don't shoot hisself in the foot to make a lot of money.

CORA   Rubin, I promise you I'll never envy Peg Ralston another thing, as long as I live.

RUBIN   Did it ever occur to you that maybe I feel like a cheapskate because I can't buy you no fur coat? Did you ever stop to think maybe I'd like to be able to send my kids away to a fine college?

CORA   All I'm asking is for you to give them something of *yourself.*

RUBIN   God damn it! What have *I* got to give 'em? In this day and age, what's a man like me got to give? With the whole world so all-fired crazy about makin' money, how can *any* man, unless he's got a million dollars stuck in his pocket, feel he's got anything else to give that's very important?

CORA   Rubin!

RUBIN   I mean it, Cora.

CORA   I never realized you had such doubts.

RUBIN   The new job is work I've never done. Work I never even thought of doin'. Learnin' about all that goddamn machinery, and how to get out there and demonstrate it. Working with different kinds of men, that's smarter than I am, that think fast and talk sharp and mean all business. Men I can't sit around and chew tobacco with and joke with like I did m'old customers. I . . . I don't like 'em. I don't know if I'm *gonna* like them.

CORA   But you just said you wanted the job.

RUBIN   I don't like them, but I'm gonna join them. A fellow's gotta get into the swim. There's nothing else to do. But I'm scared. I don't know how I'll make out. I . . . I'm scared.

CORA   I never supposed you had it *in* you to fear.

RUBIN   I s'pose all this time you been thinkin' you was married to one a them movin'-pitcher fellas that jump off bridges and hold up trains and shoot Indians, and are never scared a nothin'. Times are changin', Cora, and I dunno where they're goin'. When I was a boy, there wasn't much more to this town than a post office. I on'y had six years a schoolin' cause that's all the Old Man thought I'd ever need. Now look at things. School buildin's, churches, fine stores, movie theatres, a country club. Men becomin' millionaires overnight, drivin' down the street in big limousines, goin' out to the country club and gettin' drunk, acting like they was the lords of creation. I dunno what to think of things now, Cora. I'm a stranger in the very land I was born in.

CORA *(Trying to restore his pride)*   Your folks pioneered this country.

RUBIN   Sometimes I wonder if it's not a lot easier to pioneer a country than it is to settle down in it. I look at the town now and don't recognize anything in it. I come home here, and I still have to get used to the piano, and the telephone, and the gas stove, and the lace curtains at the windows, the carpets on the floor. All these things are still *new* to me. I dunno what to make of 'em. How can *I* feel I've got anything to give to my children when the world's as strange to me as it is to them?

CORA *(With a new awareness of him)*   Rubin!

RUBIN   I'm doin' the best I can, Cora. Can't ya understand that? I'm doin' the best I can.

CORA   Yes, Rubin. I know you are.

RUBIN   Now, there's a few more things I gotta say . . . I wanna apologize. I'm sorry I hit ya, Cora. I'm awful sorry.

CORA   I know I provoked you, Rubin.

RUBIN   You provoked me, but . . . I still shouldn'ta hit ya. It wasn't manly.

CORA   I'm not holding it against you, Rubin.

RUBIN   And I'm sorry I made such a fuss about you gettin' the girl a new dress. But I was awful worried about losin' my job then, and I din have much money left in the bank.

CORA   Rubin, if I'd known that, I wouldn't have *thought* of buying the dress. You should have told me, Rubin.

RUBIN   I din wanta make you worry, too.

CORA   But that's what I'm for.

RUBIN   That's all I gotta say, Cora, except that . . . I love ya. You're a good woman and I couldn't git along without you.

CORA   I love you, too, Rubin. And I couldn't get along without you another day.

RUBIN   You're clean, and dainty. Give a man a feeling of decency . . . and order . . . and respect.

CORA   Thank you, Rubin.

RUBIN   Just don't get the idea you can rearrange *me* like ya do the house, whenever ya wanta put it in order.

CORA   I'll remember. *(There is a short silence between them now, filled with new understanding)* When you have fears about things, please tell me, Rubin.

RUBIN   It's hard for a man t'admit his fears, even to hisself.

CORA   Why? Why?

RUBIN   He's always afraid of endin' up like . . . like your brother-in-law Morris.

CORA   Oh!
(CORA has a new appreciation of him. She runs to him, throwing her arms about him in a fast embrace. A glow of satisfaction radiates from RUBIN, to have his woman back in his arms)

RUBIN   Oh, my goodness. *(RUBIN carries CORA center, where they sit like honeymooners, she on his lap; and he kisses her. SONNY returns now with a sack of groceries, and stands staring at his parents until they become aware of him)* H'lo, son.

SONNY   Hi!

CORA   Take the groceries to the kitchen, Sonny. *(Obediently, SONNY starts for the dining-room door)* Rubin, Mrs. Stanford paid Sonny five dollars this afternoon for speaking a piece at her tea party.

RUBIN   I'll be damned. He'll be makin' more money than his Old Man. *(SONNY exits now through dining-room door)*

CORA   Be nice to him, Rubin. Show him you want to be his friend.

RUBIN   I'm nice to that boy, ain't I?

CORA   Sometimes you do talk awfully rough and bad-natured.

RUBIN   Well . . . *life's* rough. *Life's* bad-natured.

CORA   I know. And I keep trying to pretend it isn't.

RUBIN   I'll remind ya.

CORA   Every time I see the kids go out of the house, I worry . . . like I was watching them go out into life, and they seem so young and helpless.

RUBIN   But ya gotta let 'em go, Cora. Ya can't hold 'em.

CORA   I've always felt I could give them life like a present, all wrapped in white, with every promise of happiness inside.

RUBIN   That ain't the way it works.

CORA   No. All I can promise them is life itself. (*With this realization, she gets off* RUBIN's *lap*) I'd better go to the kitchen and put the groceries away.

RUBIN   (*Grabs her to him, not willing to let her go*)   T'hell with the groceries!

CORA   (*A maidenly protest*)   Rubin!

RUBIN   (*Caressing her*)   Is there any chance of us bein' alone t'night?

CORA   (*Secretively*)   I think Reenie plans to go to the library. If you give Sonny a dime, I'm sure he'll go to the movies.

RUBIN   It's a deal.
(*He tries again to re-engage her in lovemaking*)

CORA   Now, Rubin, be patient.
(*She exits through the dining-room door as* REENIE *comes running downstairs*)

REENIE   Did I hear Daddy?

RUBIN   Hello, daughter.

REENIE   (*She runs into his arms and he lifts her high in the air*)   Oh, Daddy!

RUBIN   Well, how's my girl?

REENIE   I feel better now that you're home, Daddy.

RUBIN   Thank ya, daughter.

REENIE   I've been practicing a new piece, Daddy. It's Chopin. Do you want me to play it for you?

RUBIN   Sure. I like sweet music same as anyone.

REENIE   I can't play it quite perfect yet, but almost.

(REENIE *goes into parlor and in a moment we hear another wistful piece by* Chopin)

RUBIN   That's all right. (SONNY *now returns and stands far right.* RUBIN, *center, faces him. They look at each other with wonder and just a little resentment. But* RUBIN *goes to* SONNY, *making the effort to offer himself*) Son, your mom tells me you do real well, goin' around speaking pieces, gettin' to be a reg'lar Jackie Coogan. I got a customer has a daughter does real well at that kinda thing. Gets up before people and whistles.

SONNY   Whistles?

RUBIN   Yah! Like birds. Every kinda bird ya ever heard of. Maybe you'd like to meet her sometime.

SONNY   Oh, maybe.
(RUBIN *feels himself on uncertain ground with his son*)

RUBIN   Your mom said maybe you'd like to go to the movie tonight. I guess I could spare you the money.
(*He digs into his pocket*)

SONNY   I've changed my mind. I don't want to now.
(SONNY *turns from his father*)

RUBIN   (*Looks at his son as though realizing sadly the breach between them. With a feeling of failure, he puts a warm hand on* SONNY's *shoulder*)   Oh! Well, I ain't gonna argue. (*He walks out, and as he passes the parlor, he speaks to* REENIE) That's real purty, daughter.

REENIE   Thank you, Daddy.

RUBIN   (*Opens dining-room door and speaks to* CORA)   Cora, those kids ain't goin' to the movies. Come on now.

CORA   (*Off*)   I'll be up in a minute, Rubin.

RUBIN   (*Closing the door behind him, speaking to* REENIE *and* SONNY)   I'm goin' upstairs now, and have my bath.
(REENIE *and* SONNY *watch him all the way as he goes upstairs*)

SONNY   They always want to be alone.

REENIE   All married people do, crazy.
(SONNY *impulsively sticks out his tongue at her. But she ignores him, picking up one of the favors, a reminder of* SAMMY, *and fondling it tenderly.* SONNY *begins to feel regret*)

SONNY   I'm sorry I made a face at you, Reenie.

REENIE *(Sobbing softly)*   Go on and make as many faces as you like. I'm not going to fight with you any more.

SONNY   Don't cry, Reenie.

REENIE   I didn't know Sammy had even remembered the favors until I started to go. Then I went to find my coat, and there they were, sticking out of my pocket. At the very moment he was putting them there . . . he must have had in mind doing what he did.

SONNY *(With a burst of new generosity)*   You! You keep the favors, Reenie.

REENIE   He promised them to *you*.

SONNY   Just the same . . . *you* keep them, Reenie.

REENIE   Do you mean it?

SONNY   Yes.

REENIE   You never were thoughtful like this . . . before.
(CORA *comes through the dining-room door now, hears the children's plans, and stands unobserved, listening)*

SONNY   Reenie, do you want to go to the movie tonight? It's Mae Murray in *Fascination*, and there's an *Our Gang Comedy* first.

REENIE   I don't feel I should.

SONNY   When I feel bad, I just *have* to go to the movies. I just *have* to.

REENIE   I was supposed to go to the library tonight.

SONNY   Please go with me, Reenie. Please.

REENIE   Do you really want me?

SONNY   Yes, Reenie. Yes.

REENIE   Where would you get the money to take *me*, Sonny? I have to pay adult admission. It's thirty-five cents.

SONNY   I've got all the money we'll need.
(He *runs for his piggy bank as* CORA *makes a quick return to the dining room.)*

REENIE   Sonny! Mother told you you had to save that money.

SONNY   I don't care. She's not going to boss me for the rest of my life. It's *my* money, and I've got a right to spend it. *(With a heroic gesture of defiance, he throws the piggy bank smashing against the fireplace, its pieces scattering on the floor)*

REENIE   Sonny!

SONNY *(Finding his five-dollar bill in the rubble)*   And we'll have enough for popcorn, too, and for ice cream afterwards at the Royal Candy Kitchen. *(Now we see* CORA *in the parlor again, a silent witness)*

REENIE   I feel very proud to be treated by my little brother.

SONNY   Let's hurry. The comedy starts at seven o'clock and I don't want to miss it.

REENIE   We can stay for the second show if we miss the comedy.

SONNY   Oh, I want to stay for the second show, anyway. I always see the comedy twice.

CORA *(Coming forth now)*   Are you children going some place?

REENIE   We're going to the movie, Mom.

CORA   Together?

REENIE   Yes.

CORA   Well . . . that's nice.

REENIE   Darn it. I left my rubbers out on the porch. *(She exits)*

RUBIN *(From upstairs)*   Cora!

CORA   I'll be up in a minute, Rubin. *(She turns thoughtfully to her son)* Have you forgiven your mother, Sonny?

SONNY *(Inscrutable)*   Oh . . . maybe.

CORA   Your mother still loves you, Sonny. *(She puts an arm around him but he avoids her embrace)*

SONNY   Don't, Mom.

CORA   All right. I understand.

RUBIN *(Upstairs, growing more impatient)*   Cora! Come on, honey!

CORA *(Calling back to him)*   I'll be up in a minute, Rubin. (SONNY *looks at her with accusing eyes)* Good-bye, Sonny! (REENIE *sticks her head in the door from outside)*

REENIE   Hurry up, Sonny!

RUBIN   Come on, Cora!

(CORA *starts up the stairs to her husband, stopping for one final look at her departing son. And* SONNY, *just before going out the door, stops for one final look at his mother, his face full of confused understanding. Then he hurries out to* REENIE, *and* CORA, *like a shy maiden, starts up the stairs, where we see* RUBIN'S *naked feet standing in the warm light at the top)*

CORA   I'm coming, Rubin. I'm coming.

                                                                                      CURTAIN